THE PUZZLED PATRIOTS

BRUCE MUIRDEN

THE PUZZLED PATRIOTS

The Story of the Australia First Movement

MELBOURNE UNIVERSITY PRESS

LONDON AND NEW YORK : CAMBRIDGE UNIVERSITY PRESS

First published 1968

Printed in Australia by

Melbourne University Press, Carlton, Victoria 3053

Registered in Australia for transmission

by post as a book

SBN 522 83907 X

Dewey Decimal Classification Number 3290060994

Aus 68-1625

Text set in 10 point Times type

To June, Clyde and April

Preface

THIS BOOK has not been weighted down with footnotes. So that the earnest student is not asked to take too much on trust this preface points to the origin of much of the controversial material. Many clues have been given in the limited number of notes I have provided and in the Bibliography. I have noted in the Acknowledgments that much information has been obtained by personal interview and correspondence. Much information has also come from a close study of the eight volumes of the evidence given at the Clyne Inquiry and newspaper reports of the Inquiry. The official report of the evidence is not always as reliable as it might have been. For example, on page 1385 M. C. Smith is reported as saying he attended the Yabber Club from the end of 1939 'to the time of my internment'. Mr Smith certainly attended the Yabber Club but equally certainly he was never interned. At one stage a court stenographer took down the name Curtin instead of Kirtley. The *Bulletin* went ahead with a testy piece 'I wrote to Mr. Curtin' on the basis of this mistake, which was later corrected.

In the chapter on Miles I also drew on the George Waite papers in the Mitchell Library (Uncat. MSS., set 208), the files of *Ross's Monthly*, the *Liberator* and the *Socialist,* Edward Masey's recollections and Gavin Souter's unpublished study of Bea Miles. Stephensen's valedictory address at the W. J. Miles cremation service, published as a leaflet, helped with the biography but provided rather less hard fact than Stephensen's account of his late patron in the *Publicist* of February 1942.

Stephensen's story is drawn from a far wider variety of sources. All the published works are listed in the Bibliography. For his London days, press cuttings in the *Sydney Morning Herald* library and reports in *The Times* and *Biblionews* were supplemented by

vii

letters from Jack Lindsay, Eric Partridge, Margaret Cole, John Parker, Rolf Gardiner, Rhys Davies and J. O. Prestwick (of Queen's College). Stephensen explained his part in publishing *Lady Chatterley's Lover* in an article in the *Observer* (Sydney) of 26 January 1960.

For chapter 4 I began with a study of the *Publicist* files. Additional evidence on the Yabber Club came out of correspondence with Edward Masey and a number of visitors to the club, including George Caiger and Peter Russo. S. B. Hooper had put together a short typescript account of the club and this I found in Keith Bath's papers. A few months before his death J. N. Rawling's recollections of his dealings with Miles were tapped. Among others, Hartley Grattan, Len Fox, Brian Fernandez and Clem Christesen contributed information. The 'trade secret' of Stephensen's literary collaboration with Frank Clune was publicly revealed in *Nation* (31 January 1959); subsequently Mr Clune wrote to *Nation* that there was no secret or mystery about their association.

Letters from Masey and Kirtley helped to round out the story of early war-time days, otherwise based on the *Publicist* and a handful of Sydney newspaper reports. Until he formed the Australia First movement in October 1941 Stephensen's nationalist advocacy attracted very little public attention. Press reports provide the main basis for reference to Glassop and Gilhooley (Adelaide *Advertiser*, 17 May 1945). A letter from E. C. Quicke to Gilhooley is mentioned in the Clyne Inquiry, page 1743, further justifying Gilhooley's inclusion in this book. Evidence at the Inquiry supplied most of the material about Arnold (pages 1504–20), Graham (pages 1027, 1643, 2408) and Burleigh (page 1943). The unsigned but clearly well informed two-part article on Stephensen published on 31 January and 14 February 1959 in *Nation* helped fill many gaps in this as in many other chapters.

The *Publicist* gave only the barest outline of how the Australia First movement evolved. Material on the Walshes came mainly from the Mitchell Library collection of Walsh publications, its *Empire Gazette* file and a biographical article on Adela Walsh in *People*, 9 May 1951. Masey's recollections of the evolution of the movement and Bath's voluminous file of documents (compiled after the events from memory) put evidence given before Mr Justice Clyne in fairer perspective. A copy of the shorthand report of Stephensen's address following the Adyar Hall violence is now in my possession, thus allowing a more balanced assessment of his advocacies than those based on brief and tendentious press reports.

What happened in Melbourne was difficult to discover. Many of the living witnesses appear reluctant to testify. Niall Brennan and David Pitt have been notable exceptions. W. D. Cookes's story is based firmly on evidence before, and remarks made by, Mr Justice Clyne (report page 859) and remarks made by counsel—J. W. Shand (pages 2293–4), W. R. Dovey (pages 2460–1) and H. J. H. Henchman (pages 2027, 2029–30). Several Melbourne rationalists were able to recall Cookes's activities in the Rationalist Association.

The *West Australian* report of the lower and Supreme court hearings of charges against Bullock, Quicke, Williams and Krakouer was the major source of material for this chapter. Bullock, in conversation with me, volunteered a great deal of extra detail. The actions of Intelligence officers were revealed in the evidence of Moseley (pages 1788–99), Thomas (pages 1755–88, 1805–7) and Richards (pages 1809–30) before Mr Justice Clyne.

The Clyne Inquiry evidence was vital in telling the story of the round-up in Sydney by Intelligence officers and police. Recollections of Bath and Masey helped significantly. Stephensen set down his version in an *Observer* article (22 August 1959) and also in the statement in his habeas corpus application lodged with the N.S.W. Supreme Court sworn on 21 July 1942.

Records of treatment during internment kept by Masey, Kirtley, Hooper, Bath, Matthews and Mills were used extensively. Incidents at Loveday camp involving Stephensen were canvassed at length during the Clyne Inquiry (particularly pages 661–5, 769–70).

The private papers of Bath and Hooper, Stephensen's letters to Bath and Calwell's recollections were referred to extensively in chapter 11 to supplement Hansard. Forde's former private secretary, H. V. Howe, helped me to try to establish Forde's attitude to the internments.

The chapter on the Clyne Inquiry is based firmly on the eight volumes of evidence and newspaper reports.

Mr Justice Clyne's report was sufficient for the chapter dealing with his findings. Masey's papers provided the text of F. B. Blood's submission of 13 March 1942. British newspaper cuttings (principally *The Times*, *News Chronicle* and *Daily Mail*) filed by the Press Association library in London provided much of the material on British Fascists not contained in Colin Cross's book *The Fascists in Britain*.

In the final chapter heavy reliance was placed on the papers of Bath, Mills, Masey, Hooper and Stephensen. Stephensen's manuscript of about 5,000 words, now in the possession of W. W. Stone,

X PREFACE

was prepared for the *Observer* and helped to explain his point of view. It was not the same as an article by Stephensen, referred to above, actually published by the *Observer* and which was also a valuable piece of evidence. The account of Bath's final settlement with the Commonwealth government in 1954 was told to me by Bath himself. It is not recorded in any of the papers I have seen. Stephensen's death in 1965 was the subject of a short memoir by W. W. Stone, who witnessed it. Stephensen's threat to sue Hasluck was made in a telephone conversation with Professor Henry Mayer.

Acknowledgments

ONE OF THE MAIN SOURCES of material for this account was the eight-volume transcript of evidence given at the Clyne Inquiry in 1944–5. This was made available by the late Mr Keith Bath of Sydney, who died just as this manuscript was being completed; the federal government was unwilling to allow access to the copy of the transcript of this public enquiry which is lodged with the National Archives in Canberra. Mr Bath also provided miscellaneous letters, documents, booklets and press cuttings. With this material were several well documented analyses, prepared by Mr Edward Masey and Mr Bath, of the Clyne Inquiry and its background which provided exceedingly helpful references.

Calls for information were made in person or by letter to more than 140 people in Australia and the United Kingdom. Among the many whose response calls for acknowledgment here are Mr W. W. Stone, Mr L. F. Bullock, Mr E. C. Masey, Mr A. A. Calwell, Dr Sondra Silverman and Sir Thomas Clyne.

The periodicals section of the South Australian Public Library gave courteous attention to my steady stream of requests. I must also thank the Mitchell Library, Sydney, the National Library of Australia, Canberra, and the La Trobe Library, Melbourne.

B.W.M.

Adelaide 1967

Contents

Illustrations

1

Nationalism

SINCE THE FIRST white children were born at Sydney Cove there have been people in Australia ready to see something special about their own, the newest of lands. There were also some in convict times ready enough to hate their enforced home, but as the number of 'Currency' lads grew, so national pride developed. It had in essence the same quality as the nationalism of older lands except that, until the Sudan campaign and the Boer War, it did not stem from military exploits. Love of one's own plot of soil, of one's kinsfolk, has often enough elsewhere manifested itself in devastating other people's land and hating their kinsfolk.

While some Australian-born took their birthright calmly enough, in others it became a fever. Much of the worst poetry of the eighties and nineties stemmed from Utopian visions of this 'Sunlit South'.

Australians who considered the matter held that their civilization represented a fresh start, a clean break with what had gone before.[1] To the extent that there was little room for the social conventions of the country from which they came, this was true. The absence of military fervour was fortuitous: Australia's apparent good intentions towards the rest of the world were simply a product of her distance from it; there was nobody handy to fight and anyway Australians had enough on their hands, exploring, developing, consolidating. The Malay archipelago, nearest to Australia, was not seen until the most recent years as any kind of threat, and the most offensive patriotism was not bombast in the face of Asians but the natural reaction of an untamed younger son, manifested in abuse of England and the English.

Australia has never felt moved by purely national feeling to fight other countries. Whenever governments have attempted to rally

1

opinion in favour of military campaigns it has never—not even in the case of the occupation of New Guinea in 1914—been for national aggrandizement. Australia has fought because Britain has fought or been endangered or, more recently, because America has fought or seen its interests endangered.

Thus loyalties in war have not been a simple matter of loyalty to Australia; they have been tangled with attitudes to Britain or America. For many years loyalty, whatever that much-abused word may mean, was seen as support for the British Empire. This imperial requirement did not become widely questioned until conscription for military service overseas grew to be an issue of such magnitude as to force the unthinking to think. More than 80 per cent of the enrolled electors voted in the (non-compulsory) conscription referenda in 1916 and 1917. From the time of that major rift in our society Australia has had a significant minority ready to question the wisdom of following the British, more particularly the English, in all matters.

National feeling has also shown itself in isolationism—as it did so markedly in the United States between the wars (and to a lesser extent during them). As in the United States the isolationists have commonly been people at the end of their tether, many grasping, as the 1930s progressed, at anti-Semitic and Fascist straws. These were similar people to those who, in *The Times*'s description of the participants at the mass Fascist rally at London's Olympia in June 1934, 'have tired of passing through difficult times, in which hope has been strained.' In the United States a vast, frightening upsurge of vocal political minorities (from William Dudley Pelley's Silver Shirts to Huey Long's Share our Wealth movement) plagued Roosevelt's early years in power. These had no echo in Australia except for the mushroom growth of the right-wing New Guard in Sydney to oppose J. T. Lang's Labor government of New South Wales.

As Australians grew in awareness of the world the Utopian content of their nationalism diminished. Millennial Eden, that fine sentiment of Bernard O'Dowd (who, however, was realistic enough to note that there was also a possibility that Australia could turn into a 'new demesne for Mammon') was understood to be hyperbole. But the Anglophobia remained, showing up most strongly in J. F. Archibald's *Bulletin* where it developed as shrill a note as had been heard up to that time or for decades after. English reluctance in the early years of the century to agree to Australia having her own naval squadron fed this fire a little. English generals such as Haig, who uselessly sacrificed Australian bodies on the pyres of Flanders, also contributed, especially when Australians could look more calmly in retrospect at what had happened. Larwood's bodyline tour of 1932–3 brought much previously unspoken anti-English sentiment into the open.

Inevitably those who grew to suspect the English and their political, economic and social dominance of the young Commonwealth came in time to see new virtues in England's enemies.

In World War I the Irish Republican Brotherhood had seven members interned in Australia. Reporting in 1918 on their internment, Mr Justice Harvey said that the view of these men was that any means were justified to injure Britain whom they saw as the enemy and oppressor of Ireland. They were hardly Australian nationalists. One of them, Frank McKeown, a Melbourne bricklayer, had no interest in Australia (according to Mr Justice Harvey) as Ireland occupied the whole of his thoughts. These were the extremists who were willing to help finance the purchase of German arms for use in Ireland against the English. Others among Australia's considerable community of Irish descent, less bitter, put Australia first and the Empire second—to use Archbishop Mannix's words. Mannix's fight with W. M. Hughes over conscription crystallized many issues of loyalty. It no longer become axiomatic for Australians to respond unthinkingly to the calls of the British War Office. Many, of course, clung more closely than ever to the imperial connection, frightened by the Roman Catholic menace of Archbishop Mannix and that Sinn Fein bogey which so scandalized the Protestant middle classes.

It would be true to say, though only in very general terms, that while the middle and upper classes in Australia felt reassured by the British ties, the working class began to develop definite reservations. These suspicions appeared better founded when Sir Otto Niemeyer of the Bank of England, invited to Australia in 1930 by the Scullin Labor government to help solve the problems of economic depression, urged social economies in the sacred name of balanced budgets. Here was a representative of English finance suggesting that Australia's standard of living was too high and should be reduced. Sir Otto's support for deflation brought him under bitter attack from Lang, Premier of New South Wales, who spoke for a considerable section—and that the most nationalist-minded—of the labour movement. The name of Niemeyer is still firmly fixed in the popular imagination as that of an unfeeling agent of an economic imperialism which put pounds before people. He became a handy scapegoat for the sadly crippled working class and an unfavourable advertisement for the British connection.

The Depression knocked most of what remained of the Utopian

stuffing (which was little enough) out of sentient Australians. Russel Ward has fairly described 1919 to 1939 in Australia as 'an uncertain, cautious and shabby era'. What nationalistic feeling there was tended to concentrate on suspicion of British and international finance. Misanthropy tended to provide a nucleus for the new type of nationalism.

One vigorous new nationalist, a man who took good care to broadcast his opinions widely, was Percy Reginald Stephensen—but the Percy Reginald Stephensen of 1934 onwards. He had the restless energy, and a Sydney businessman, William John Miles, had the money and disciplined determination to insist that this new nationalism get a hearing. Joining forces in Sydney, they provided six years of cantankerous opposition to the English influence on Australia but not, curiously, to the monarchy. In time this pair added to their causes a mild but persistent anti-Semitism and a growing sympathy with the German, Italian and Japanese governments.

Their nationalism was of a kind that has been described as narrow and tribal-minded (by T. G. H. Strehlow)[2] and as local clannishness (by Brian Fitzpatrick).[3]

Miles and Stephensen attracted some support, enough to earn them the wholehearted opposition of the Labor Left, and also, though less publicly, the distrust of the Anglophilic Right. For the Right the strong anti-communism that went with the new nationalism did make it more palatable.

The Australia First movement, the final political structure erected by Stephensen (without Miles's backing), ended its five months' existence with its leaders, some of its members and a few of their friends behind barbed wire in an internment camp in their own country in March 1942.

2

Miles

IT HAS BECOME a commonplace to observe that Australians visiting England often adopt, and some of them retain, a nationalistic feeling that they failed to show at home. The crowds of young tourists who sailed for Britain and the Continent in the past twenty years may have shown this attitude in its most heightened and easily mocked form with kangaroo emblems and Australian flags, but the phenomenon existed in earlier years. When the Australian encounters the 'true' England with its crowded streets and accommodation, its warm beer and quaint customs, a suddenly discovered chauvinism is a frequent response. Xavier Herbert said in 1958 that he had been to Britain and 'it was my visit to that country that made me conscious of my true nationality.'

Both W. J. Miles and P. R. Stephensen returned from trips abroad anything but Anglophiles.

Miles, the only son of wealthy, very 'English', parents, was born on 27 August 1871 in Woolloomooloo, first went to England at the age of eleven and while there saw the first cricket Test played in England. This was the game dominated by Spofforth, the demon Australian bowler, who collected seven English wickets in each innings, and the game in which the term 'the Ashes' originated. The young Miles was delighted when the colonials won by seven runs. As Stephensen later remarked, Miles 'barracked for Australia, then and always thereafter'.

As Miles avoided personal publicity little is known about his early life. It is mainly through a lengthy obituary comment by his far less reticent protégé, Stephensen, that we have any substantial record. From this it appears that it was in Miles's teens that he developed his consciously Australian bias.

He spent his younger days in a luxurious home at Ashfield and for four years went to one of Sydney's great public schools, Newington College, where, according to one of his rare backward glances committed to print,[1] he did not receive one lesson in Australian history. Miles became a public accountant and was admitted as a partner into his father's firm of Miles Vane & Miles. (The other partner was H. D. Vane.) This practice was merged in 1908 with that of F. N. Yarwood, under the name of Yarwood Vane & Miles. In 1912 Miles retired from this notable firm, which then became the present Yarwood Vane & Co. Miles set up on his own as a consulting accountant and financial adviser in an office in Challis House, Martin Place. He became, and was until his death, a director in the high-class George Street men's-wear store which his father had bought as Peapes and Shaw, and is now known as Peapes Pty Ltd. He owned 70 per cent of the total shareholding of that company, and at various times he was a director of the British General Electric Co. Pty Ltd in Australia, the Sydney Meat Preserving Co. and several other enterprises.* In his later years his income came from dividends, director's fees and from specialized accountancy. He gave up his Martin Place office when he began his association with Stephensen in 1935.

Partly by his own efforts, and partly helped by his inheritance, Miles was a business success. He was, according to all accounts, most determined and methodical, and a man never to be trifled with. He played chess at interstate level, and unlike many Sydney businessmen took a wide interest in community politics and culture, not shunning causes because they might be unpopular. Indeed his forthrightness and controlled drive seemed to ensure that the less popular the cause the more energy he would devote to its support. The many calls he allowed to be made on his time caused him to develop an insistence on punctuality that became habitual.

It was not in his nature to join any organization or back any cause lightheartedly. As an Australian he was very far from typical, and the national failing of being content with 'near enough' was entirely absent from his endeavours. To Miles, compromise was alien, so this put him out of normal party politics. In any case he habitually scorned parties and objected to compulsory voting on the ground that it forced him to support one or other of them, though none reflected his own views. Miles always lodged an unmarked ballot paper at elections as his form of protest.

---

* One enterprise that more often than not did not make a profit was his betting on the totalisator at Randwick. A regular attender at the races there, he bet heavily to a losing system.

Physically he was a man of barely middle height with a thick grey moustache and, ironically, a nose that caused strangers occasionally to mistake him for a Jew. His speech was carefully precise, rapid and usually loud. When he found, as he did increasingly, that colleagues or business associates were less well organized and were liable to upset his careful timetable, his small reserve of tolerance was often unequal to the strain. Less and less, as the years went on and his health deteriorated, was he able to suffer fools gladly. By 1937, with some of his business interests put finally aside but his time fully occupied, he was revealingly signing himself 'Yours tiredly' in a brusque letter to Xavier Herbert, whose *Capricornia* he was publishing.[2]

Even before Miles decided to devote most of his money and almost all his spare time to asserting Australian values and disparaging the imperial link, he had made a considerable impact on Sydney society with his work in the Rationalist movement. Largely through the pioneer efforts of people such as Joseph Symes and Thomas Walker, this cause lagged hardly at all in organization, zest and influence behind the British free-thinking groups, and Miles contributed to its progress.

Although his education at school was not extensive and had been interrupted by his overseas trip, Miles collected a large and broad-ranging library which he studied systematically. To T. H. Huxley, J. S. Mill and Charles Darwin, those liberating gods of pure reason, he was a ready convert, and he founded, became first secretary of, and for years directed the affairs of the Rationalist Association of New South Wales.

This 'district' of the Rationalist Press Association at that time had more members than any other except London. It was a fighting, free-thought body, largely because of its blunt and intellectually uncompromising secretary. Even today his annual reports make stimulating reading. He was never above upbraiding his members for their intellectual shortcomings. In 1918 he remarked that Melbourne was very much ahead of Sydney and other capitals in the quality of its rationalist activity. After detailing five possible reasons for this he added in a comment, typical of him in those years: 'Archbishop Mannix has, doubtless quite unintentionally, been a rationalising factor for some time'. Miles was also chiding rationalists for their too narrow concern with secularism, reminding them, rightly, that rationalism was a method of thought applicable to all human affairs.

In the first *Sydney Rationalist Annual,* published in August 1914, he contributed an article on Sir Oliver Lodge (Miles was a bitter opponent of Lodge and other members of the British rationalist movement who were then tinkering with telepathy); later followed a leaflet entitled *The Myth of the Resurrection of Jesus, The Christ,* one of his favourite themes.

As Miles was welding his Sydney rationalists into the successfully argumentative body he wanted them to become, his attention was diverted by W. M. Hughes's move for conscription for overseas military service. Ever suspicious of imperial motives and jealous of Australian independence,* Miles joined a team of speakers organized in the Sydney Domain by the Anti-Conscription League of New South Wales. When referenda in 1916 and 1917 finally killed the conscription issue, Miles was ready for the next imperial threat.

In 1871 Sir Julius Vogel, Treasurer and later Premier of New Zealand, had advocated a southern Pacific federation of New Zealand, Fiji, Tonga and Samoa under British rule, and in addition suggested the federation of the whole British Empire. Subsequently other Empire statesmen, from Joseph Chamberlain at the first meeting of the Colonial Conference in 1897 onwards, spoke of the idea as one of practical politics. How thoroughly the proposal was debated in cabinet, parliament and at conference tables is shown by this passage of truly intercolonial length delivered at the 1917 Imperial Conference by the New Zealand Premier, William Massey:

I know that numberless opinions have been expressed upon what ought to be done, innumerable pamphlets have been written and innumerable speeches have been delivered, and I am bound to say that all this writing and all these speeches and all these changes of opinion which have taken place during the last dozen years, particularly since the War commenced, have done a very great deal of good, inasmuch as they have set the population of the Empire thinking, and they have impressed people who have never studied the question previously with the potentialities of the Overseas Dominions and with the necessity of taking advantage of the present opportunity to bring the different parts of the Empire more closely together than ever before, and to bind them in such a way that they will not be likely to separate for many centuries to come, and I trust they will never separate.

During the war it was agreed to leave this question of imperial federation until peace-time. W. J. Miles was ready for it. In October 1917 he had tried to get his Advance Australia League with its 'Australia First' slogan organized in Sydney, Melbourne and Bris-

---

* He opposed Australian participation in the Sudan campaign when he was only a boy of fourteen. He was against involvement in the Boer War and opposed conscription in 1916–17. We must take Stephensen's word on his attitude to the first of these three wars.

bane, but no evidence is available of any significant public response. Years later, Miles admitted that his 1917 move was premature. The first of his League's four objectives was 'to resist any reduction of Australian autonomy'. The others were to maintain a White Australia, to foster Australian national sentiment and to urge Australians to make the most of their country's resources. In practice the immediate driving force was opposition to imperial federation, under which, it claimed, Australia's self-governing powers would be heavily reduced.

Miles's poster propaganda and his public meetings were at pains to stress that opposition to imperial federation was a plank of the Australian Labor Party platform though Labor M.P.s had been silent on the question. Through the early years of the labour movement Miles (according to Stephensen) 'shared in its enthusiasms and hopes, but, earlier than most, he lost those hopes'. A recent writer, Peter Coleman, notes incorrectly in his *Obscenity, Blasphemy, Sedition* (1962) that Miles began with the revolutionary Left. This common mistake stems from confusion of W. J. Miles with J. B. Miles of the Communist Party. Certainly Miles was ready enough to work with the radical Left to oppose conscription and he did not mind helping R. S. Ross with his socialist *Ross's Monthly*, although the reason he urged fellow-rationalists to subscribe was because of its secularist content.

There is no record of the adult Miles saying or doing anything he did not believe just because it was expected of him. Once his course was set he used any and every means short of violence or fraud to achieve his end. Thus the Rationalist Association was turned, for a time, into a mouthpiece against imperial federation. It was in justification of this that he exhorted members to see rationalism as something wider than mere opposition to the churches.

Before long—and perhaps it was inevitable—Miles's thoroughgoing scepticism brought him into conflict with fellow-rationalists, many of them undoubtedly less rigorous in their disbelief. Like Symes and J. S. Langley, two of Australia's greatest free-thought advocates, he had grown more than a little autocratic. Like them he seemed as destined for trouble with colleagues as with opponents. After having been honorary secretary of the N.S.W. Rationalist Association for seven years he fell out with Joseph McCabe, that tireless former Franciscan monk, who had made several proselytizing tours of Australia and New Zealand for the Rationalist Press Association in London. Miles suspected McCabe of being a secret political agent of the imperial government. Listing a host of matters

over which he and the RPA were in disagreement, Miles resigned
early in 1920. One point of rupture, he said, was that most of the
writers in the Association's official journal, the *Literary Guide,* spoke
of the war as being within the 'will of man' and not biologically inevitable. This 'biological inevitability' was already a weary old Miles
hobbyhorse in issue after issue of *Ross's* in 1917, and was to stay
with him until his death. Miles saw war as a 'law' of life; pacifism
was thus a waste of time.

Miles also objected to what he considered to be the anti-Roman
Catholic and pro-Protestant nature of the RPA, and often showed
that he had a lot more time for Archbishop Mannix than for some
fellow-rationalists. Mannix was anti-imperialist, and Roman Catholics in Australia, being generally Irish-orientated, often had little
stomach for the English.

Over the years many people could have counted themselves
Miles's associates but few became friends. Those who came closest
to him admitted he could be very 'difficult', and his continual attacks
on what he regarded as mental complacency cannot have made him
an easy companion. He married in the 1890s and had five children,
one being Beatrice ('Bea', or 'Bee' as she insists), a famous Sydney
eccentric. She and her father clashed, and when a psychiatrist examined her after she had been wrongly committed to a mental asylum
he found her to be suffering from a neurosis which was 'the direct
result of attempts to repress an uncontrollable child'. Bea's asylum
episode brought her early (aged twenty-four) into the public eye.
Smith's Weekly did its best with a headline: 'Madhouse Mystery of
Beautiful Sydney Girl'. She added to her notoriety by thirty years of
uninvited public readings of Shakespeare in Sydney streets, plus an
unrelenting war on taxi drivers and bus conductors, frequently ending
in court appearances.

In an unpublished biography, Gavin Souter has said that her
naturalism was all her own but she may well have acquired her
rationalism and nationalism from her father. She found her Sydney
school (Abbotsleigh) inadequate in its teaching of Australian subjects, but nevertheless developed something of an Australian bias,
although her favourite writers, after Shakespeare, were the icono-
clasts Swift and Mencken. Her father never spoke to her about his
campaign with Stephensen to promote Australian self-reliance,
although she was well aware of it. He left her £5 a week in his will.[3]

Miles had been an official of the Sydney Shakespeare Society, and,
not surprisingly, a devotee of Pope. He did not discover Joseph
Furphy's *Such is Life* until 1920. This was late enough but still well

before most literary Australians realized what a classic it was. Later
Stephensen was to call the book 'talismanic to Australians'. To Miles,
writing in 1922, it was 'the greatest and finest piece of Australian
fictional prose'. His discussion of it in the *Socialist* became the
occasion of an anti-imperialist homily.

if an Australian wrote a great masterpiece which brought the
world's regard, he would be treated as a disloyalist towards the
British Imperial King and Government. The mass of the people
in Australia—the great majority of all classes—believe themselves to be inferior to their prototypes in Britain. Australian
sentiment only shows itself in small matters; when they are big,
the people's imperialism causes them to kneel in reverence of spirit
and bow towards the land where their King lives. We are a
colonial people in spirit, thought and act.

This was the truth only slightly exaggerated, for the twenties were
hardly a time of great national spirit. Australians had lived through
two decades of nationhood, including the failure at Gallipoli, and
they were showing far more obsequious respect for the Crown
than had the colonials of the nineties. The change could hardly be
blamed entirely on the inauguration in 1904 of annual Empire Day
celebrations.

As always, exactly what loyalty and patriotism meant was totally
different for different people. To Miles, patriotism, or 'Australia
First', meant watchfulness against imperial encroachment. To James
Howard Catts, too, Labor M.H.R. for Cook (N.S.W.) until 1922,
another anti-conscriptionist and the man largely responsible for the
commemoration of Anzac Day, 'Australia First' was a worthy
slogan. He had 'Advance Australia Fair' sung at all Labor Party
meetings in his electorate, encouraged the display of Australian flags
and was proud of his country's coat of arms. Was this what Miles
meant when he referred to 'Australian sentiment in small matters'?
Catts's wife, in a biographical study of her husband, noted that 'no
man was more patriotic to the British motherland'.

To Miles, if Australia was first the Empire was necessarily second.
He did not talk of 'cutting the painter'; to him it was inevitable that
the painter would break.

To Professor Mungo MacCallum, Australia First meant something very different. A war-time conscriptionist, he insisted, in an
address to the Empire Literature Society in 1921, that 'if we put
Australia First in a really long-headed and intelligent way, we shall,
for Australia's sake, be utterly loyal to the Empire'. MacCallum
admitted that it could not be ignored that the phrase 'Australia First'

'came into vogue in the dark days of the war, and in the mouths of some meant, whether affection for Australia or not, certainly antagonism, or at least, indifference to Britain'. Miles kept out of public controversy between 1923—when he contributed an article on rationalist propaganda to the *Liberator,* a Sydney free-thought journal (not to be confused with its more famous namesake in Melbourne between 1884 and 1904)—and 1935 when he began his own small occasional magazine, the *Independent Sydney Secularist,* which combined nationalism and agnosticism. There is no evidence to suggest that his ideas had changed, so it must be assumed he gave his attention to his business activities. He made several trips abroad, the last about 1929.

By 1935, with the world once again starting to rearm for a further settlement of its troubles, Miles put most of his business interests aside and, at the age of sixty-four, prepared for another bout of public advocacy. He was ready to finance anything that attacked either Jesus Christ or the British Empire. It was at this seminal time that he came across 'The Foundations of Culture in Australia', or at least the first section of it, written by P. R. Stephensen and published in Stephensen's literary magazine, the *Australian Mercury,* in July 1935. This essay, subtitled 'An Essay towards National Self Respect', Miles saw as an attack on the British Empire—and in a way it was. Miles did not put his own new *Secularist* entirely aside, but with Stephensen he went off in a different direction, dropping secularism and taking up politics.

Stephensen knew Bea Miles (an attractive girl), but not her father, until Miles wrote to him in June 1935. They met in Miles's office in Martin Place. Miles wanted a younger associate with similar ideas; Stephensen wanted financial backing. Both clearly found what they sought in the resulting partnership (if it could be so called while Miles kept paying the piper and calling the tune), which involved their association almost daily for the next six years. Stephensen had been canvassing several wealthy Sydney people for finance to publish his lengthy essay, with two extra instalments hurriedly added, but without success. It was part of their deal that Miles should publish this book and clear it out of the way so that they could settle down to their venture.

With Stephensen believing that 'Britain's impending decline' meant Australia's gain, he was very much Miles's man. He sat comfortably in the position that Miles had shortly before advertised as vacant, that of a secretary or research officer, who must be 'Aryan', to help him in a new political organization. This advertisement, in the

Sydney Morning Herald, had resulted in the Communist Party send-
ing along one of their unknowns to apply to see what Miles was up
to. Such skirmishing aside, Stephensen clearly was the man Miles
wanted. He became Miles's 'literary adviser' at £5 a week, at a time
when the adult male basic wage in Sydney was £3 9s.

Miles introduced him to a handful of close associates—S. B.
Hooper, a bank manager and a fellow anti-conscriptionist; the book-
ish C. W. Salier, by inclination an historian, by employment a senior
official of the Australian Mutual Provident Society, and Edward
Masey. Masey, at thirty by far the youngest of the group, was a
family friend. He was a foundation member of the Australian Institute of Political Science, formed in 1932. One other associate was
Valentine Crowley, a widely travelled engineer with republican ideas
partly arising from a six-year stay in the United States, who not long
before had been introduced to Miles by Salier. Crowley had retired
in 1920 but had been forced by the Depression to seek work as an
agent with the Australian Mutual Provident Society in 1931. He
found much in common with Miles and they traded ideas. It was not,
of course, a balanced trade, for Miles exported more than he imported. Crowley submitted a credo for an Australia First League to
Miles in June 1936 which included the adoption by Australia of a
republican form of government. It also called for the removal of all
statues of English kings and queens. His belief, however, was not
strong enough to hold out against Miles's counter-persuasion. Miles,
that most surprising of pro-monarchists, gradually prevailed on
Crowley to change his views.

Miles told his circle that he intended to start a new monthly paper
with a strongly political nationalist policy. It would run at a loss for
a considerable time, but he would meet that loss. Stephensen would
help to produce the paper while Salier and Masey would provide
some literary contributions. Salier, a long-time rationalist, had often
contributed to such journals as the (Sydney) *Liberator* under the
pen-name of 'H. Bruno Thomas', and was to continue using this
cover at times. Masey had been writing for the *Australian Quarterly,
Current Problems* and the *Australian National Review* on problems
of Australian trade and population.

Miles was ready enough to support Australian literature, as witness his backing of *Capricornia* after Stephensen had been unable to
finance its publication, but his central interest was now elsewhere.
The old fear of imperial federation with its threat to Australian
independence could hardly have been very real by 1936 but he still
mistrusted the English and hoped to diminish their influence. While

in the popular view Stephensen was largely held responsible for the new journal, the *Publicist,* since Miles's name did not appear, Miles was still firmly in control and he never left anyone in any doubt about this. He was willing to spend heavily to make his new venture an influential organ of opinion. It was to start strongly pro-Australian and, to use Miles's words in an early editorial, holding 'no illusions about the British of Britain'. The journal gradually developed an interest in Hitler and a general sympathy with the Axis powers and their policies.

The *Publicist*'s Anglophobia was novel in that it remained in favour of the monarchy, faithfully echoing Miles's sentiments, as it did in all things up to his death. Traditionally, Anglophobia had been, from Wentworth to John Dunmore Lang and then in the *Bulletin* of Archibald and Traill, fiercely, almost offensively, republican. This seemed natural while the Crown appeared the fountainhead of the worst, most snobbish and least egalitarian features of the English system. Though the *Publicist* every now and then reminded its readers quite explicitly that the paper supported the monarchy, it continually demonstrated that it had little time for the monarch's subjects in Britain, and even less for what the paper derided as 'the English garrison in Australia'—a phrase that had already appeared in *Stephensen's Circular* of March 1934.

Miles, who had an income of about £6,000 a year, was willing to meet any expense that would publicize his *Publicist.* He must have spent at least £2,000 annually printing it, providing it with premises, and advertising it in newspapers, other journals and on the radio. Few, if any, minority-interest journals in Australia can have been so generously endowed. Few indeed have rivalled the *Publicist*'s record of five and a half years of unbroken monthly publication. The *Publicist* stated editorially in number 1 of volume 1 that 'the rock upon which the foundation of this paper's policy rests is the rock of "Australia First".'

By March 1939 Miles, writing as 'John Benauster', was able to state what none could challenge: *'The Publicist* is non-democratic and extremely anti-Leftist; *The Publicist* is positively pro-monarchical and pro-Rightist'. How easy for such a paper to get tagged as Fascist, and how surely its policies would justify such a tag.

3

Stephensen

STEPHENSEN DESCRIBED HIMSELF, and rightly, as a 'man of letters'. Few Australians, whatever right they had to the appellation, would choose to use it, probably because its flavour of 'putting on airs' is hardly a widespread national characteristic. It was one mark of Stephensen to insist, more so as the years wore on, that nobody regard him lightly. It was his tragedy that he grew to be consistently underrated.

His achievements were, in fact, considerable. His literary career, running from 1926 to his death in 1965, was marked by verve, assiduity and variety. He helped others more than he helped himself. P.R.—or 'Inky' (to use a family name that stuck)—Stephensen wrote no novels and, apart from some lampoons in younger life, no poetry. These were about the only fields of literary endeavour he did not explore.

He wrote biographies, criticism, short stories and often acted as 'ghost' for others less gifted in literary composition or unable to spare the time to process their material for publication. His central role was that of promoter. Xavier Herbert's view was that 'Australian writers were just sneaks until "Inky" stood up and yelled for them'.

His own self-evaluation, confided to me in a letter written in 1952, was that when the political and literary history of Australia's thirties was written, 'my name will follow that of A. G. Stephens as a striver towards the full Australian nationalism that will have become taken for granted, say, by the year 2000 A.D.'

Stephensen acted as a spur in the thirties to flagging Australian literary creation, without receiving full credit for his achievements. He was one of the notable omissions (Brian Fitzpatrick was another) from Who's Who in Australia. Miles Franklin has noted, with justice, that Stephensen's key critical work, *The Foundations of Culture in Australia,* is 'more assiduously consulted than acknowledged'.

Stephensen's cultivation of Australian literature and his preoccupation with national self-reliance began on his return from eight years in Britain in 1932.[1] Earlier, there had been signs aplenty that whatever he decided to do in life he would do it wholeheartedly.

Born in November 1901 at Maryborough, Queensland (though occasionally he gave as his birthplace his father's home at the time, nearby Biggenden) he attended Maryborough Boys' Grammar School, having won a State scholarship from Biggenden State School. At Maryborough, where Vere Gordon Childe taught him Latin, he captained cricket and football teams and was a prominent school athlete. In his teens one recorded exploit was to ride a pony that towed one of Bert Hinkler's experimental gliders with its ibis-like wings down the sandhills at Bundaberg. More significant was his action at the age of fourteen in renouncing religion by walking out of a church service. This was possibly his first revolt against majority opinion. From Maryborough he went on from matriculation in 1919 to study arts at the University of Queensland, taking up residence at St John's College.

Throughout his three years at the university he was active in undergraduate affairs. Fellow-students were impressed by the exuberance and *élan* with which he plunged into those extra-curricular activities that go so much further than lectures towards making men out of boys. Herbert Burton, later to become a Professor and Principal of the School of General Studies at the Australian National University, entered St John's at the same time. Life, he found, was never dull while Stephensen was around. A year after his graduation the university magazine, referring jokingly to Stephensen as 'the live-wire blonde', commented on his 'abnormal energy'.

Stephensen did not display any well-defined nationalism as an undergraduate, although he did change the name of the *Queensland University Magazine* to the Aboriginal *Galmahra,* meaning poet, seer, teacher or philosopher among the tribes. At the time Stephensen rejoiced that the magazine had been 'freed at last from the incubus of that cumbrous three-word title'. Much later (1954), he saw his action as 'an Australian retort to Sydney University's Europocentric *Hermes*'.

Among his student friends was Jack Lindsay, several years ahead of him, who attacked the idea of nationalism in Australian literature in 'Satyrs or Kookaburras', an article in the *Queensland University Magazine* in August 1920. Subsequently Stephensen and Lindsay published subtly differing accounts of their relations and developing political opinions, which is hardly surprising in view of their widely diverging courses. At all events, both agree that Stephensen was a far Left radical during his student days. Lindsay began by being absorbed in poetry, and the Dionysian philosophy of his father, Norman. Eventually he developed revolutionary ideas but he maintained them and did not, like Stephensen, veer sharply away to the Right.

Argumentative from his earliest adult days, Stephensen found great stimulus and satisfaction in university debating and he represented Brisbane in inter-university contests. With Eric Partridge, another of his fellows to make his mark in the world of letters, he helped select poems for an anthology entitled *Australian University Verse: An Undergraduate Anthology 1920-1922* (Melbourne, 1922).

In 1921 he became one of the first members of the infant Australian Communist Party, later claiming to have held ticket no. 45. Though he was most unlikely to have been a passive, merely dues-paying member there is no public record of his party activity. Historians of the party, such as J. N. Rawling, would have been ready enough to refer to it. What he did in England a few years later is another matter.

After graduating in arts at Brisbane in 1922 he left to teach, like 'Jersey' Burton, at Ipswich Grammar School. There he formed a communist association which met monthly for lectures and debates, but was probably not connected with the official party organization. Stephensen did some enthusiastic work in Ipswich among industrial workers for the Workers' Educational Association. For part of the time he was at Ipswich, D. H. Lawrence was at Thirroul on the south coast of N.S.W., busy on *Kangaroo,* which was to be published the following year, 1923. As a freelance reviewer for Brisbane's Labor newspaper, the *Daily Standard,* Stephensen wrote what was probably the first notice of any depth and consequence published about the book in Australia. Later he was to have personal dealings with Lawrence.

In 1924 he was selected Queensland's Rhodes Scholar, following Burton in 1922 and R. L. Hall in 1923. That other 'odd man out' in Queensland politics, Fred Paterson, who turned to communism in 1923, had been Rhodes Scholar in 1918. Reaching Oxford in October 1924, Stephensen enrolled in the School of Philosophy and Political Economics (P.P.E.). He also discovered new and exciting scope for his political enthusiasms. As it had been in Brisbane, so too in England his prime aim was, as he told a friend, to startle the *bourgeoisie* who, in their post-war gloom, were only too easy to shock. The success of the 'Zinoviev letter' in October 1924 which put Baldwin in power showed this.

As a member of the Oxford University Labour Club and, according to a fellow-student, one of the four members of the Communist Party at Oxford, he was busy propagandizing. One of his most explosive exploits was to spread Gandhian anti-imperialist leaflets among the seventy or so Indian students. *The Times* of 9 December 1925 referred to 'two non-Indians at Oxford who had been engaged in secret propaganda among members of the Majlis, the university Indian society'. Eight days later in the House of Commons[2] Lieutenant-Colonel Cuthbert James, M.P. for Bromley, asked the Home Secretary, Joynson-Hicks, whether it was true that communist leaflets of an indictable nature, printed in a foreign country, had recently been circulated among Indians at Oxford University. 'Jix' replied that he was aware of this but trusted that he would not be pressed for a further statement—one of those classic 'gentlemanly' evasions by those in power who believe that democracy is all very well so long as the governing is left to them.

Stephensen's part in the leaflet incident had apparently been discovered from papers seized when police raided the Communist Party headquarters in London in 1925, an event confused in the memory of many contemporaries with the more notorious Arcos (All Russian Co-operative Society) raid of 1927, an incident yet to be adequately chronicled.

Lord Birkenhead, a man whose main pleasure at that time was looking under beds for Bolsheviks, was the Conservative government's Secretary of State for India. Predictably, he wanted all students involved in the attempt to influence the Indians to be expelled. As a friend and former student of the University's Vice-Chancellor, Dr J. Wells, he could expect considerable support. Wells, a crusty Tory, first approached the students' colleges—Stephensen was at Queen's—and asked them to take action. J. R. Magrath, Provost of Queen's, then in his nineties and once a pupil of J. S. Mill, stood up to Wells with a characteristically forthright refusal. Wells had then to call in the undergraduates himself and ask them to sign the following undertaking on pain of expulsion: 'I solemnly promise that, so long as I am a resident member of the Oxford University, I will hold no communication, direct or indirect, with any organised Communist association, and that I will not endeavour to propagate Communist ideas either directly or indirectly.' After signing, an unabashed Stephensen told a reporter that the action of the Vice-Chancellor in compelling him to sign a promise not to propagate communist views was 'quite in accordance with the conservative traditions of Oxford authorities who are notorious for their resistance to new vital ideas of each succeeding generation'. The Vice-Chancellor, he added, had unlimited power. His word was law and he, Stephensen, wished to continue his studies.

Other students objected to the Vice-Chancellor's action and a lively meeting of protest at the Union Society saw an overwhelming majority against it. Under society rules a ballot of the whole society, including life members, dons and clergy, could be called for, and this was arranged, resulting in a vote of 367 in favour of censuring the action of the Vice-Chancellor and 403 against.

All this was manna to the still untamed young man from Queensland, who found he was the centre of attention for his political activity. He was then the subject of a leader in *The Times* of 16 February 1926: accepting a scholarship for a 'career of Communist organisation' might be an act of thoughtlessness but was none the less 'palpably dishonest'. *The Times* maintained that the University authorities had been excessively tolerant over the whole affair.

Stephensen said that he left the Communist Party in 1926 over this incident. In later years, according to his audience and mood, he was to find differing explanations of this parting. As time went on he became more concerned about his place in history; his self-consciousness had become more acutely developed. In 1944 he stated that he had resigned from the party completely after his talk with the Vice-Chancellor, and that he had had nothing to do with it after that, except to oppose its policies. In 1954 he wrote that he had discarded Marxian communism in 1926 having found it 'only banditry disguised as a political philosophy'. But back in 1939 his version had been that he had resigned 'following the fiasco of the British general strike of that year, which was a Communist fiasco.' Jack Lindsay's brother Philip, a more detached observer, wrote in his autobiography that Stephensen was a 'volatile Communist' as late as the autumn of 1929.

Stephensen's part-time work for the communist *Sunday Worker* outlasted his 1926 'break' with the party. There are several contributions signed with his name, though not on political matters, in 1928 and 1929, and several of its book reviews, signed only with initials or pen-names, look suggestively like his (it can be taken no further than this). There was one Tomais Aodh, whose identity nobody at the present *Morning Star* can recall, who wrote of the 'forgivable' luxury of gloating over beautiful books. This appeared just at the time that Stephensen was busy producing beautiful books.

There was another, 'Percy Flage', thought not to be Stephensen, who contributed verse on Birkenhead and Oxford.

There is ample evidence to back Stephensen's claim that while he was a communist he was an effective one. In Paris during Oxford vacations, as well as taking delivery of the leaflets 'Jix' and Birkenhead found so objectionable, he translated Lenin's *Imperialism* and *On the Road to Insurrection* from the French.

Three years after Vere Gordon Childe published his restrained but sour view of the internal power struggles of the Australian labour movement in *How Labour Governs,* Stephensen 'looked back in anger', though with less first-hand knowledge, on the same subject in a *Communist Review* article (February 1926) entitled 'The Democratic Arcadia—Some Reflections on the Australian Labour Movement'.

Britain's general strike of 3 to 12 May 1926 gave Stephensen a welcome chance for activity. He was one of the leaders of the University (pro-) strike committee. Though many students acted as strike-breakers mainly for the fun of it, some, including the Labour Club, supported the strikers. These included Hugh Gaitskell, A. J. P. Taylor and John Parker. Parker, now Labour M.P. for Dagenham, remembers Stephensen speaking at meetings in the surrounding Oxfordshire villages. Taylor[3] recalls Stephensen devising errands and inventing tasks for undergraduate volunteers to give them something to do when in truth there was nothing significant to be done in Oxford. Taylor said that Stephensen referred to having had experience of 'Wobbly' strikes on the Sydney waterfront and was prepared for similar rough times. It is hard to see how this could have been so, as Stephensen had never been a member of the Industrial Workers of the World, although he had known some who were members. At the time he would have been in Sydney there were no 'Wobbly' strikes.

Stephensen took second-class honours in P.P.E. (or 'Modern Greats') in 1927, but he did not bother to pay the fee and take out his degree. Although his academic record was a creditable achievement, he felt that England had more to offer. He was not ready to return to Queensland, if indeed the thought of persevering with his original intention of teaching there still remained. Seeking an occupation permitting him to 'display his panache in a stormy wind' (to use Jack Lindsay's colourful phrase) he fell in with Jack Kirtley, an amateur publisher of limited editions who was operating as the Fanfrolico Press, a book-publishing venture he had begun in Sydney. Kirtley, 'a quite reserved chap who could be jovial and Australianly sardonic now and then' (according to Lindsay), had become tired of the

English and wanted to get back home. He handed over all the assets, which consisted of Fanfrolico editions of Norman Lindsay, to Jack Lindsay. Stephensen willingly filled Kirtley's vacancy and became manager.

In their nine months together Kirtley and Lindsay had published only four books. Between late 1927 and early 1929 Stephensen vigorously expanded the enterprise. One joint venture was the production of the *London Aphrodite* literary magazine along lines similar to the Sydney magazine *Vision,* which Lindsay, Ken Slessor and Frank Johnson published in 1923–4. *Vision* had run for four issues, the *London Aphrodite* for a planned six. High-spirited, it was devised largely as a counterblast to J. C. Squire's comparatively pedestrian *London Mercury.* Stephensen saw Squire as 'the leading representative of a deplorable type (the critic) in the contemporary world of English letters—he is an apotheosis of the average.'

In their *Aphrodite* Stephensen and Lindsay provided an outlet for Aldous Huxley, Rhys Davies, Liam O'Flaherty, W. J. Turner, T. F. Powys, Brian Penton and Karel Capek and blew off a certain amount of steam. Some verse in the fourth issue showed that politics still concerned Stephensen:

> The middling class, the piddling class, they feed the brutes a bit:
> and the working men of England, they ain't satisfied with it.

If this and other Stephensen offerings sounded a trifle light-weight they had much in common with his taunting satires on contemporary English and political absurdities: a preface to Beresford Egan's *The Sink of Solitude* (Hermes Press), and his *Policeman of the Lord* (Sophistocles Press) and *The Well of Sleevelessness* (Scholartis Press, belonging to Eric Partridge). There was no limit to the invention of these proliferating presses which did no actual printing and owned no actual machinery. Fanfrolico, however, was different (though it, too, had no printing press) in that it succeeded in publishing many fine books, some in limited editions on very costly paper with matching prices. There was Jack Lindsay's translation of the *Lysistrata* (1926) illustrated by Norman Lindsay, Hugh McCrae's *Satyrs and Sunlight* (1928) and Ken Slessor's *Earth Visitors* (1926). These are now collectors' items. Norman Lindsay's Dionysian view of life was, according to D. H. Lawrence, more than adequately represented. Lawrence regarded the seven massive Fanfrolico volumes given to him by Stephensen as 'a waste of good printing'. Even so, he was pleased to have the offer by Fanfrolico to publish a volume of his paintings, though before this project became reality it was handed to a new concern, the Mandrake Press. This consisted of Stephensen as manager, financed by a London bookseller, Edward Goldston, a Jew. Stephensen left Fanfrolico, and another Queenslander, Brian Penton (whom he had met at the University of Queensland in 1920 but had never liked) moved in.

Stephensen has noted with some pleasure that Fanfrolico collapsed nine months after Penton took over. In later years Stephensen sued the *Bulletin* in Sydney over a comment by Penton on a book Stephensen had published, but their disagreement had begun before that. Looking back, Stephensen saw the colourful Fanfrolico venture as 'an example of Australian striving, though its emphasis was away from Australia'. An account of Fanfrolico written by Lindsay and Penton was regarded by Stephensen as an instance of 'senseless malice' as it entirely omitted to record his work and minimized Kirtley's pioneering role. (This fugitive publication is unavailable even in leading Australian libraries; Stephensen's account is the sole reference.) Philip Lindsay has noted that the final failure of Fanfrolico must be largely blamed on his brother Jack.

How Mandrake, Stephensen's second press, began is also a matter of dispute. Lindsay's version is that he handed over Lawrence's paintings and the backing of Goldston, who had earlier been interested in Fanfrolico, to ensure Stephensen a good start. Stephensen said that the press was formed because Lawrence did not wish to be associated with the Lindsays.

Mandrake's edition of Lawrence's paintings made a good profit. An edition of five hundred at 10 guineas, plus an extra ten on special paper at 50 guineas, sold out in a week, bringing Lawrence a much-needed £577 in royalties. Lawrence had been sanguine about the future of Mandrake: 'I hope nobody will ever try to pull it up by the roots', he wrote on 14 May 1929. Later, on 20 February 1930, the tired novelist, angry with most of the world, frustrated and in ill-health, took a different view: 'Oh, that Mandrake, vegetable of ill omen.'

Stephensen helped to publish an undercover edition of *Lady Chatterley's Lover* in a London basement in November 1929, the first English edition printed in England but with a protective 'Printed in Italy' tag. He also published, under the Mandrake imprint, Lawrence's essay, *Apropos of Lady Chatterley's Lover* and, under his own name, a limited edition for five hundred subscribers of Lawrence's poems, *Pansies*.

So acutely perceptive in his vision of Australia during his 1922 visit, as shown both by his letters and by *Kangaroo,* Lawrence took little time to sum up Stephensen. His main complaint grew to be that Stephensen would 'pop up like a bubble', was 'another sort of mushroom—he grows too fast', was 'a bit of a windbag' and had 'unreasonable antipathies'.

Lawrence told his wife Frieda that Stephensen was not an artist but a businessman. Lawrence's estimate of one side of Stephensen's character fits in with that of others like Philip Lindsay who saw him as 'tall, fair, handsome, noisy, generous, but a trifle deaf . . . in manner and appearance, the typical Queenslander, the Cornstalk from Banana-land, a turbulent merry fellow, whom no-one could dislike'. Another friend, Herbert Burton, saw him as 'never dull', and Jack Lindsay, who had definite reservations about Stephensen in other matters, admitted freely that the man had a 'breezy magnificence of manner' and an 'unfailing panache'. He impressed the novelist, Rhys Davies, as 'a most likeable man' with 'a sort of over-forceful interior pressure'. Davies was present when Stephensen met Lawrence at Bandol in the south of France. Lawrence seemed to find the young Australian attractive but overwhelming. They stayed up talking late one night, and the next morning Lawrence remarked to Davies that after Stephensen left his room the walls still shook and he could not sleep. Another observer at Bandol was Barbara Barr, née Weekly, Lawrence's stepdaughter. Lawrence, she said, had been looking forward to this visit of the 'cheerful colonial'. She herself found him a 'jolly, go-ahead sort of person'. Stephensen read aloud to the Lawrence ménage one of his short stories about an older woman leading a beautiful woman astray. Lawrence 'demolished it for him at once', according to Barbara Barr, for its unreal emotions and situations. Such a rejection must have hurt Stephensen but he went ahead and not long afterwards published his only volume of short stories, The Bushwhackers. He subtitled these Sketches of Life in the Australian Outback and many years later referred to them as 'a burst of Australianity uttered at a time when Australian literature was down in the dumps', but even Morris Miller, a great admirer of Stephensen, could not manage to say more of these stories in his survey of Australian writing than that they were 'partly humorous and partly satirical' (page 775).

Mandrake did not last long, even though, according to Stephensen, it lost no money. It became entangled with Aleister Crowley, that English dabbler in the occult, the self-styled 'Beast of the Revelation', whom Stephensen described as 'difficult to handle'. Worse, times were becoming harder. Limited editions, as Eric Partridge also found with Scholartis, were a luxury people found they could do without during the Depression. Stephensen and Goldston sold out to Crowley's friends.

Stephensen had married a classical ballerina, Winifred Lockyer. It was her second marriage, and she stood by him loyally to his death. Almost ready to return to Australia, his final literary endeavours in England were to compile a book on *Harry Buckland, Master of Hounds* for Faber, and a biography, *Pavlova,* in collaboration with Walford Hyden, for Constable.

It is more than likely that he tackled these books in a purely commercial spirit. He can have made very little money out of the Fanfrolico Press and even less from Mandrake. In his final years in England he found it a struggle to earn enough for food and lodgings. At one stage he edited a small greyhound racing paper to make a few pounds.

Why did he want to leave Britain? Was he just short of money, or homesick, or did he believe that Britain was played out? In 1938 he wrote that he left Britain at the end of 1932 'partly because I believed an impending British decline to be inevitable . . . partly because I believed, or hoped, that an Australian resurgence would be possible.' Whatever the reason, he left for home after having received an invitation to carry on his work as a publisher in Sydney.

Norman Lindsay had seen him in 1931 in London where they had discussed publishing prospects in Australia. Lindsay returned to Australia early in 1932 and, assured of backing, Stephensen followed. By October he was in Sydney telling reporters that British publishers preferred novels with American settings. A mild Anglophobia was already apparent. Did it hide a deeper hatred? Did he feel he had been a failure while in England? An unkind editorial comment in the *Australian Quarterly* for October 1938 suggested something of the kind. Though not named, Stephensen is certainly the target: 'It has not been unknown, for instance, to find advocates of Australian culture embrace Australian culture only after they failed to make money out of English culture. It is not unknown that Australian Nationalism should be the outward cover of antipathy to Britain.'

Though he may not have made money, Stephensen had hardly been a failure. He had gained academic honours. He had a fine record in the publishing of good literature. He had had an exciting time in British politics. Mandrake may have been a disappointing side-alley after the dashing Fanfrolico affair, but it was hardly enough to sour a man for long. After eight years away and the prospect of a new start in Sydney he had reason to be cheerful. His later battle to get finance for his Australian book-publishing plans and his fight with British publishers over access to the Australian market could have been, and no doubt were, embittering.

Stephensen in his years as an active Australian nationalist tended to rationalize his departure from Britain as being due not to the fact that he was at a dead end and interested in Lindsay's Sydney proposition, but rather to a vision of imperial decline. He was pleased to be able to note that his course had gone parallel to that of the earlier Queensland bookfellow, A. G. Stephens, who had also, thirty-eight years earlier, come to Sydney, via London, at the invitation of the *Bulletin*. Between 1897 and 1906 Stephens saw through the presses twenty-three Australian books, including *Such is Life*. Stephensen's association with the book publishing ventures of the *Bulletin* was much shorter; he stayed only a year. Both were blamed for wasting time and money over the format of books, though Stephens more than Stephensen. In a lecture on Stephens to the Fellowship of Australian Writers in 1940, Stephensen referred to his near-namesake as 'an Australian critic and patriot', adding, 'We need more patriots and critics if our Nation is to survive'.

Soon after his return from England in October 1932 Stephensen was made managing director of the Australian Book Publishing Company which had The Endeavour Press as its trademark. With finance from the *Bulletin* the press turned out more than thirty volumes, including Norman Lindsay's *Saturdee*. The directors of the new enterprise were S. H. Prior (who died in 1933 and was replaced by Cecil Mann), H. K. Prior, Norman Lindsay and G. F. L. Bombelli.

With characteristic confidence and vitality Stephensen plunged into a publishing programme for Endeavour, convinced that it must succeed. Unfortunately his estimate of local literary talent awaiting publication was higher than our hindsight now suggests was realistic, but he had reasonable grounds for his optimism. After all, did not Henry Handel Richardson, Leslie Meller, Vance Palmer and others have to go to London to be published? Did not poetry by Christopher Brennan, Hugh McCrae and William Baylebridge remain unpublished? Surely we were ready for a literary renaissance? Anyway, it was high time we gave up the role of a literary Crown colony. So Endeavour published *Saturdee,* G. B. Lancaster's *Pageant,* stories by 'Kodak' (Ernest O'Ferrall), Banjo Paterson's *The Animals Noah Forgot,* Bernard Cronin's *The Sow's Ear* and republished Louis Stone's *Jonah.* Brian Penton's *Landtakers* was added to the list after Stephensen left late in 1933.

With the unpublished manuscript of *Capricornia* under his arm,

Xavier Herbert, believing that the millennium had at last come for Australian letters, set off to see Stephensen. Meeting him at the *Bulletin* office, he found him 'obviously unimpressed'. It took five years and many disappointments before the first edition of Herbert's classic eventually appeared as a book, financed by Miles. However in 1938, the year of publication, Stephensen maintained that the long delay was proof that Australia was 'a literary boghole'. About twenty years later he saw the Endeavour Press as 'a striving by Australians to get out of the colonial groove.'

At the end of his one-year contract Stephensen parted company with the *Bulletin*. An argument with Bombelli, the printer, was apparently the main reason for this. (They often argued about matters of style.) Stephensen insisted on the destruction and reprinting of 3,000 copies of Paterson's *The Animals Noah Forgot,* against the protests of Bombelli who maintained that the book was well printed. Stephensen had other differences with the board.* When he left, he took some books with him to publish by agreement.

After leaving Endeavour the ever-optimistic Stephensen looked around for backers for another publishing house. His ideas remained grandiose. (When he was starting Endeavour he told Harley Matthews that he intended to publish a book a week by Australian authors.) Some of the *de luxe* edition atmosphere of Fanfrolico had certainly taken a shaking from the Depression but Stephensen was still 'thinking big'.

In a preliminary announcement for his new publishing house, P. R. Stephensen & Co. Ltd, he said that a former Governor of New South Wales, the Earl of Beauchamp—the man who had befriended Henry Lawson—would be chairman of directors. Its headquarters would be in Canberra with branch offices in all States and in New Zealand. This grand plan was not realized. P. R. Stephensen & Co. began publishing from Bond Street, Sydney, with a slight offering by Henry Handel Richardson, *The Bath,* her first book published in her homeland. Other worth-while books, plus a few dull makeweights, followed. One notable venture was the launching of Eleanor Dark with her *Prelude to Christopher.* There was also Randolph Hughes's study, *C. J. Brennan—An Essay in Values,* one of the first contributions to what has now become a vast academic industry, the dissection of the great master's works. Another Stephensen book, Vivian Crockett's *Mezzomorto,* was treated coldly by Brian Penton in a

---

* Harley Matthews, the Sydney vigneron-poet, remembers being told by H. K. Prior of the *Bulletin* that the Endeavour Press under Stephensen showed a loss of £10,000.

review for the *Bulletin* under the name 'Con Bennett'. Stephensen sued the *Bulletin,* claiming that the criticism was malicious, and after a week-long hearing in October 1936 was awarded £750 general damages.

In 1934 Stephensen went to Canberra, planning to incorporate a new venture, his National Book Publishing House with £50,000 nominal capital. However he was unable to proceed with flotation, and vainly cast around for finance. At one stage in 1935 he had to declare himself bankrupt, and he was perennially hard up until he met Miles. Hal Porter recalls how Stephensen wrote to him about this time suggesting that Porter's work was ideally suited to a real literary magazine and did he have £200 to help finance such a magazine?[4]

Capricornia, originally advertised for publication in May 1934, did not appear under the Stephensen imprint. The two tons of type it involved had to be melted down to meet the creditors of the collapsed company.

Stephensen was on to a good thing with *Capricornia* but his attraction to the work of William Blocksidge, the Brisbane poet-philosopher who adopted the name 'William Baylebridge', did not reflect the same perception. Stephensen met Baylebridge, who gave him £100 to help set up his Bond Street publishing venture,[5] in 1933 and in the following years acted as his literary sponsor and typographical adviser: most of Baylebridge's works were privately printed.

Baylebridge had swallowed a heady draught of Nietzsche (whose *Antichrist* Stephensen had translated and published in 1929 when he was with the Fanfrolico Press) and, as Hugh Trevor-Roper has neatly remarked, 'many people . . . have been rendered almost insensible on reading Nietzsche'. Baylebridge was certainly our 'oddest' writer, to use the expression of Judith Wright who was not impressed by his 'paranoid rhetoric'. Reviewing a collection entitled *Salvage,* published in 1965, Gustav Cross wrote that 'nobody who was really a poet could have written these stilted, ungainly verses, full of archaisms, ejaculations and false poeticisms'. The *Bulletin* in 1912 thought Baylebridge's *The New Life* was an astonishing thing to have come from Australia—'astonishing in its crudeness and occasional strength, equally astonishing in its gassy rhetoric and its foolishness'.

Stephensen thought highly of him and the reason is fairly apparent: there is, in Baylebridge, an aggressively nationalistic content. At all events Baylebridge became with Stephensen almost as great an obsession as another philosopher, Morley Roberts, became in 1940 with W. J. Miles. Stephensen did not easily drop an idea, a friend or an enmity.

By 1935, when his publishing ventures were lying in ruins, he was still in the literary mainstream, still on good terms with the literary fraternity, a vice-president of the Fellowship of Australian Writers, not yet naggingly Anglophobic and in most ways seemingly a good liberal. He agreed to chair a public meeting of welcome in Sydney to the radical Czech author, Egon Kisch, apologizing to Kisch for the churlish attitude of the Lyons government in refusing him permission to land. R. G. Menzies, the Attorney-General, had said that Kisch would be barred 'because of his subversive views and his association and affiliations with Communist organisations'. Kisch managed to get ashore by the simple expedient of jumping off the ship and breaking a leg. Before the Sydney welcome Stephensen characteristically prepared himself thoroughly for his job as chairman, consulting an encyclopedia at the Czech consulate about Kisch's qualifications. According to Kisch, Stephensen's revelations constituted the first occasion that his literary bona fides had been established. Unfortunately the encyclopedia was very old and its contents consequently dated, but the thought was there.

In July 1935, about the time he met Miles, Stephensen chaired a meeting called to form a New South Wales branch of the Book Censorship Abolition League. He was also writing section 2 of *The Foundations of Culture in Australia,* in which he railed against 'developments in the Sydney Domain and on Yarra Bank, the fantastic proceedings against Egon Kisch, the banning of periodicals by the Post Office solely on political grounds . . . the prohibition of anti-war meetings and processions in Sydney and Melbourne'. He was also setting down an even more significant paragraph:

Fascism is a greater menace to us than Bolshevism could ever be; for Fascism is a schoolboy bully, armed. It has no intellectual pretensions, aims at imposing discipline 'from above', is a Junker-idea, a Hun-idea which Australians have fought to abolish from the earth. Bolshevism at least has a humanitarian goal, a cogent philosophy and a professed respect for ideas.

He called on intellectuals to give the common man a lead in proclaiming 'Australia First' as the only constructive national idea.

This essay was to be probably his final public statement as a liberal. It is more than suggestive that his change of attitude to political and social questions from there on coincided with his association with Miles.

4

The *Publicist*

OFTEN INFURIATING, more often dully repetitive, always argumentative, at times childish, the *Publicist* was all these things from its start in 1936 to its final issue in March 1942. It badly needed a good sub-editor with authority, but as most of the tediousness came from the editor (who also paid the bills) its rank growths went unpruned. If Miles wanted to use page after page for a speech by Hitler, who was to stop him? If he felt like arguing his old *Ross's* favourite of 'Is war biologically inevitable?' there was nobody to deny him. Miles, not Stephensen, was master and fully so until illness kept him away. At times Stephensen had something bright and even original to say; Miles was invariably unoriginal and wearisome. Only once in all his contributions did there seem a prospect of something entertaining—in April 1941 he commented on having seen police spying on four men and two women nude in the bush at Heathcote Creek— but even this fizzled into nothing after its promising beginning.

Planning for the *Publicist* began in the first half of 1936 at informal conferences between Miles and Stephensen and one or other of Miles's associates, Salier, Hooper and Masey. According to Masey, it was at a dinner Miles gave in March to celebrate the publication of Stephensen's *Foundations* that he announced his plans to produce the *Publicist,* starting in July.

Miles set up the journal's office at 209a Elizabeth Street, in the T. & G. Building. He engaged a typist, and a boy to make daily calls for him at the Stock Exchange. Miles was to have full and sole editorial discretion, but Stephensen was taken on as his literary assistant for £20 a month (rising to £42 after the first year). (Stephensen was also able to earn money doing what he acknowledged to be 'hack work' for other authors. He estimated this brought between £100 and £200 annually.)

The *Publicist,* sixteen unillustrated pages set between yellow covers, was sold partly by subscription and partly on news stands, mainly in Sydney. To say it was unillustrated is near enough to the truth but, in fact, five pictures were used between 1937 and 1941: portraits of Xavier Herbert and Morley Roberts, a bust of A. G. Stephens, a candid shot of a girl at the 'disgraceful' school at Wanaaring (one hundred miles 'back o' Bourke') and, most entertaining of all, a picture of Stephensen with an Aboriginal captioned, 'One of these two is P. R. Stephensen'. Normally 3,000 copies of each monthly issue were printed though never more than 2,250 were sold. War-time paper rationing forced the monthly print down to 1,000 copies. In its final stages it had 258 subscribers on its books. Miles expected the publication would make a loss—and make a loss it certainly did, with no advertising from start to finish. Cantankerous and polemical, it never provided temptation for the businessman with a commercial message to announce. But although Miles spent heavily on it, this may not have been without its compensations. He once told an acquaintance, and he was not a man given to either idle or boastful chatter, that the shop, the typist, the boy and Stephensen all figured as tax deductions. In effect, the *Publicist* was jointly financed by Miles and the Commonwealth government.

Miles, writing first as 'John Benauster' and later also as 'Alcedo Gigas', set the querulous tone that many other contributors came increasingly to adopt. In March 1939 Miles, who did not once write under his own name, explained his pen-names. 'Benauster' came from 'ben' meaning 'well' or 'good', and 'auster' was the root of Australia, the south or the south wind. 'Alcedo Gigas' was a slight rearrangement of *Dacelo gigas,* the ornithological name for the kookaburra. Occasionally, too, he wrote as 'L. M. Veron', the name, he said, of a political writer who married into the Miles family in the nineteenth century. There was in fact a Mrs Leah Margaret Veron living at Epping who complained she had been wrongly identified with the writer and had been visited by police. Stephensen, who usually had little objection to being known publicly for his opinions, also came to affect pen-names. One was 'Rex Williams', evolved from King Billy, a typical example of *Publicist* humour. Cecil Salier mainly appeared as 'H. B. Thomas'; Mrs Dora Watts was 'Anna Brabant'. Mercifully, Stephensen was usually given extensive space, thus ensuring that the *Publicist* was, on balance, worth buying by those con-

The Publicist

THE PAPER LOYAL TO AUSTRALIA FIRST

No. 50.   SYDNEY   1st AUGUST, 1940.   MONTHLY, 6d.

Rightist Number

Price, 6d.

cerned about the growth of an Australian national spirit and able to put up with a fair amount of hectoring.

Like most minority journals, the *Publicist* was extremely self-conscious and any mention of it in the columns of its contemporaries was welcome, however abusive the notice. The *Publicist* was forever explaining its *raison d'être* and eternally haggling about unimportant passages in the criticisms it attracted elsewhere.

The editorial in the first issue stated: 'No writer will be a writer for this paper unless he stands definitely for Australia First'. It further explained that the aim was not to found a new political party. 'Our aim is limited to arousing in Australians a positive feeling, a distinctive Australian patriotism of a thoroughly realistic kind'. Miles noted, and he repeated it several times later, that Australia First, the paper's masthead slogan, necessarily relegated the remainder of the British Empire to second place.

'We believe', ran the editorial in the fifth issue, 'quite 80 per cent of people in Australia cannot think in terms of Australia First. That belief of ours created *The Publicist*.' So the journal, consciously a minority opinion organ, which once suggested it could fairly be described as 'Australian Tory', pushed the Australian barrow in all matters, large and small. There was nothing particularly high-minded in its advocacy, petty rancour being all too often involved. The *Publicist* gave the impression of saying things that badly needed saying but which others were either not saying at all, or not saying loudly enough. Yet, searching for detail to buttress this opinion, surprisingly little can be found. There were, in fact, very few notable contributions. One of these was 'My Army, O, My Army', by Harley Matthews, a plea typical of his forthrightness, for a more democratic army with less saluting, less servility and less paraphernalia, such as swords, from earlier ages.

Stephensen generally supplied a budget of varied comment under the heading of 'The Bunyip Critic'. Often he had something worth saying but blunted its impact by including it in a deluge of verbiage. Behind all his praise of things Australian and gibes at what he saw as attacks on Australia lay his opinion that Australia had a 'differentness' able to be imparted to those born here. (Exactly what was involved in this 'differentness' he never satisfactorily explained.) 'If not,' he wrote in July 1938, 'there is no hope for us, and we are merely "citizens of the world".' He thought, in 1936, that 'no cause, outside Australian boundaries, is worth the spilling of a single drop of Australian blood.'

Miles was more prone to preach in a pale imitation of the speeches by Hitler that the *Publicist* began to publish in 1938. Both Miles and Stephensen lacked a sense of proportion; most unsuccessful political proselytizers do. They flogged the same tired arguments through edition after edition. Anyone who annoyed them, or slapped their favourites, or was seen to 'insult' Australia (whatever that meant) was pursued with columns of petty abuse. The *Publicist* amassed enemies and gained very few friends. Some simpler patriots were won over. Enemies came faster when Miles broadened the range of his comment to include discussion of German, Japanese and Italian policies. Hitler's Reichstag speech of 30 January 1937 was favourably compared with the attack by W. M. Hughes on German repudiation of the Versailles Treaty. Most, though not all, references to the Axis powers and their right to behave as they thought best came from Miles. However the first *Publicist* references to Japan came from Salier (as 'H. B. Thomas') who sought friendship with that country and, in March 1937, dismissed the idea of any Japanese invasion in force of Australia. Stephensen gradually followed Miles, at a distance. At one stage he commented to Kirtley that Hitler was a damn nuisance—he took too much space in the *Publicist*. But before long he was taking up the Miles line; a typical comment in June 1939 being, 'Why need Australians bemoan the absorption of Czechoslovakia by Germany when Australia is already "absorbed" by British and American Jew-Capitalists?'

'Alcedo Gigas' in July 1937 saw Germany's Count Felix von Luckner, that not universally welcomed visitor to Australia, as 'a good German', and contrasted the complaints of intellectuals about his visit with their protests at Egon Kisch's exclusion.

The *Publicist* was far from being alone in its pro-Axis policy of the thirties. When Eric Baume[1] broadcast violently anti-Nazi views in his 2GB radio commentaries in 1938 the controllers of that station gave in to pressure from the German Consul-General, Dr Asmis, and had the criticism stopped. A number of political figures who are still living had their mild flirtations with Fascism, as had Lord Rothermere of the London *Daily Mail* early in 1934. One military intelligence officer who had visited Japan and written pro-Japanese articles before the war became a prisoner of the Japanese on Amboina. It would be quite wrong to imagine that Stephensen and Miles were the only publicists being cultivated by German and Japanese officials in Sydney. What was special about their fondness for Fascism was that it was combined with a raucous chauvinism.

Particularly in the early issues of the *Publicist,* there were a number of contributors outside the inner circle of backers who had little or nothing to do with the political 'line' of the publication. These included George Farwell (who wrote on early Australian theatre), Randolph Bedford and John Manifold, and, later, H. E. Holland, Alistair Kershaw and Rex Ingamells. Among the less frequent contributors, Hardy Wilson and Kirtley were, however, clearly sympathetic. Randolph Bedford was *persona grata* until he clashed with Miles over the inevitability of war.[2] Masey was another substantial *Publicist* contributor from 1936–42, tackling serious matters of economics and demography. If not the most exciting of writers, he was never insulting, petty or objectionable.

The propaganda load came to be borne principally by the editor, his assistant and that Gallipoli veteran and World War I Military Medallist, Martin Watts from Liverpool, New South Wales, who was interested, like Kirtley, in defence and allied matters. Watts was influenced by his wife Dora who was more intensely political. How far the increasingly intransigent racial note of his contributions was due to her is hard to assess, although she maintains that she only helped to correct his poor spelling and grammar. An army Intelligence officer who called on Watts referred to 'petticoat government' and noted: 'He was quite prepared to be frank and open and would have told me considerably more than he did but his wife kept a very good check on him'.

A list of those who annoyed Miles or Stephensen and thus generated *Publicist* attacks reads like a directory of Australia's principal inter-war intellectual stimulants. H. G. Wells was a 'septuagenarian superficialist' and a 'British bounder'. Professor Ernest Scott was 'quite undeep as a historian'. Stephensen found it necessary to count the number of Australian-born among the people mentioned by Scott in footnotes in *Australia During the War* as being important or prominent in Australia from 1914 to 1918 and found only 286 out of a total of 558. He found that 120 of the non-Australians were 'agents and representatives of Britain'. Others to be ground in the *Publicist*'s mill were Bishop Burgmann, Professors S. H. Roberts and G. V. Portus, Eric Baume, Hartley Grattan, Vance Palmer, Cyril Pearl and R. G. Menzies (seen as standing for 'Britain First').

The *Publicist* not only welcomed criticism of the harshest kind as a sign that it was getting attention but published large sections of the unfavourable comment, followed, of course, by longer sections of comment and reply. Thus scanning its columns enabled one to discover not only what the paper was saying but also the response of its critics. Bishop Burgmann, attacked by Stephensen for being an Australian in the Church of England, replied: 'I have never had to

endure Oxford and therefore Englishmen do not get on my nerves
as they do on those of Mr. Stephensen. My Nationalism is not speci-
fically anti-British.'

Hartley Grattan, that tireless American student of Australia, was
startled by Stephensen's reaction to an address he had given in
Canberra on 30 January 1938 before the summer school of the
Australian Institute of Political Science.* Grattan had been discussing the likelihood of Australia remaining neutral in a world war
involving Britain.

Neutrality was a subject which had greatly concerned the United
States; Neutrality Acts had been passed in 1935, 1936 and 1937.
In Australia, as Grattan pointed out, the notion had hardly been
considered ('In foreign affairs, the Australian point of view has yet
to run the gamut of expression from A to B'). Grattan told the
summer school that he had been unable to discover any reason for
doubting Australia's technical legal right to declare herself neutral.
However no neutrality policy that would stand the test of practice
could violate the national interest for any significant period. He had
been unable to find any support for the idea that Australia wanted to
be neutral. Australian neutrality was a figment of the imagination of
metaphysicians of politics. He could only conclude that 'while the
legal right of Australia to declare itself neutral exists, the impulse
towards neutrality is almost totally lacking in Australia today.' Australia could not remain neutral in any general war likely to break
out in the visible future.

All this was a matter of central concern to the *Publicist,* with its
strong isolationist sentiment. Though Grattan had not in fact
expressed himself for or against isolationism, Stephensen chose to
regard the address as an attack on his nationalist-isolationist position. In an exasperating comment in the *Publicist* in March 1938 he
discussed Grattan's argument. He met reasoned historical narrative
and calm conjecture with a tedious rodomontade. Grattan, he said at
one point, 'ought to have more sense than to be taken in by the
abstract arguments of jurisprudence, which are of no more value
than the crackling of thorns under a pot. When Britain declares war,
Australia is automatically at war. Get that!'

At the time of the original argument Grattan defended himself at
length, and in April 1938 the *Publicist* allowed him four and a half

* Stephensen apparently did not attend this four-day symposium on 'Australian Foreign Policy'. Some *Publicist* supporters, including Valentine Crowley, did. Mrs Adela Pankhurst Walsh, later to enter this story, also spoke up
at discussion time to appeal for stronger Empire ties and an extension of the
Ottawa imperial preference trade agreements.

pages to reply. He complained about Stephensen's 'brawling manner' and called him, quite accurately, a 'staggeringly florid rhetorician'. He went further:

> What holds your attention in Stephensen's work is a feverish wonderment as to what will be said next. Mr. Stephensen's occasional side remarks and terminological inventions like 'Jew-Yank', John Benauster's full-dress articles and the weird cryptograms of Alcedo Gigas, all point, in my mind, in the wrong direction. I don't like the smell of the social program they seem to forecast.

Grattan wrote that Stephensen appeared to see nationalism as some sort of elixir of life which would transform Australia, whereas the essence of the matter was how Australian nationalism was to be implemented.

Another embattled critic of the *Publicist* was John McCallum who, like Masey, was a director of the Australian Institute of Political Science. McCallum referred in the October-December 1938 issue of the British *Political Quarterly* to the *Publicist* as a 'little known' mouthpiece of the 'inconsiderable' separatist opinion in Australia. What it advocated, he wrote, was important because it showed a shrewd appreciation of tendencies current in Australia but of which most Australians were unaware. In reply, Stephensen observed that where the editorial board of the *Political Quarterly* was not British it was Jewish. When this kind of response became habitual, as it did, there was clearly very little of his former liberalism left.

Although few Australian journals can have been so generous with space for those of opposing views there was at least one attack that was ignored. Was this because it was too well documented and too well aimed, with Miles for once, and not Stephensen, as the target? A former rationalist associate of Miles, J. N. Rawling, then a communist, launched this criticism in the August 1938 issue of *World Peace,* the organ of the Australian League for Peace and Democracy, a 'front' organization. The article, headed 'Loyal to Fascism First', named Miles as 'a man with a bee in his bonnet and with money to spend'. It noted that in the *Publicist* bookshop, alongside copies of the *Publicist,* there were copies of the Italian Fascist paper *Italo-Australian,* the German Nazi paper *Die Brücke* and pamphlets published by the Japan Pacific Association under the title *Japan-China, Who's it all About?*

Gradually, as more of the obvious nationalist bullets had been fired, the *Publicist* turned to the world scene, at a time when it was fairly clear that Spain would not be the last battleground. (Stephensen had prophesied a world war, involving Australia, for 1937.) First German policies were taken up to be admired, then Japanese.

Stephensen filled an odd corner of the journal in May 1937, at Miles's request, with a letter on Japan signed 'James White'. He chose 'White', he explained later, because it dealt with colour, the Asiatic question. 'As an Australian', he wrote in the letter, 'I say let the Japanese have a free hand in China.' Then in November 1937, as 'Rex Williams', he wrote that it was 'far better that Australia should rise with Japan in the Pacific than decline with Britain in the Atlantic.' This comment came after a call by the Sydney Trades Hall Council for a boycott of Japanese goods. Stephensen believed that Australia's 'irrational Japanic panic' a phrase that he was never to tire of using, was inspired by British propagandists. (Stephensen may have had some consolation in his final years in noting that Australia was in fact rising with Japan in the Pacific while Britain was going through difficult economic times in the Atlantic.)

Miles was more interested in Hitler but eventually commented (in July 1939, as 'L. M. Veron') that the 'pro-Japanism of *The Publicist* in the present great war between Chinese and Japanese is warranted on all the historical facts, and by the advantages that a Japanese victory should have for Australians.' He claimed that a 'stupid' Chinese attack on 7 July 1937 had begun the conflict. This was the notorious 'China Incident' engineered by the Japanese who had troops out on manoeuvres near a Chinese outpost on the Marco Polo bridge near Peking. Plainly looking for an excuse, any excuse, to develop their gradual, filtering movement across China into active aggression, outright war, the Japanese demanded permission to enter the walled town of Wanping. They claimed that one of their soldiers was 'missing'. When the Chinese authorities refused, the Japanese attacked with mortars. The incident was exploited further and before long expanded into full-scale war.[3]

It is difficult to know what sparked the pro-Japan policy of the *Publicist*. It was hardly in the Australian tradition.* Miles had been annoyed at government action in 1936 against Japanese textile manufacturers which favoured similar but dearer goods from Britain. Stephensen provided one clue in his March 1939 piece on Japan's 2,599th anniversary when he noted: 'Japan was, and remains, the only country in the world that is completely free of International Jew Finance.' For more than a year at this stage Miles had been

* D. H. Lawrence had noted in a letter written at Thirroul in June 1922: 'They are terribly afraid of the Japanese. Practically all Australians, and especially Sydney, feel that once there was a fall in England, so that the Powers could not interfere, Japan would at once walk in and occupy the place. They seriously believe this: say it is even the most obvious thing for Japan to do as a business proposition. Of course Australia would never be able to defend herself. It is queer to find these bogies wherever one goes. But I suppose they *may* materialise'.

publishing references, never complimentary, to the Jewish people. It began with a comment on S. H. Roberts's book on Germany, *The House that Hitler Built,* written after his study leave there in 1935–7. Said Miles: 'Roberts' summary of Hitler's case against the Jews appears to us to be a very good one.'

Miles thought that if the Jews were to obtain as great a relative influence and power in Australia as they did in Germany in the decade following 1918, anti-Semitism would increase proportionately in Australia. The *Publicist* decried the Jews for advocating internationalism and thus rivalling Australian or any other nationalism. Martin Watts and Hardy Wilson, Miles's architect, echoed him on this theme. (Hardy Wilson, like Miles a product of Newington College, had done little actual designing of buildings. He practised as a partner in the firm of Wilson, Neave and Berry for some years before retiring at the age of forty-six to devote himself to drawing and writing. He has been described as 'an 18th century man in the 20th century'.[4] He had a special interest in Greek and Chinese architecture.) Gradually the Jews became more hateful to *Publicist* writers and the peak was probably reached in 1939 when Hardy Wilson wrote that 'all the fuss' about Jews being persecuted was 'rubbish'. This was a full year after the widely publicized Jewish pogrom in Germany and at least five years after the aggressive anti-Semitic policy of the Nazis had become unambiguously apparent. War with Germany stopped the *Publicist*'s praise or excuses for German policies but it failed to stop its anti-Semitism.

The *Publicist* refused to be frightened by the word 'Fascist', though one must realize that in the thirties the word was not always used in the pejorative sense that it is now, but was then applied in a more naïve way. As the thirties progressed, however, there was less justification for this *naïveté*. Stephensen saw Fascism and Nazism —this was in the late thirties—as examples of regenerative Gentile philosophies emerging to combat international Semitism. He may not have believed this originally, but just wrote it to please Miles; however there was nothing in his later life to suggest he wanted to reconsider.

Had the *Publicist* confined itself to stressing the joys of things Australian and the achievements of Australian culture, plus a steady but unhysterical emphasis on the drawbacks of the imperial connection, it would hardly have attracted so justified an obloquy.

An early Stephensen contribution to the *Publicist,* to be much quoted later as an example of his antagonism to Britain, and stretched so as to be equated with disloyalty, expressed a valid opinion. This was his first satirical 'advertisement' in the first issue:

WANTED 500,000 young Australians, must be physically fit, perfect in wind and limb for use in Europe as soil fertilizers. Apply, stating nitrate content of body, to No. 10 Downing Street, England.

This was fair, if pungent, political comment. Obviously based on Australia's huge casualty figures in World War I, when 59,342 soldiers out of 331,780 on the battlefield were killed or died of wounds, it was a warning against any repetition. Many of the Australian losses arose from the orders of British commanders almost entirely out of touch with front-line reality, who ordered assaults involving casualties quite incommensurate with tactical gain. Yet some of Stephensen's colleagues took fright and ran for cover when this 'advertisement' was disinterred and offered as evidence of disaffection at the Clyne Inquiry (see chapter 12).

The *Publicist* also ran a satirical recruiting poster in 1936 and repeated it in five issues in 1937. It referred to the 'Great' European War expected in 1937, proclaiming:

DON'T GO!
Your Country Needs You
Australia will be Here!

Stephensen was rarely able to leave well alone and thoughtful comment gradually gave way to inanities such as: 'I prefer any Australian noise to any European noise.' Referring to the hated G. H. Cowling, Professor of English Language and Literature at the University of Melbourne, whom he saw as anti-Australian, he wrote: 'I do not know whether Cowling means "a little cow" or "a little cowl", but he does not cow or cowl me in the slightest.'

In September 1937 Stephensen opposed a request from the University of Sydney to the State government for a £1 million endowment on the ground that the academic staff had a fixation on Europe and neglected Australian literature and history. This had some basis in fact and he had discussed it all before in his *Foundations*. It was fair enough, but he probably overdid the attack on 'Europocentric' academics. He observed: 'Take any Sydney University B.A. and behold a mental dead fish, a kippered herring, smoked in European smoke and salted in European salt.'

Allied with the anti-Semitism and kindness towards Axis policy came another unwelcome note, one firmly in the Fascist tradition, and part of Fascism's flight from reason. The psychologist would refer to it as 'authoritarian submission'. It was implicit in this passage of Stephensen's in July 1939:

We need here a Mahomet, a Hideyoshi, a Cromwell—or a Hitler —a man of harsh vitality, a born leader, a man of action, not one sicklied o'er with the pale cast of thought. Fanatics are needed, crude harsh men, not sweet and decorous men, to arouse us from the lethargy of decadence, softness and lies which threatens death to White Australia.[5]

A. E. Bennett, a younger brother of Major-General H. Gordon Bennett and general secretary of the Who's for Australia League (founded on Armistice Day 1929 with many high-sounding aims but principally to encourage people to buy Australian-made goods), had said much the same thing. Australia, he proclaimed in 1930, badly needed a Man to lead the people. He went on to say this so often that critics could hardly be blamed if they thought the implication was that Bennett should lead the people. Much the same thought must have occurred to some readers of Stephensen's articles in 1939, even if he did protest that he was not really interested in politics and wanted only to help create a society in which Australian literary endeavour was given a fair chance. 'My personal interests are not political; they are "literary" ', he wrote in November 1938. Had Stephensen any real ambitions as a leader he should have realized that there were better ways of going about it. He had alienated the unions by his attacks on the Labor Party ('decidedly loyal—to Britain and Sir Otto Niemeyer first'); he had upset the conservatives by his attacks on Britain and the Empire; he had stirred the intellec-tuals by his dalliance with anti-Semitism and Fascism and had per-turbed those of the middle class who had become aware of his existence by declining to see anything wrong with German and Italian policies. Nationalism in Australia had largely been associated with the forces of social change but there can have been very few of the Left in the late thirties who had any time for Stephensen's message.

Month after month the *Publicist* plugged on, Miles replenishing its treasury, never stinting to make the paper more widely read. At least seven articles in the *Publicist* were subsequently issued as leaflets, including Stephensen's exposition of fifty points of Australia First policy and W. C. Wentworth's 1822 prize poem *Australasia*. The journal was also sold in six-monthly bound sets. For five years the *Publicist* was advertised every Saturday in the *Sydney Morning Herald*. It advertised regularly in the Sydney University students' paper *Honi Soit*, in the pro-Nazi German-language paper *Die Brücke*, in Lang's *Century*, in the Australian Railways Union N.S.W. branch monthly journal *Railroad*, and on cinema screens. Miles also bought radio time on the Roman Catholic station 2SM every Monday morning for two and a half years to early 1940. This cost £5 for a ten-minute session; Stephensen spoke and Miles filled in when Stephensen was on holiday. Station 2KY ran *Publicist* advertisements from October 1936 to November 1937. After 2KY deleted the words 'opposes boycott against Japan' from an announcement, the *Publicist* changed to 2UE but in January 1938 2UE declined the contract. The *Publicist* complained that the Council for Civil Liberties showed no interest when 2KY and 2UE banned its announcements. The New South Wales *Education Gazette* refused a *Publicist* advertisement as 'political propaganda'.

The text of one of Stephensen's radio talks (on 12 December 1938) has been preserved. It ended on this note: 'We oppose democracy, as a political system, because we believe it can never evolve the bold leadership that will be necessary to guide Australia through the difficulties of the coming year.'

H. L. Mencken was saying much the same sort of thing in the United States. Stephensen, who admired Mencken, had other ideas in common with him. There is some evidence of correspondence between them. Mencken is supposed to have written of the *Publicist:* 'We could do with a paper like it in America.'[6] Making all allowances for their vastly different backgrounds, there appears to be some, though not much, point in comparing the two men. Both were literary figures with aspirations which neither could achieve. Both were agnostics and political isolationists. Both developed in the later years almost pathological hatreds of the leader of their country's political Left, Mencken being infuriated by Roosevelt and Stephensen by Evatt. Both showed an equivocal attitude to the Jewish race while both (but particularly Mencken) retained friendship with individual Jews. This was about as far as it went. Mencken had an immeasurably greater influence on the Americans, especially on the intellectuals of the twenties who responded enthusiastically to his 'stirring the animals', than Stephensen ever had in Australia. Mencken's *American Mercury,* a monthly which began publishing in 1923, had a wide circulation, reaching a peak of 77,000 in 1927, whereas Stephensen's *Australian Mercury* ran for one issue in 1935. Most important, Mencken had a sense of humour which was reflected in his prose. He coined scores of sparkling aphorisms (pensioner: 'a kept patriot'), and was, and still is, a joy to read, however unpalatable his opinions. Mencken's mental horizon was wider than Stephensen's; the latter had the pedagogic itch; if

Mencken had any consuming itch it was to deflate the pompous and overblown.

Stephensen did not limit his journalism to the *Publicist*. He contributed articles, for instance, to the *Australian Quarterly* in March 1940 and to the *Australian Rhodes Review*, the organ of Australian Rhodes Scholars. He had described the *Australian Quarterly* in a moment of pique in 1938 as a 'characterless periodical which nebulously meanders, without point or focus or parabola of direction', but later sent it his 'A Reasoned Case against Semitism'. There was nothing particularly reasonable about his argument. As Stephensen pointed out in his *Foundations* (page 85), Australia lacked, and badly needed, social critics like Mencken (and Shaw, Wells, Chesterton, Nathan and Lewis). Stephensen himself lacked their stature. A. K. Chesterton had written much the same sort of thing—that anti-Semitism was purely a reaction to Semitism—and Hilaire Belloc had covered the ground in *The Jews* (1922). The *Australian Quarterly* was stretching to the limit its devotion to democracy and freedom of expression to publish such a provocative piece, despite all its qualifying clauses and Stephensen's claim that he did not intend to malign the Jews.

In the first issue of the *Australian Rhodes Review* (March 1934) Stephensen complained of slapdash craftsmanship in Australian book publishing. The third (1937) carried his article on 'The Decline and Fall of the British Empire'. He suggested that the £1,200 involved in Rhodes scholarships did not carry with it the obligation to 'think imperially' in the manner of forty years before. He looked back on Oxford and his 'delightful' three years there. Warming to this theme, he continued:

> The English at their best are the best people in the world, the nicest; but when a man has a country like Australia for a motherland, his primary allegiance could not be to any other country . . . the kindest thought we could have for the Empire is to hope, sincerely, that its demise will be as painless as possible for those charming people who were our hosts during the three most carefree and callow years of our lives.

By the third year of the *Publicist*, Stephensen in his nationalist advocacy was looking beyond merely writing articles and giving radio talks. He began thinking of forming a movement or party. The *Publicist* started to publish a series of suggested policy points so that the aims of such a movement could become clarified. In August 1936 Stephensen had put forward fourteen points for Australians; no. 1 being the abolition of State Parliaments, no. 2, reafforestation, and no. 3, water conservation. In July 1937 came ten vague policy points, starting with 'Development of Australian Culture' and ending with 'Australia for the Australians'.

Then, in September 1938, came twelve more detailed points to be used as a basis for discussion by informal groups of *Publicist* readers. These dealt with the party system, compulsory voting, monarchism, conscription, military control, defence policy, finance, overseas trade, population, homogeneity, public works and Australian culture. Stephensen called for correspondence: he wanted to discover if there was any real desire for an Australian resurgence, and asked readers not to write with comments until they had formed a small discussion group of no fewer than three or more than seven members.

Urging the formation of an Australia First party, Stephensen reported in December 1938 on the response he received. Twenty letters were chosen for inclusion in a *Publicist* symposium of comments. Of these, twelve came from New South Wales, four from Queensland, two from Victoria and one each from South Australia and Western Australia. Some came from individuals who had not formed a group. To a comment on homogeneity from a Vaucluse reader Stephensen added this rhetorical query: 'Would 'Vaucluse' state whether 4th or 5th generation Australian-born Jews are 100% Australian? Are Jewish immigrants an assimilable element, or do they forever remain Jews first?' To a Melbourne reader who suggested segregating non-detribalized natives in reserves: 'Why not segregate the Jews also?'

By January 1939 Stephensen could say that groups had been formed in all mainland States, but a month later the blood had gone out of the idea. It was explained as being 'my idea only' and merely 'preliminary and exploratory'. Miles, who had not been enthusiastic, had allowed Stephensen a trial run and it had not been good enough. Stephensen explained that most correspondents would not accept the full implications of an Australia First policy when concretely represented.

Much later, in May 1940, the *Publicist* came up with yet another list of policy points; this time, fifty points for an Australia First party to be formed after the war. It appeared that Stephensen had been reconciled to waiting until then. Some correspondence was kept up with a few interstate contacts, but the group idea was let slide. Stephensen had admitted in March 1939 there was only the slightest chance that an Australia First party could then be formed with any prospect of immediate success. That was in Sydney. Elsewhere in

Australia there was even less nationalist ferment of the kind from which political parties are formed. There was a rudimentary organization in Melbourne, mainly, but not exclusively, of Roman Catholic students. In Brisbane the Queensland government publicity officer, C. B. Christesen, had received a letter in 1938 from S. B. Hooper, asking him to organize a discussion group, but he had taken no action. In no other Australian city or town were there enough sympathizers to achieve anything.

How small an impact the *Publicist* had on Australian society may be gauged from a comment by H. L. Harris, a Sydney economist, in *Australia's National Interests and National Policy,* published in Melbourne in 1938. After a brief reference to an 'incipient fascist movement' (clearly the New Guard), he remarked: 'apart from the small group of Communists, there is no organised or recognised movement which declares itself opposed to the British connection, although there are individuals who are, or so emphasize their Australianism as to give the impression that they are opposed to it.'

Different people found different things to please them in the *Publicist*. The German consulate in Sydney and the German newspaper *Die Brücke* (published in Sydney) liked its attitudes to the Axis powers. Simple patriots like Brian Fernandez, a lad who had just left school at Riverton, South Australia—directed to the *Publicist* by Ian Mudie, the poet—was attracted by its strong nationalist tone and could see nothing sinister about it. He sent a letter about the lack of teaching of Australian literature in schools which Miles, who had complained of the same sort of thing in his own schooldays, published. Fernandez, full of youthful idealism and a devotee of Henry Lawson, responded to Stephensen's ideas and wrote confiding his ambition to become a writer. Stephensen encouraged him and suggested he concentrate on the local scene. Fernandez wrote a small book of intensely patriotic poetry entitled *Australia Awake* (1941) but alas for the *Publicist*'s Briton-baiting it contained more than a hint of Anglophilia. Fernandez joined the Royal Australian Navy, became a commissioned officer, served overseas during the war and afterwards returned to take up a soldier-settlement block on Kangaroo Island, still puzzled over all the hullabaloo about Australia First.

Some of the more complicated souls who backed the *Publicist* met weekly in Sydney to discuss its ideas and current political and social movements. Australia First thought gradually developed at these meetings which came to be given the jocular name of 'Yabber Club'. This label bestowed on the occasions rather more formality than they possessed. They began when Miles, Salier, Masey, Hooper and Stephensen left the *Publicist* office each Thursday afternoon to discuss the paper's editorial content over tea or coffee in a corner of the nearby Shalimar Café.

In the twenties in Sydney there had been many such private literary, artistic and political clubs in teashops, coffee lounges and back rooms of hotels. By the thirties they were less common but still numerous. There was nothing sinister or conspiratorial in them. Miles and Stephensen thought that the Shalimar Café, in the basement of the building in which the *Publicist* was situated, would be a convenient place to meet. Proceedings were informal. There were no rules and no chairman, although Miles was usually deferred to. There were no 'banned' topics. Other people began to join in, mainly friends and associates of the five 'foundation members', plus visitors to the *Publicist* office-cum-bookshop who showed sympathy with the journal's ideas. People regarded as 'grossly hostile' were not invited.

First to join the five was Valentine Crowley, an electrical engineer who, as mentioned earlier, had retired in 1920 but was forced back into employment in 1931. Crowley, like Miles, had been an ardent anti-conscriptionist in World War I but had not met Miles until introduced by Salier, his senior in the Australian Mutual Provident Society, soon after the first edition of the *Publicist* appeared. If Miles wanted lively argument, Crowley was the man either to provide or to provoke it, being a person of violent opinions, many of them enthusiastically anti-British. What he saw as Australia's continuing colonial status enraged him.

Stephensen invited Harley Matthews, who in turn brought his Liverpool neighbour, Martin Watts. Watts's attachment to the club and then to the *Publicist* grew far stronger than that of Matthews, who attended only two or three times in all. Xavier Herbert came at times. He was always a lively arguer and helped sustain the iconoclasm that Miles craved.

J. T. Kirtley, the stockbroker's clerk turned fine book publisher, came in once from Woy Woy. Miles Franklin, another friend of Stephensen, often attended, as did Ian Mudie and a Sydney public accountant, Malcolm Smith, who found the discussions the most invigorating in which he had ever taken part.

'Yabber' was not solely devoted to lamenting Australia's reluctance to shed its colonial status. Miles insisted on *general* conversation to discourage fission into competing groups. Art, religion, morals, agriculture, architecture and literature all came up for dissection. Without doubt some made highly shocking and seditious remarks, heretical by the standards of Sydney in the late thirties, and almost invariably they were challenged immediately in the intellectual free-for-all. It was, in a way, rather touchingly undergraduate.

Attendance at the Yabber Club grew gradually. There was no fixed membership and people dropped out or renewed their attendance just as they liked. The largest membership ever to get together at one time for the session, which usually lasted for two hours from 4.30 p.m., was about seventeen, while sometimes it was down to three or four. Occasional visitors—such as Peter Russo, then Professor in the Modern Languages department of the Tokyo University of Commerce—dropped in. Russo was introduced, at Stephensen's request, by Frank Clune, whom he had met in Tokyo.

Others with motives rather less disinterested than Russo's listened in. Various branches of the country's Intelligence services sent agents to check if any sedition was being hatched. This was surely reasonable curiosity, especially after 3 September 1939. The Commonwealth government had an informer planted there who was unable to find anything very objectionable to report. He thought the club was 'as harmless as a curate's tea party and loyal as a Primrose League.' When World War II broke out, surveillance became more thorough but Army Intelligence sent along a man whose reports were discarded as unreliable. Late in 1940 he was replaced by agent 222, Sergeant Alan Clement Panton, who went to Miles to say he was a journalist interested in the *Publicist*'s ideas, so Miles invited him. Stephensen subsequently claimed that he knew Panton's true role and accepted him as a bona fide investigator, not an *agent provocateur*. Panton sat quietly, took no active part in the discussion and went away to make notes from memory of anything he thought should be recorded.

Stephensen was not so happy about George Caiger, a fellow-Queenslander who had been to Oxford. Caiger had spent the thirties in Tokyo as a lecturer in English. Returning in 1940 he was taken along to the Yabber Club as a civilian. Soon afterwards he joined Army Intelligence as a junior officer, to find he was the only one there with any first-hand experience of the group. He reported the movement as consisting of 'harmless individuals sharpening their wits on each other.' Stephensen saw Caiger as an *agent provocateur* —perhaps because he did not emulate Panton's quiescence. No Germans, Japanese or Italians ever attended the Yabber Club.

In all there were more than 200 meetings, the last few being held at Ann's Pantry, a teashop in Hunter Street close to the *Publicist*'s new address in February 1942. Several Sydney men who later served with distinction in the A.I.F. and R.A.A.F., which is surely one—and perhaps the most practical—criterion of loyalty, attended the Yabber Club at one time or other. Several of those present at the Shalimar Café tried a little organizing within the Australian Natives' Association, and the result was an ANA luncheon club which outlived Yabber. This new club was chaired by P. C. Lang of the Yabber Club, a public accountant who had become the president of an ANA suburban auxiliary. Six of the club's foundation members came from Yabber.

In 1938 Stephensen began to give some of his time that was free from the *Publicist* to profitable collaboration with Frank Clune, helping him with his numerous travel books. He had met Clune originally in 1935 at meetings of the Fellowship of Australian Writers. Clune was only one of the writers whom Stephensen helped, but he was certainly the most notable in terms of work done and books published. Stephensen had several times commented favourably in the *Publicist* on Clune's highly individual literary style. According to Clune, he first consulted Stephensen over collaboration in 1938 when they did weeks of research together for Clune's *Free and Easy Land,* a discursive account of Queensland. Thereafter Stephensen shared the work in most of the other Clune books, each a good seller. Stephensen referred in the November 1938 issue of the *Publicist* to Clune's 'amazing factual flair and capacity for research' in a brief mention of Clune's *Sky High to Shanghai.* Later, when few were willing to acknowledge Stephensen, when his world had collapsed and Australia seemed united against him, his former partner was one of the few to stand by him.

The *Publicist* group often expressed sympathy with the Aborigines. Miles once wrote: 'We Kookaburras prefer the Blacks to the Whites'. Stephensen served as Secretary of the Aborigines' Citizenship Committee, pledged to support the Aborigines' Progressive Association which had Aboriginal membership only. When J. T. Patten, a part-Aboriginal, was the association's president in 1939, the *Publicist* reported his organizing activities. Patten was arrested while addressing a meeting of Aborigines at the Cumeroogunga mission near Barmah, New South Wales. Patten, who edited the association's paper, the *Abo Call* (published by the *Publicist* and on sale at the *Publicist* office) was charged with having enticed Aborigines to leave the reserve—but there had been little harmony at the mission before he came and the inhabitants needed small encouragement to depart.

The police could not say anything very damning against Patten when he was before the court at Moama, and he was released on a bond. Some days afterwards an inflammatory report appeared in the Sydney Labor newspaper, the *Daily News,* boldly headlined: NAZIS BEHIND PANIC. It suggested that the reason the Aborigines fled from the mission was 'to provide the German press with material to further Nazi claims for the return of colonies'. According to the *Publicist,* Patten 'sued' the *Daily News* for this report, but there is no record of the action reaching court.* Stephensen helped Patten organize the Aborigines' Day of Mourning on Australia's 150th birthday, 26 January 1939, a day for which they said the Aborigines had no reason to rejoice.

* The *Daily News* soon afterwards went into receivership, to be bought and closed by Consolidated Press.

5

War-time

THE DECLARATION OF WAR against Germany in September 1939 meant several changes for the *Publicist*. It had to become circumspect, to say the least, in its references to Germany. As Stephensen noted, 'a state of belligerency necessarily alters the basis of political discussion in combatant countries'. Now that it was officially disloyal to be, or even to be suspected of being, pro-German, the paper was far more vulnerable. A physical assault on its Elizabeth Street premises was not long delayed. Less than an hour after Australians heard Mr Menzies say that Britain had declared war and that therefore Australia was at war, red-painted letters a foot high appeared on the glass shop window of the *Publicist* proclaiming it to be the 'Nazi H.Q.'.

Stephensen wrote in the delayed September *Publicist* that before the war he had done his best to create goodwill between Australia and Germany, 'not because I held a brief for the Germans, but because I thought Australians were being mentally weakened by the revengeful Jewish campaigns of anti-Hitler hate which for years has flooded our Australian news press. If we are to fight against Germany, let us at least fight for an Australian, not a Jewish, reason'.

The *Publicist,* like the Australian Council for Civil Liberties (also founded in 1936), attacked the repressive National Security regulations gazetted under the Defence Act on 25 August 1939 and re-gazetted under the National Security Act when it was passed in September. Otherwise the *Publicist* did not criticize war preparations and stated, though without obvious enthusiasm, that it could see no valid reason against Australia giving voluntary help to Britain in any war in which Britain was involved. The core of this attitude was expressed by Stephensen in March 1940: 'Australia is not an ally of Britain, but is a dependency of Britain, and it is for this reason that we are at war'.

While sympathetic references to Germany might no longer appear, the paper went on in much the same way as before although, from May 1940, it was required to submit all articles for censorship. Paper rationing forced it to reduce the monthly printing order to 1,000 copies. The only article recorded as having been banned by the censor was Kirtley's 'Logic of Maginot,' which discussed the futility of the French frontier defences along the German border.

A new contributor appeared, a Melbourne solicitor, A. Rud Mills, whose preoccupation with Nordic mythology made him readily acceptable to a paper so concerned with 'Aryan' survival in the face of Semitic onslaughts. A new subject for harangue was the 'philosophy' of the English writer, Morley Roberts, to whose work Miles had been introduced by S. B. Hooper. Roberts, who had toured Australia in his youth, was the author of more than sixty works of fiction, and in his later years had turned to theorizing on the nature of life. As his conclusions strongly supported Miles's favourite thesis that war was 'biologically inevitable', Miles adopted him with enthusiasm. Any and every comment, however dated, he could gather concerning his new hero went into the *Publicist*. When Sir Frederic Eggleston described Roberts in a review as 'the perfect Hitlerite', Sir Frederic at once went on to Miles's black list.

From his late twenties Miles was troubled by angina pectoris. In his final years one foot became gangrenous but, although increasingly irritable, he hobbled daily to the office. From June 1941 onwards the pain he was suffering grew acute and, confined to his bed, he began to plan what would happen after his death. His article in the 'resurgence number' of the *Publicist* (September 1941) foreshadowed changes involving greater responsibility for Stephensen.

As the war progressed, attacks from the Left on Stephensen increased. He had taken court action against the communist *Workers' Weekly* on 7 April 1939 over an article and an accompanying street poster bearing the words 'Sydney's Nazi Underworld', complaining that he had been portrayed as a paid traitor and agent of another nation. The *Workers' Weekly* said in defence that the matter complained of was true, published for the public benefit and fair comment on a matter of public interest. Stephensen, who gave short evidence, was cross-examined at length during the proceedings before the New South Wales Supreme Court. No evidence was given for the defence. The jury found for Stephensen but awarded the insulting one farthing in damages.

As usual the *Publicist* obliged everybody, friend or foe, by publishing a seven-page report of the court case.

The year 1941 was notable for the campaign, only marginally successful, to draw the Jindyworobak non-political literary nationalists into the *Publicist*'s orbit. Jindyworobak, founded in Adelaide in 1938 by Rex Ingamells, was a movement to free Australian art from 'alien' influences. The word 'Jindyworobak', used to mean 'distinctive Australian quality', was taken by Ingamells from the glossary to James Devaney's book of Aboriginal tales, *The Vanished Tribes* (1929). Ingamells freely acknowledged the considerable influence that Stephensen's *Foundations* had had on him, though he maintained in the first Jindyworobak publication that Stephensen was not Australian enough! He refused to concede, as he claimed Stephensen did, that imported British culture was the most important element in Australian culture. Still, Stephensen and Ingamells had much in common, though Stephensen felt this more strongly. Ian Mudie, who has been described by Dr Brian Elliot as Ingamells's 'most vigorous disciple', was an important link between the *Publicist* and the Jindyworobaks. Mudie's poems were published regularly in the *Publicist* after October 1937 and he was also the target of the type of criticism commonly aimed at the *Publicist*. A. D. Hope, reviewing Mudie's *This is Australia* for *Southerly* in November 1941, said that Mudie's poetry had 'traces of the fanaticism of the Hitler Youth Movement'.

Stephensen, badly needing allies, scratched around for superlatives to describe the Jindyworobaks' work and suggested that the time had come for them to join forces—'a combination of politicals and poeticals is formidable'. Mudie induced Hooper and Val Crowley to make a cash donation to Jindyworobak. Financial aid from this source, according to Ingamells, 'dwarfed the little we had previously received from anywhere'. Ingamells added, in 1948: 'Subservience it was never thought to thrust upon us.' There is no evidence that, whatever Stephensen may have desired, Jindyworobak was ever further involved than receiving this 'no-strings' finance for its publishing programme.

After having decided that the early numbers of C. B. Christesen's *Meanjin Papers,* a new Brisbane literary venture begun in 1940, were worthy, the *Publicist* grew to regard succeeding issues as less welcome. The fifth issue of *Meanjin Papers* must have cheered Miles with its reference to Morley Roberts's *Biopolitics* as 'a really important book'. Though the sixth number gave Stephensen space for an article on Queensland culture, it also contained a review by

'Mopoke' (Brian Vrepont), attacking Mudie's *This is Australia*. Vrepont criticized the 'inelegance of his missionary spirit' and apologized to Australia, on poetry's behalf, for Mudie's 'seriously purposed intellectual and emotional sterility'. Stephensen complained that *Meanjin Papers* had cut his own article and marred it by a grotesque misprint. He castigated Vrepont's review as 'a rotten attack', one that 'must rank with the most cowardly attacks ever made upon poets by critics.' Christesen fired back in the following issue and another enmity was sealed.

Stephensen also found a foe in Cyril Pearl, editor of the Sydney *Sunday Telegraph,* who had asked the government to act against the *Publicist* as it had done against Cyril Glassop's National Guard organization—to be referred to later—declared illegal by the Attorney-General, W. M. Hughes, in September 1941. Pearl said of the *Publicist* that 'month after month it churns out a stale mixture of rabid anti-British nationalism, Nazi-inspired, and anti-semitism and windy Fascist pseudo-philosophy.' Stephensen's counterblast had in it a certain inevitability: 'We of the *Publicist* do not know whether or not the editor of the *Sunday Telegraph* is a Jew'.

Max Harris of Adelaide, without whom few literary controversies in the past twenty-five years have been complete, was another to tackle Stephensen. From the full height of his twenty years of age he lunged furiously, words tumbling over themselves, in the columns of Cecily Crozier's *avant-garde* journal, *Comment*. He found the *Publicist* anti-Australian, and an article by 'Anna Brabant' especially offensive in its acceptance of Lionel Lindsay's attack on the influence of Jewish art dealers. So in the next *Publicist*: 'We do not know whether "Max Harris" is a Jew'. When the *Publicist* clashed with the University of Melbourne students' paper *Farrago,* some of the office-bearers, according to the *Publicist,* were seen to have 'decidedly Jewish names'.

As war against Japan appeared more likely through 1940 and 1941—the Australian 22nd Brigade was sent to Singapore in February 1941 to guard against no other eventuality—the *Publicist* gradually became more guarded in its comments on Pacific affairs. In 1940 Kirtley, in his role of commentator on military strategy, had written that Japan would be incapable of attacking the south Pacific in strength. He was far from being alone in holding this view. Stephensen, who in April 1939 had mildly chided W. C. Wentworth (how could he speak more harshly to a man with such forebears?) for 'inexcusably' naming Japan as a potential invader, was still in 1941 advocating 'friendly reciprocity' between Australia and Japan.

He welcomed the appointment of Tatsuo Kawai, the Japanese envoy, in March 1941. When war did come in December 1941 the *Publicist,* after looking back as it had in 1939 on its endeavours to maintain peace with Germany, called on its readers to back their government. It suggested that hostilities were the result of 'a failure of diplomacy'. In the new war Stephensen considered that 'distance, no less than time, operates in our favour'; in 1936 and 1937 he had discussed Australian defence in realistic terms. If the Japanese bogey did exist we should plan to meet it. Our aim should be to destroy enemy troopships. He criticized the scuttling of the battle cruiser H.M.A.S. *Australia* and advocated buying or building 300 diesel motor torpedo boats instead of buying, as the navy did, three cruisers from Britain.

The last three issues of the *Publicist,* in January, February and March 1942, were edited by Stephensen. Miles died on 10 January 1942, having handed over the paper to Stephensen, Val Crowley and Hooper from 1 January. The final numbers of the *Publicist* contained forthright editorial appeals against defeatist war planning. Stephensen poured scorn on a reported statement by the Minister for the Army, Frank Forde, that 'if England goes down, Australia will go down.' He thought Forde should have phrased his oratorical flourish rather differently: 'Even if England goes down, Australia will NOT go down.'

As early as 1939 there had been some pressure on the federal authorities for action against the *Publicist.* A comment in the *Daily Telegraph* in November 1939 suggested that a watch was being kept on 'underground activities which are anti-British but not directly pro-Nazi'. Then on 17 April 1940 Eric Harrison, a United Australia Party M.H.R., asked the Minister for Information, Sir Henry Gullett, whether he had seen the seditious and disloyal articles appearing in the *Publicist,* and Sir Henry assured him that articles of such a kind would not appear again. The Minister was possibly depending on control through censorship. From the opposition benches, on 25 November 1941, S. M. Falstein of the A.L.P. drew the attention of Dr Evatt, Attorney-General in the Curtin government, to the 'anti-war, anti-democratic, pro-fascist' Australia First organization.

For some time communist speakers in the Sydney Domain and on Melbourne's Yarra Bank had been urging suppression of the *Publicist* and internment of its supporters. After the Russo-German non-aggression pact even less notice than usual was taken of these 'demands' of the extreme Left. (One communist at least has since admitted that this was 'a difficult and nerve-testing period'.)[1] After

Hitler's march into the Soviet Union on 22 June 1941 the communist voices gained a new authority. The State Labor Party, a New South Wales manifestation of the banned Communist Party, called for internment of the Australia First group at a Sydney Town Hall rally on 18 November 1941. The State Labor Party's paper *Progress* on 21 November called for public trial of individuals connected with the group.

Creatures well out of the mainstream of Australian political life who came to the surface during the country's most desperate days of early 1942 had a disturbing way of attaching themselves to the *Publicist* group, or of giving the impression of some connection. Some were splenetic anti-Semites, others were pro-Japanese, while a few were merely confused. A lone Sydney political aspirant, Cyril Glassop, had nothing to do with Australia First but perhaps it was inevitable that his endeavours would be mistakenly coupled with those of Stephensen and Miles. The *Sunday Telegraph* under Cyril Pearl had suggested that the *Publicist* group was similar to Glassop's National Guard, 'a little fascist seedling', and should be similarly banned. Glassop, a perennially unsuccessful federal parliamentary candidate, had a penchant for forming organizations with imposing titles, minute memberships and fleeting existence. In 1939 there was The New Front, which opposed democracy because, he explained, the Communist Party was using democracy to further its own ends. Then in 1941 he thought up the National Guard, which was dedicated to reconstruct rather than to destroy democracy. Glassop chose as its emblem a coiled whip on a black background. At the time that W. M. Hughes proscribed this organization, Glassop admitted it had 'hung fire' a little because he had hurt himself in a fall while working as a fitter on a warship and had been unable to enrol members. Though his National Guard was banned he was not interned.

About the time this National Guard paper tiger had been officially crushed, the *Sydney Morning Herald* noted the apparent existence of a National Socialist Party of Australia. A typewritten circular had been mailed in Sydney bearing its name, and stating, *inter alia*: 'the fact that Australian officers command our overseas troops matters nothing; they have been replaced before and will be again by dim-witted, cocktail-drinking society boys from English public schools.' The circular was signed 'Heil Hitler'. Was this just a joke? It is possible, although a member of the Australia First movement, Edmund Arnold, was found by police to possess some literature containing the ten points of the National Socialist Party. It could have been one of Arnold's phantom organizations, and he may well have been the sole member of this 'party'. He was a little like Glassop in this. A fervent anti-Semite with an interest in theosophy and the occult, he thought that the world's Jews should be sent to Madagascar, at their own expense. In 1944 he was pottering around with a plan for an Australian League of Greater Empire, involving Australia, south-east Asian countries and the Pacific islands. He believed before and during the war—when the notion had surely achieved some unpopularity—in the inherent superiority of the 'Aryan' race. He advertised in the *Sydney Morning Herald* in February 1942 for people to help him form the World Aryan Federation, which would deal with the Jews. Six people, including two police officers, responded to his call. The officers persuaded him against going on with the idea. This sole meeting was held in Adyar House, which at the same time accommodated downstairs a public meeting of the Australia First movement.

An earlier attempt to form much the same sort of organization had been made, with a similar press advertisement, in 1940. This announced without euphemism that it would be an anti-Jewish association. The New South Wales Minister of Justice, Vernon Treatt, later recalled that within forty-eight hours this 'movement' was scotched. [2]

Thomas Hugh Gilhooley was only marginally involved with Australia First, and probably only to the extent of being a subscriber to the *Publicist*. He was arrested in Western Australia (according to one account this was connected with an army signallers' strike) and sent to South Australia for internment, to be provisionally released on the understanding that he stayed there. Twice he left South Australia and was as a result twice before the courts. At his second appearance the prosecutor, F. D. Green, replied to a charge by Gilhooley that he had been offered an appeal against internment before a 'secret' tribunal. Internee cases were kept from publication, said Green, to protect the people involved so that their histories should not come out, 'otherwise their whole future in Australia might be problematical'. Gilhooley met some Australia First internees when he was behind barbed wire but they were not friendly.

Because Stephensen published in pamphlet form his *Publicist* article on Japan's 2,599th anniversary about the same time as a laudatory book on Japan by 'Myles Chequin' (John Sleeman), Stephensen was blamed by some for this book. Sleeman first burst onto the public scene when accused in 1922 of an attempt to bribe a Queensland M.L.A., F. T. Brennan. He became a leading light in Beckett's Newspapers which published the notorious *Beckett's*

Budget (1927–31). He befriended the Japanese and one uncon-firmed report suggests that he helped the Japanese consul in Sydney to burn documents just before Pearl Harbor.

Another shadowy figure who, like Arnold, was actually on the Australia First membership roll, was English-born Thomas Potts Graham, a fanatical anti-Semite. Early in 1942 he distributed pam-phlets which claimed American troops were in Australia as part of a diabolical plot by international Jewry to govern Australia from America. Australians, he said, should join the Japanese in fighting their common enemy, Jewry. The authorities interpreted the dis-semination of these pamphlets as a breach of National Security regulation no. 42, an act likely to prejudice the defence of the Commonwealth. Graham was convicted and given six months' gaol, the magistrate commenting that the internment camp was the right place for him. At the end of his gaol term he was interned and held until the end of 1943. His leaflet was frowned on by the Australia First movement which issued a disclaimer of responsibility. In internment a group of Australia First internees, not including Stephensen, petitioned the camp commandant to have Graham kept away from them. (Graham had once sent a manuscript dealing with the introduction of national socialism in Australia to Miles, who replied that he thought something might be made of it.)

Associated with Graham in pamphleteering was Gilbert Cochrane Burleigh of Bondi, given six months' gaol for having attempted to send an insulting cable to Churchill.[3] In court the prosecutor said it was believed Burleigh was acting for the Japanese. Mr Atkinson, S.M., remarked on Burleigh's 'long and unfavourable' record, calling him a 'go-getter of a very bad type'. Burleigh, when questioned by police, denied he was a member of the Australia First movement. A police report, of a credibility impossible now to determine, later stated that Burleigh was friendly with Stephensen.[4]

Miles, Graham, Arnold and Stephensen were beyond question anti-Semitic, and their increasingly unpleasant attacks on Australian Jews constituted one of the least savoury and defensible aspects of *Publicist* and associated Australia First propaganda. When the flow of Jewish refugees from Europe increased from 1938, the *Publicist* became more offensive. Miles and Stephensen, who gradually became as adept as his master in Jew-baiting, had little to learn from the Melbourne Douglas Credit weekly, the *New Times,* which was commending to its readers the notorious *Protocols of the Elders of Zion.* Miles and Stephensen accepted the authenticity of that rank and dubious document. Miles, who went so far as to sell copies of it, had a further outlet for his feelings in his *Independent Sydney Secularist.* It has proved impossible to discover by what means and to what sort of people this publication circulated. Neither the National Library in Canberra nor the Mitchell Library in Sydney holds copies.

Although few are keen to admit it, Miles's attitude did in fact touch a sympathetic nerve in a substantial minority of Australians. There was an undercurrent of anti-Jewish feeling in the late thirties and early forties, some, of course, engendered by ignorance and thoughtlessness, some founded on slightly more justifiable grounds, as noted by A. E. Mander in *The Making of the Australians*:

> we are compelled to recognise that some of the new arrivals, quite unconsciously, provoked dislike. Some had habits of thrusting themselves forward when they wanted anything, more than Australian manners and customs allowed. Some seemed, to Australian eyes, greedy. Some were openly contemptuous of the people they had come to live amongst. Such individuals were very conspicuous. They made it hard for themselves—and at the same time they made it hard for others, the more adaptable and better mannered of their kind—to win acceptance.

These less attractive migrant characteristics described by Mander explain to some extent why the new word 'reffo' (refugee) had such a derogatory tone around the years 1938–40. Not all Australians welcomed those fleeing from the Nazis with quite the generosity that polite myth suggests. Nevertheless, though there were some Australians whose welcome was reserved or even mistrustful, very few doubted that the European Jews had good reason for leaving Germany, Austria and Czechoslovakia. The *Publicist,* among a very small minority, appeared unconcerned. In mid-1939 Martin Watts thought that German concentration camps were only 'possibly uncomfortable'. We heard, he said, 'only the accusation and not the defence'. Hardy Wilson went further, as has been noted already, with the opinion that 'all the fuss about Jews being persecuted is rubbish'. To him the Jew was 'the drone of humanity'.

Lionel Lindsay with his *Addled Art* (1942), and Norman Lindsay with similar attacks on the influence of the Jew in art, contributed to the atmosphere in which the *Publicist*'s attitude was not found universally objectionable. Yet Norman's son Philip was belligerent in the opposite direction. In his autobiography, *I'd Live the Same Life Over,* he recounts meeting three Australian soldiers in London and discovering them to be unredeemably anti-Jewish.

'Hitler's propaganda,' he commented, 'had eaten into that Liberty-loving land and I was sick to hear it.'

The *Publicist* remained unregenerate about its attitude to the Jews. Miles, in attacking Len Fox's pamphlet *Australia and the Jews* in February 1940, said that no Jewish refugees should be admitted. There was no solution to the Jewish problem, he went on, none, that is, 'while a Jew lives'.

Anti-Semitic Australia First activists campaigned against the appointment of Julius Stone, a Jew from New Zealand, to the Chair of International Law and Jurisprudence at the University of Sydney. They also objected strongly to the Freeland League scheme to settle a Jewish colony in the Kimberleys in Western Australia.[5]

How Stephensen became disenchanted with the Jews is something that puzzled many of his friends and well-wishers. He fended off all enquiries about this as he did about his simultaneous movement away from liberalism. Could it all have been due to the influence of Miles? It is rarely possible to be certain why a man changes his opinions. A man may not himself know.

6

Movement

DESPITE SEVERAL quite unambiguous *Publicist* references to the
necessity of leaving the formation of any Australia First party until
after the war, a sudden gathering of forces in September 1941 saw
the Australia First movement brought into being. Its founding manifesto noted that the association had been formed 'in view of the
extreme gravity of the military situation abroad and of the political
situation at home.' This indeed fitted the facts. Germany occupied,
and was not seriously challenged in its possession of, most of Europe
and had a firm foothold in North Africa. In Australia, Menzies of
the U.A.P., Fadden of the U.C.P. and Curtin of the A.L.P. had each
been Prime Minister in quick succession from August to October.
On 7 October John Curtin took over the federal government; on
15 October the preliminary meeting called to consider forming an
Australia First movement was held. On 20 October the movement
was formally constituted at a general meeting and held its first
public meeting on 5 November.

The *Publicist* or Yabber Club group, although they were certainly
its main strength, did not on their own constitute the Australia First
movement. There was representation from Melbourne in L. K.
Cahill, a former communist, who had been pressing for months for
some such organization to be formed, though Cahill did not so much
represent Melbourne as represent himself. A further and most
unlikely element in the movement was a group of members of the
recessed Women's Guild of Empire in Sydney. On the face of it a
more unexpected ingredient in the new alliance could hardly be
imagined. The guild had been active in criticizing the *Publicist* in
1937 for its hostility to Britain. The *Publicist* had fired back that
'English women in Australia are, almost to a woman, active propa-

gandists for Britain First in Australia.' One of the six objects of the guild was to assist in the development of Australia as a part of the British Empire. Its campaign director and principal spokeswoman was Mrs Adela Pankhurst Walsh, a woman with a political past every bit as varied and colourful as Stephensen's. A member of the famous English suffragette family, whose female members all went to gaol for their beliefs, she came to Australia to campaign for socialism in Melbourne. In 1915, as a member of the Women's Peace Army, she wrote *Put Up the Sword,* a vigorous attack on war as a means of settling quarrels. In the traumatic national rift over conscription for overseas service she was a zealous 'No' campaigner. Like Miles she had been a contributor to *Ross's* in those turbulent years. In 1917 she married the militant Tom Walsh of the Seamen's Union; it was his second marriage. Miriam Dixson in *Labour History* (Sydney), no. 10, which wrongly describes Walsh as secretary of the Seamen's Union, notes that he and his new wife were foundation members of the Communist Party of Australia (page 22). Walsh was the Irish-born president of the Seamen's Union whom S. M. Bruce, the Nationalist Prime Minister, tried to deport in 1925, together with the union secretary Jacob Johnson, as a strike leader. Not long after this Walsh broke with the union (or the union broke with Walsh—it all depends on the point of view) and the once firebrand radical moved right to become a bitter anti-communist. Mrs Walsh moved with him. Both became great speakers against communism. Adela switched her attentions to the Guild of Empire which had as its primary objective the combating of communism; Tom joined Eric Campbell's New Guard, often lecturing on communism at its Locality meetings.

Then about 1939 the Walshes discovered Japan. Articles about it began appearing in the Empire Guild journal, the *Empire Gazette.* After a visit to that country, subsidized by the Japanese, the Walshes became even more fervent publicists and, again with Japanese backing, published several pamphlets on what they had seen on their tour.[1] On her return Mrs Walsh said:

> When I reached Brisbane I learned that Australian soldiers were in the Near East and I say solemnly and with a full sense of responsibility that it will be the height of madness for Australians to play any role in Asia unless the general public knows far more than they appear to do of Japan, China and Russia . . . People who glibly say Japan will conquer the Philippine Islands and then come to conquer Australia can be speaking of some remote possibility a thousand years hence, but not of present day politics or possibilities.

Soon after war broke out in Europe in 1939 the Women's Guild of Empire, announcing an extraordinary meeting to decide its future, also made it public that Mrs Walsh was no longer actively associated with them. For a short while she was at a loss to know in what field of politics or social endeavour she could exercise her still considerable energies, and tried to continue some of her guild work under the name of the People's Guild. In September 1940 she stood as an (ungrouped) candidate for the Senate but gained only a handful of votes (about 1,700 to the U.A.P. no. 1 candidate's 223,000). The U.A.P. included her as no. 4 on their twenty-one candidate ticket; Labor put her as no. 16.

According to Stephensen it was Mrs Walsh who suggested amalgamation with the *Publicist* group. It is very difficult to imagine that any initiative from Mrs Walsh and her colleagues would have led to amalgamation had not Stephensen been looking for some pretext to start an organization. It was Stephensen who invited Cahill to leave his Yarra Bank soapbox and come to Sydney to speak in the Domain. Cahill could be relied on to contribute to the pressure on the ailing Miles to drop his opposition to starting a movement. Miles had nothing to do with the movement and had he not been confined to bed it is almost certain that he would have stopped Stephensen. He had no respect for Mrs Walsh, having once told Masey that she was a woman 'with the utmost contempt for the truth'. But he was dying and, if he knew what was happening, let Stephensen go his own way.

Stephensen drafted a ten-point manifesto as a basis for the merger, by-passing the fifty points that he and Miles put together early in 1940 because the Guild women would not accept some of them.

Between twenty and thirty people attended the preliminary meeting on 15 October 1941 held at the North Sydney flat of one of Mrs Walsh's colleagues, Mrs Marjorie Corby. Stephensen gave his ten points an airing and read out a proposed thirty-clause constitution and rules. Five days later a general meeting, held at the Shalimar Café, adopted this constitution and the new movement elected its executive. Stephensen, who took the chair to open the meeting, was voted president. Other foundation members were Cahill, Ian Mudie, G. T. Rice (a *Publicist* reader and Yabber Club member), his wife Sheila, Mrs Walsh, her colleagues Mrs Vera Parkinson, Mrs Corby and Miss Elaine Pope, and W. F. Tinker-Giles who ran a shoe shop at Cronulla and had been drawn into the Yabber Club after a visit to the *Publicist* bookshop to buy a copy of *Capricornia*. Mrs Rice was made honorary secretary and 10s was set as the annual membership fee. An office was rented at 26 O'Connell Street which Mrs Rice attended at regular hours and from which the new joint organizers, Mrs Walsh and Cahill, operated.

Miles did not join, but his daughter Beatrice and a son, J. B. Miles, did. The ten foundation members became the executive committee which met weekly. Finance came from membership fees (about £40), collections at public meetings and donations (£20 came from Tinker-Giles and £20 from Miss Pope). Public meetings were arranged at Sydney city halls—seven at the Australian Hall in Elizabeth Street and three at the Adyar Hall in Bligh Street. Except for the first two at the Adyar Hall in January and February 1942, these meetings were well attended—by hecklers. A study class for members was begun with Masey and P. C. Lang as tutors.

Little serious objection could be taken to any of the ten points which served the movement as a manifesto. There was no reference, as there had been in the fifty points of the *Publicist,* to anti-Semitism or to national socialism. There was no mention of communism. Supplementing the manifesto was a dodger issued later which listed two points: the recall to Australia of all troops overseas and independent Australian action in international discussions and negotiations.

At a time when it was becoming increasingly clear that war with Japan was inevitable, the movement at its first public meeting on 5 November made opposition to United States bases in the western Pacific one of its main points. Mrs Walsh and Cahill, who could be guaranteed to stir the Sydney Left, objected to what they called an 'American invasion' of Australia.

Cahill, unable to resist jibes at Russia, provoked interjections. Stephensen, less combative, was applauded for saying that the movement claimed the same measure of independence for Australia as the people of Britain claimed for their country in external affairs. Estimates of the size of the audience at the first public meeting ranged from 212 (Stephensen) to 100 (*Daily Mirror*). The *Mirror* report was unflattering, so Stephensen thought its reporter must be either a Jew or 'a particular sympathiser with Jews against Gentiles'. Stephensen claimed an attendance of 231 at the second meeting, held on 12 November, at which that serious student of economics, Edward Masey, was an additional speaker. His speech, the least provocative, went unreported in the press. Masey had disagreed with some early contributions by Stephensen to the *Publicist,* calling them unnecessarily offensive, illogical and too long. He and Cecil Salier, who shared these views, decided early in 1937 not to offer any further contributions to the journal. Masey had contributed six articles in 1936–7, one of them, 'Australian Trade Policy', being issued as a pamphlet. Then for more than three years he wrote nothing for the *Publicist*. He returned in August 1940 with articles on finance. Though unhappy about the involvement of Mrs Walsh with the new movement in 1941, he and Salier decided it would be ungracious to stand aside and joined at the end of the first public meeting. At the subsequent Yabber Club gathering he criticized Stephensen, Cahill and Mrs Walsh for baiting communists instead of being constructive. His own public address of 12 November was the result of a challenge to put his theory into practice. Mrs Walsh told this meeting that economic pressures had been responsible for the Russo-Japanese and 1914–18 wars. An interjector asked her whether the movement was Australia First or Japan First. Cahill, operating with that special licence which apparently allows fervent nationalists to be insultingly outspoken about their fellow-countrymen,[2] called Australians 'emotionally weak'. At the first meeting he had seen them as 'physically lazy'. Now they were 'colonial children' who had been easily led and 'rushed with enthusiasm into this European war, which is not theirs.' Cahill stirred up the large body of opponents in the audience including some uniformed R.A.A.F. men, and proceedings had to be closed hurriedly. Other meetings at the Australian Hall followed much the same pattern. The social irritation they caused undoubtedly had much to do with the subsequent sad history of the movement.

On 19 November Stephensen, asked if he was a Communist Party renegade, replied, according to a press report: 'I gave the Communists up when Russia joined the League of Nations in 1926 and proved itself a humbug.'[3] The same press report added that a woman in the audience pointed out (correctly) that Russia did not join the League until 1934. Among other things Stephensen told the meeting he objected to were the introduction of Jewish refugees and limitation of trade relations with Japan (this was at a time when Japanese forces were known to be concentrating in Indo-China). Hecklers accused Stephensen of being pro-Axis. What Stephensen replied to this far from novel complaint went unrecorded except perhaps in the inaccessible archives of Army Intelligence which probably had a shorthand writer there.

Stephensen told the meeting that his movement did not yet have 100 members. If it gained 50,000 or 60,000 members it would then consider nominating candidates for Parliament.

Valentine Crowley caused a minor stir at the following meeting by airing the orthodox nationalist, and surely justifiable, objection to Australians calling England 'home'. Mrs Walsh, rather vulnerable on this point, explained that though she had been born in England, Australia was now her home. She could not resist taking it just that little further: 'Australia is my "home" just as it is the home of naturalized Germans and Italians. Would you say that these people are not loyal to Australia?' Dissenting voices informed her that she was mistaken, Germans were loyal only to Hitler. At the final meeting before Pearl Harbor, held on 4 December, Cahill advocated national unity 'on the Portuguese model' and Stephensen admitted a preference for 'national socialism' to 'international communism'. One of the audience responded: 'Heil Stephensen!'

The Australian Hall meeting of 19 December was held with Cahill no longer on the platform. He had not been happy working with Mrs Walsh and he had argued with Stephensen about conscription for service abroad. Cahill had wanted the movement to go into recess for the war's duration. He argued that Australia's separate declaration of war against Japan altered everything and he thought Stephensen should back the government in the new circumstances. So though he was present at the meeting it was as a member of the audience to hear Stephensen opposing conscription. Cahill's term as organizer, at a weekly rate of £5 (paid out of Tinker-Giles's pocket), had lasted about one month. He resigned about the time of Pearl Harbor and joined the militia.

Mrs Walsh was expelled (or left) about the same time mainly because of her embarrassing support for the Japanese. Her version was that 'the people with wild ideas [in the movement] had loud voices', and she resigned. However, the weight of evidence suggests that she was pressed to leave.

At the last meeting before the Christmas recess, on 19 December 1941, Stephensen was greeted by organized opposition. Masey, his supporting speaker, who dealt with Australia's external relations, was more calmly received.

Miles died on 10 January 1942, three days after the movement's first public meeting for that year. He was cremated at Rookwood the next day with Stephensen delivering the valedictory address. Miles maintained his peculiarly stark sense of humour in personal matters to the end when, knowing he was dying, he ran a sweep on the time he would finally go.

Stephensen's speech on 5 February so impressed Keith Bath, a Manly real estate agent, a former Nationalist and U.A.P. activist and a *Publicist* reader for two years, that he discussed joining the movement on 17 February and came along to hear more on 19 February.

The Australia-First Movement

Public Meeting

will be held in

Adyar Hall

Bligh Street, Sydney, on

Thurs. 5th Feb.

at 8 p.m.

Advance **AUSTRALIA** *First!*

Bath had already been involved with Army Intelligence, who had called on him in January 1942 to inspect his radio, on which, according to a business competitor, he had been getting excellent reception from Japan. This was a time of several radio 'scares', with allegations, almost invariably unfounded, that Sydney people were transmitting messages to Japan—H. K. Prior, managing director of the *Bulletin,* was accused of this in Parliament. References on Radio Tokyo to Australian beach-front defence preparations seemed to people to verify fears of home-front spies. In Bath's case, Sergeant George St Heaps, a police friend of his, came to explain that enquiries made about his radio had not been authorized and there was no reason why he should not listen to Japanese broadcasts. Sergeant St Heaps told him to keep listening and report anything of interest. Bath subsequently invited the sergeant to lunch at home to meet Stephensen and discuss the Adyar Hall incident. St Heaps was later to be one of the party which went to arrest Masey.

Whether by accident or design it is hard to say, but the public meetings of 7 January and 5 February in the Adyar Hall had been orderly and quiet. Were the customary interjectors saving up for something special? Certainly 19 February, the third meeting, was very special. Although distracted from domestic news by the previous day's Japanese bombing of Darwin, the *Sydney Morning Herald* still found space on page 6 to describe this Australia First meeting as 'one of the worst brawls ever to occur in a Sydney public hall.'

It began with between 200 and 300 people in the hall, about half of whom were soon to reveal themselves as opponents of Australia First. Masey and Stephensen had been advertised as speakers, with Valentine Crowley as chairman. Miles Franklin, whom Stephensen had first met and befriended in London in 1932, was among those on the platform. She was a writer whose sympathies caused her naturally to gravitate towards nationalist movements. After the opening anthem, 'Advance Australia Fair', Crowley made a few general remarks, being heard in silence only until he mentioned Stephensen. This proved the spark needed to ignite audience emotion. Thus the first speaker, Masey, billed to talk on Australian nationalism, got only as far as 'Ladies and gentlemen . . .'. After an interjector shouted that the Australia First movement was a Fascist organization, violence took over. Rotten eggs were thrown, chairs were smashed, stinkbombs let off, brawls began and one man swung a large wooden hammer as a weapon. Gordon Rice, one of the movement's executive, walked up to the first interjector to ask him to sit down and keep quiet. A group of about a dozen men at once set upon Rice. Another, smaller, group advanced on the platform where Stephensen was vainly appealing for order. Miles Franklin was quickly bundled to safety out to the back of the building. Movement supporters went to join battle with Rice's assailants and some, including Stephensen's twenty-four-year-old brother, Eric, and Richard Ludowici, went to aid Stephensen. One man smashed a water carafe over Stephensen's head while others were punching him. He was knocked to the floor and kicked. Keith Bath hurried out to call the police, who proved surprisingly hard to find.

After about fifteen minutes of all-in fighting at Adyar Hall, police appeared. If a police shorthand writer had been present, as was the custom, he had not attempted to quell the disturbance. By the time the police did come, 'the villainous bruisers, who had obviously been hired by some person or persons'—to use Stephensen's melodramatic but in the circumstances justifiable words—had gone. Order restored, a bloodied, black-eyed and considerably battered Stephensen took over the meeting. Although most of the hostile element had gone, some dissenters remained, for interjections resumed almost immediately. Stephensen responded by inviting a waterside worker to the platform to have his say. On the rare occasions when this tactic has been tried in Australia at election meetings it has usually resulted in the general collapse of the invited party into truculent speechlessness—but not this time. The far from tongue-tied opponent spoke pungently about the Walshes and their free trip to Japan, accusing them of being quislings. Another interjector supported him, trading insults with Stephensen whom he called a 'filthy Japanese agent'. Again the meeting dissolved into an uproar but without the earlier violence. Police arrested James McLoughlin, a wharf labourer, and Andrew Dove, a labourer, on charges of having behaved offensively. When McLoughlin and Dove were removed, the interjecting group, perhaps one hundred strong, left in a body. Stephensen then spoke for about eighty minutes. When the demonstrators went they took with them the movement's subscription receipt book which two of them found on Mrs Rice's table. Confirmation of this incident has been given by Tom Nelson, a communist and an official of the Waterside Workers' Federation, in *The Hungry Mile* (1957):

> One night in 1942 a body of wharfies went to the Adyar Hall where Australia First leaders were meeting, to rout out and wind up the pro-Japanese movement. We managed to capture most of their records in that raid and handed them over to the Curtin

Labor Government which subsequently interned many members of that organisation for the duration of the war.

Stephensen, who refused to be silenced by his physical ordeal, maintained in his speech the right of his organization to hold meetings even at such a time of national peril. He complained about the loss of Rabaul because of its insufficient garrison at a time when the main bulk of Australian strength was in Palestine. Stephensen was not to know that the Prime Minister, John Curtin, was then battling against the considerable opposition of Churchill to get I Australian Corps (the 6th and 7th Divisions) across the Indian Ocean without diversion to Burma or Java. Stephensen asked that U.S. soldiers coming to Australia be placed under an Australian commander-in-chief. We should not, he said, allow U.S. publicists to say that their forces came to protect us when in truth they came only to use Australia's position for their own sake. Half a dozen questions politely asked and as politely answered closed the meeting. It was the last the movement held.

Next day Keith Bath, who had not returned to the hall, assuming that the meeting would not be going on, read in his morning paper that Stephensen had in fact delivered his speech. Full of admiration for this feat he immediately went into the city to see Stephensen at the Australia First office. Stephensen told him that he had just received a cheque for £25 from Sir Thomas Gordon[4] to be used for the hire of the Sydney Town Hall for a meeting of protest. It happened, and not for the first or last time, that a political group hitherto ignored began to attract support when it became widely known as being actively anti-communist or as having attracted the opposition of communists. Bath said he knew the Lord Mayor, Alderman S. S. Crick, and arranged for Stephensen, Hooper and Crowley to see him the following day. Alderman Crick told them their application would have to go before the next council meeting. Some delay clearly seemed likely in getting a decision on a matter which was of some urgency. To the movement it was important that the protest should follow the original disturbance as soon as possible. As the Adyar Hall authorities said they did not want any more meetings, Bath, who had long been associated with civic affairs in Manly, suggested an early meeting there at the Arcadia Theatre, which was booked for 5 March. Bath asked for, and was promised, police protection from any invading basher gangs. Inspector Christensen of Manly gave him this assurance.

Early on the day of the meeting Stephensen was approached by the New South Wales Police Commissioner, W. J. MacKay, who asked him to call it off because of the likelihood of civil disturbance. Stephensen replied that it was up to MacKay to stop this happening. MacKay said he could not spare the men, and insisted that if Stephensen did not cancel the meeting he would have to make it an order. Then, after Stephensen finally gave in, MacKay incautiously admitted he was acting under instructions from the federal Attorney-General, Dr Evatt.

Stephensen went to Manly to chalk a notice outside the theatre announcing that the meeting had been cancelled by the police, who had reason to fear a breach of the peace. As there had been extensive advertising—3,000 leaflets plus advertisements in the *Sydney Morning Herald* and the *Manly Daily*—a large crowd converged on the theatre that night, sufficient, according to its caretaker, to have filled it. While Stephensen and his brother Eric were outside assuring people that the meeting really was off, Bath and his wife waited inside the theatre. About 8.20 p.m. Stephensen went in to see the Baths with Inspector Christensen and two detectives. According to Bath, it was at this point that Stephensen said to him: 'Thank you very much for all you have done, Mr. Bath. I am afraid the Australia First movement will now have to become a mere social group until after the war, now that the authorities have seen fit to ban our meetings.' The membership at this stage was about eighty.

Stephensen next circularized members of the New South Wales Legislative Assembly denying an allegation made on 25 February by the member for Bondi, Abram Landa, that his movement was pro-Fascist or anti-Semitic. Landa had called for the suppression of the movement, saying it was ironical that an Australian had been fined £5 for having interrupted Fascist propaganda. (Several days before, McLoughlin and Dove had appeared before a Sydney magistrate on their offensive behaviour charges. McLoughlin, who was fined £5, told the court that he had three times tried to enlist, had three brothers in the army and the views expressed at the meeting were repugnant to him and most of the audience. In his opinion the Australia First movement was doing immeasurable harm.) Landa asserted that the movement was anti-Semitic, adding: 'If Mr. Stephensen maintains that the Government of Australia has been guided by any policy dictated or even suggested by Jews, he is indulging in the type of propaganda used by Nazis everywhere.' Stephensen's circular outlined ten points—not the same ten points as in the movement's original manifesto—he had intended putting to the Manly meeting:

1. A national non-party government and no party legislation during the war emergency.

2. Active defence against air raids by fighter planes rather than passive defence by blackout.

3. Fighting spirit instead of 'deep shelters', 'scorched earth', 'evacuation', 'Maginot mentality', and retreatism.

4. Courageous and positive war leadership instead of 'scare advertising'.

5. A public inquiry into ministerial responsibility for the insufficient defence of Rabaul.

6. No formation of an irregular 'People's Army'.

7. Recall when practicable of the AIF and RAAF for Australia's defence.

8. Aid for Australia first (i.e. before Russia).

9. An independent voice for Australia in Pacific war councils.

10. Immediate transfer of all Commonwealth Government departments to Canberra.

In his reply to Landa, Stephensen claimed the right to oppose Jewish policies as such whenever these policies appeared inimical to Australia's welfare.

Without the reassuring buttress of Miles and his bank-book, Stephensen was meeting attacks with spirit but he must surely have been increasingly aware of Army Intelligence interest in his organization. Another worry came from quarrels within the movement's ranks. Mrs Walsh and Cahill had departed, but this did not end dissension. Masey and Salier had become reconciled, though not entirely, to the movement's policy and the way the *Publicist* was being run. Tinker-Giles, the treasurer, resigned partly through pressure of private business and partly because of a disagreement with Mrs Walsh. He was not to be wooed back although he agreed, after several requests by Stephensen (the last on 6 March) to come to the movement's office and check some items in the books and sign cheques. When Giles did arrive, on the morning of 9 March, Stephensen told him that he was 'putting the movement in abeyance' and a new treasurer would not be needed.

Mrs Walsh and Cahill were replaced on the executive by Martin Watts and Miss Phoebe Walton, a schoolteacher. Miss Walton contributed several articles to the *Publicist* on her experiences in the London blitz, contributions that sat oddly in that company. She was a regular attender at the weekly study and speakers' classes held for movement members and was, like Masey and Salier, far from convinced that Stephensen was following the best policy. A Sydney printer, W. A. Cummins, and his wife joined the committee some time in its final weeks.

When Stephensen submitted the draft of a three-point leaflet to a movement study class at the end of January he met a rebuff. Masey, backed by the class, strongly objected to point three which stated Australia's right to make a separate peace. He felt that among other things it would be falsely interpreted as advocating a move towards signing a separate peace with Japan and Germany and not just a claim for increased national status. He told Stephensen after the class that he would take no further part in the movement if the third clause was left in the circular. The clause was dropped and the dodger reduced to two points dealing with the recall of the A.I.F. and the upholding of Australia's independent status.

In February the *Publicist* vacated its Elizabeth Street office and took less costly premises in Hunter Street.

7

Melbourne

WHEN LESLIE CAHILL came to Sydney to help Stephensen as a rough and ready public speaker and organizer he left behind in Melbourne an Australia First group of indefinite purpose and shape. It had no Miles to pay its bills and no Stephensen to provide enthusiasm, and perhaps for this reason it had little impact on the politics of that austere southern capital.

Melbourne had long had a group of Catholic radicals whose feeling for the British Empire was rather less than enthusiastic. Like Dr Mannix, whose followers they mainly were, they put Australia first; that is, if they felt Ireland no longer commanded their primary allegiance. The Empire was very definitely second, if it rated any priority at all. Cahill, though his parents were Sinn Feiners, was not a typical member of this group. Once a communist, he had become a zealous opponent of his old comrades and had also adopted anti-Semitism.

Cahill signed up another Victorian as a member of the Sydney movement: A. Rud Mills, a Tasmanian-born solicitor who went through the University of Melbourne Law School at the same time as R. G. Menzies. Mills was no Catholic and was not even greatly concerned, on the evidence of his public statements, with Australia. He was not a member of the group in Victoria. In his own special way he was anti-Semitic, but he was also anti-Christian. His thoughts tended to be shrouded in Nordic mists and it was in such an 'Aryan' atmosphere that he came to have something in common with the more German-biased Australia Firsters. A third important figure in Victoria, also outside the Catholic-Irish group, was W. D. Cookes, the controller of the large shoe manufacturing and retailing business of Ezywalkin, who was an old friend of W. J. Miles and acquainted with Rud Mills. He had absolutely nothing to do with the Victorian group—as far as can be discovered. Cookes tried, with no significant success, to get support for Australia First ideas within the Victorian rationalist movement—he was a director of the Rationalist Association of Australia Ltd, and the Rationalist head office was in the Ezywalkin building. At one stage all the members of the Rationalist Society began to receive Australia First literature through the post, but this was the total extent of the involvement of the society.

The main body of nationalists, the anti-imperialist Irish or descendants of Irish, were more in the nature of a study group. Many were, or recently had been, undergraduates at the University of Melbourne. Articles appearing in the literary magazine *Design* in 1940 and editorials in the Catholic weekly *Advocate,* both edited by P. I. O'Leary, reflected their position. *Design* and the *Publicist* had a small bout of mutual admiration, *Design* calling the Sydney monthly 'pungent' and the flattered *Publicist,* unused to much praise, referring to O'Leary's short-lived review as 'piquant'.

In the *Advocate* 'Pericles' offered some friendly criticism of the *Publicist* early in 1939 and the *Publicist* (probably Miles, realizing that here was a possible source of valuable support) commented: 'Although regular writers for *The Publicist* are not Catholics, it has been clear that Catholics have shown a more spontaneous sympathy and understanding of our propaganda than any other section of the community.' This was not the first time the hard-headed Miles had leaned towards the Catholics. In 1920 one of his objections to the Rationalist Press Association was that it was 'sectarian', that is, anti-Catholic and pro-Protestant. Miles admired Mannix for his success in showing up the Empire as being fundamentally very weak.

The Melbourne group, centred mainly in industrial Richmond and middle-class Malvern, held several meetings including a mock parliament at the Temperance Hall in Russell Street. (W. M. Bourke, a young solicitor, later to become a fiercely anti-communist Labor M.H.R. who was expelled from the A.L.P. in 1955, and his brother Daniel, were among those to take part. Daniel Bourke, a *Publicist* subscriber, was a great admirer of Stephensen's nationalist advocacy.) Being far less provocative, the Melbourne group did not encounter anything like the opposition offered to the Sydney movement, except in the response to Cahill's boisterous Yarra Bank campaign against the communists. Richmond group meetings ran from about August 1940 to March 1941.

E. L. Kiernan, a Legislative Councillor whose father was an Irishman, claimed to have formed a Melbourne Australia First group which consisted mainly of men much younger than himself. (Kiernan was a politician who broke with the Labor Party over the Premiers' Plan in 1932.) But in a letter to a Perth sympathizer, Mrs O'Loughlin, in July 1940, Miles said that there was 'no relation between the young men in Melbourne and us—but they circulate *The Publicist* to our mutual advantage.'

Cahill claimed to have founded Australia First as a Melbourne organization in 1939 on the Yarra Bank but his handful of supporters were united more by their anti-communism than by any fervent nationalist feelings. They affected an armband when taking up collections. Cahill had some strange ideas on campaigning. One scheme was to canvass Melbourne suburbs with a mobile amplifier advertising a list of Australian books. His reasoning was: 'If Australians could be induced to read Australian books it would only be a matter of time before they would think Australianly—and once they began to think Australianly they would act Australianly.'

Niall Brennan, son of the federal parliamentarian Frank Brennan, belonged to a University group called the Eureka Society, mostly Irish Catholics who were opposed to involvement in England's wars and who regarded themselves as 'faintly affiliated' with the Australia First group. They held some Japanese cultural friendship functions and saw the worsening relations with Japan as being due to English policies. The society had no 'attitude' to Jews or Germans. David Pitt, one of Brennan's colleagues, felt strongly that Stephensen's *Foundations of Culture* deserved more attention and used it as a basis for discussion with students in 1937–8. About this time he published in *Farrago* a series of 'Provocative Paragraphs' urging greater national self-dependence. These items, signed 'Percival', caused a considerable stir in the paper's correspondence columns, with members of the University Labour Club such as Helen Palmer (now editor of the independent socialist journal *Outlook*) taking issue. Helen Palmer was also anti-imperialist, but she and Pitt had little else in common; she was strongly anti-Fascist and Pitt strongly anti-Communist. The nationalist argument tended to be lost in the continuing student debates over the Spanish Civil War that had engaged the attention of B. A. Santamaria and S. J. Ingwersen (a *Publicist* contributor) on the Franco side.

Cahill had little to do with these young Catholics. Brennan, for example, met him only once—and was not impressed. Cahill was accepted by Miles as the spokesman for the Victorians and was given space in the *Publicist,* though his opinions were always presented there as his own. In far more of a hurry than the other Victorians,

Cahill was urging Sydney to form a political party, despite a cold response by Miles. Even so, Miles gave Cahill space in the *Publicist* to publish material supporting Rud Mills's candidature for the Fawkner seat in the 1940 federal elections. Cahill also wrote in the *Publicist* that there was an Australia First campaign to win Kooyong from R. G. Menzies. In fact Menzies faced an A.L.P. opponent and four independents, none of whom declared themselves for Australia First. Mills stood in Fawkner as the nominee of the Motorists' Protection League, polling 2,152 votes to 38,387 for H. E. Holt (U.A.P.) and 22,558 for A. E. Fraser (A.L.P.).

What appears to have been the central Australia First organization in Melbourne (ignoring University groups or Yarra Bank cabals) was, at least for a time, chaired by an Ansett Airways executive, R. D. Collins, who held some meetings at his home. He is now a *restaurateur*.

Rud Mills met Cahill on the Yarra Bank and sent him 10s 6d in 1941 to join the Sydney movement. Mills, who became a *Publicist* contributor, had himself published several small political papers, the *National Socialist* in Sydney and the *Angle* in Melbourne in the thirties, to publicize his belief in 'racial purity'. Commonwealth Investigation Branch officers and Victorian police had had Mills under observation since the outbreak of war because of his earlier interest in Germany and his sympathy with English Fascists. He had been to the Soviet Union—on an Intourist trip with Sidney Webb as one of the party—and, according to his wife, on his return wrote a book (never published) attacking the Russian system. He gave lectures on this subject in Melbourne to the annoyance of local communists. Mills had also written poetry under the pen-name of 'Tasman Forth' (he was born at Forth in Tasmania) in 1934, and a discussion of the Christian ethic in politics, *And Fear Shall be in the Way,* in 1933. In 1936 he published books expounding his ideas for an 'Odinist' church, a new Nordic-based religion with Mills probably its sole true believer.

Mills may have been the only Victorian connected with Australia First to know Miles's friend Cookes. Mills approached Cookes for a subscription to the *Angle*. He knew that Cookes, being a rationalist, was interested in religion and he (Mills) wanted to discuss his ideas with him. Cookes subscribed to and helped to finance the *Publicist*; his opinions carried weight with Miles. Stephensen did not have much to do with Cookes, who, like Mrs O'Loughlin, was one of Miles's private contacts. However, after Miles died Stephensen wrote to Cookes for a donation to keep the *Publicist* going and received

£250.[1] In soliciting this contribution Stephensen, perhaps sensing the best line to take, told Cookes that the *Publicist* was the only paper which had consistently opposed British, American, Jewish and communist attempts to undermine Australia. Cookes approved of the Australia First movement but was not a member. He was among the lucky ones to escape detention when the storm broke in March 1942.

Niall Brennan and fellow-students had been warned, as the war went on, to spend their time in other company. Brennan's father was an old friend of Frank Forde, the Minister for the Army from October 1941, and passed on this advice, which was taken. It was becoming more apparent, in any event, that the Fascist label, increasingly applied to Australia First, meant real danger.

8

Perth

WHILE MELBOURNE NATIONALISTS were busying themselves else-where and the Sydney movement was deciding whether anything should be done until after the war, events that would settle their future were taking place 2,000 miles to the west. What happened in Perth in those days constitutes one of the least credible episodes in Australian history; it was also among the least creditable, and invites comparison with occurrences in the England of 1816–20, when an easily alarmed Home Office flooded radical organizations with government spies and *agents provocateurs*.*

In Perth in 1942 the *agent provocateur* was Frederick James Thomas. His principal victim was Laurence Frederick Bullock, a man of Gallipoli. Bullock's fellow-conspirators were an insurance agent, Charles Leonard Albert Williams, a dairy-farmer, Edward Cunningham Quicke, and a postal assistant, Nancy Rachel Krakouer. These four Western Australians became the first people to be tried before an Australian court on a charge of having plotted to aid their country's enemy. Their misfortune swiftly brought disaster to the Australia First movement in Sydney, with which it was falsely alleged they were associated.

There had never been an Australia First organization in Western Australia although a few copies of the *Publicist* were sent to individuals, one of whom was Madeline Labouchère Eva O'Loughlin of Nedlands, an Austrian who had married an Australian and had lived

---

* Oliver, Castles and Edwards were the most notorious of these *agents provocateurs*, experts in manufacturing and encouraging conspiracies which they then denounced. George Edwards concocted a plot for Arthur Thistlewood and his small group of associates in the radical land reform society of Spencean Philanthropists, talking them into a scheme to kill Ministers gathered at a cabinet meeting. He then arranged for them to be raided as they met before the plan was due to be executed, in a barn in Cato Street, London.

in Australia for more than three decades. She corresponded with W. J. Miles; this was the extent of her connection with the Australia First movement. Her accent and nationality suggested prudence in political campaigning in war-time. She had once been a member of the Anglo-German friendship group known as The Link, and was anti-Semitic, a circumstance she claimed stemmed from her early days in Vienna when she saw Jews hoarding food in times of starvation. When Hitler marched into Vienna in 1937 she hoped everything in Austria would change for the better. Mrs O'Loughlin knew Laurence Bullock at least as early as 1939 when, she said, he approached her with a proposal about forming a political party with a £2 annual membership fee, to include a subscription to the *Publicist*. Mrs O'Loughlin passed this idea on to Miles who replied that he was not in favour and did not want Bullock as his agent in Western Australia.

Bullock, a strange, restless figure, was throughout the thirties deeply involved in Western Australian domestic politics. Born in Richmond, Surrey, he joined the British Army in World War I, aged sixteen. His mother soon had him out, but within a month he was back in uniform again. He served in Egypt and Gallipoli with the British Expeditionary Force, being attached to the 1st Battalion, Northants Regiment. He was honorably discharged at the war's end, medically unfit, on a 29s a week life pension. Deciding to emigrate from Britain, he went to Canada under the Prince of Wales scheme for British Legion men and worked for a time on a cattle train. He returned to England, only to leave shortly afterwards as a migrant to Western Australia in 1924. Until 1929 he worked on the ill-fated group settlement dairying scheme. When, like so many others, he was eventually driven off the land, the Depression struck and Western Australia with its heavy reliance on exports of wheat, wool and butter was severely affected. Bullock spent the early thirties living on sustenance and relief payments. A fully paid-up member of the Returned Servicemen's League, he was refused aid because he was a British, not an Australian, ex-serviceman: he had forfeited his 29s pension on migration. He occupied himself in his time of hardship in political and industrial organizing, forming the Sustenance and Relief Workers' Union in this exceedingly unhappy time in the State's history. F. K. Crowley, in *Australia's Western Third,* has told how for a time Perth and its suburbs looked like one vast unemployment depot. Economies forced on the State government, which meant sackings, led to clashes between police and the desperate unemployed men seeking to demonstrate in Perth. Bullock was one of the human items tossed around in this current of social despair. But unlike many of the more helpless victims he looked around for political solutions. He worked with T. J. ('Diver') Hughes, the colourful Labor M.L.A. for East Perth from 1922 to 1927 and later (1936) an Independent M.L.A., chairing and organizing many of his meetings. Bullock has claimed that he and Hughes were directly responsible for prodding the State government into legislating for the State lottery which began in 1933. Bullock was always interested in community affairs and political ideas and when the *Publicist* came his way he found its message attractive. He thought of forming some sort of organization to propagate its ideas in Western Australia.

When World War II broke out Bullock became an object of suspicion to the State political police. Detective-Sergeant G. R. Richards,[1] who was in charge of the Special (political) Bureau of the Perth C.I.B., later told Bullock: 'You were always a person of interest to me in the job I was in.' He tried twice to enlist in the forces—in Motor Transport in 1939 and the Air Force in 1940—but was rejected. War for him brought employment after his lean years. One job was with a small farmers' supply firm which virtually folded under him. As he found himself left with its office furniture he decided to use it to run a similar agency himself. It was in this capacity that he met the local German consul, Ittershagen. When police searched Bullock's flat in 1940 they discovered correspondence with him. The searchers, Richards and Constable Baseley, also found some letters addressed to Ittershagen that had not been sent, one of them being the constitution of a new political party, the People's Party, in which Bullock suggested that the consul might be interested. Whatever was found was insufficient to warrant his arrest or internment on any charge. Bullock maintained that his connection with Ittershagen was solely concerned with a car agency. It was probably through Ittershagen that he met Mrs O'Loughlin.

Finally Bullock became established in a good job and one at which he proved adept. He became organizer for the butterfat section of the Primary Producers' Association in the south-west region. Gradually he established himself, and the prospect of Country Party preferment came into view as a possibility. But it came to nothing because, perennially restive, he kept talking politics, often Australia First politics, much to the interest of Richards's section.

At Balingup, Bullock met E. C. Quicke who, like himself, had been associated with the Douglas Credit movement. Finding Quicke opposed to the Primary Producers' Association, Bullock, looking for common ground in an attempt to woo his support, showed him

the *Publicist*. As Quicke liked what it had to say, Bullock, rarely one
to leave well alone, went on to say that he was the leader of the
Australia First movement in Western Australia. This was not the
case, however much he wished it; he just wanted to encourage
Quicke.

After the Japanese entered the war, Bullock, most unwisely—
though it would have been useless to have warned him—began telling acquaintances that a negotiated peace with Japan should be considered. He had been reading Edgar Snow's *Red Star over China,*
and interpreted its meaning for Australia as being that Japan supplied a buttress between the United States and the 'eastern Bloc'.
Japan was thus important to Australia, and if there must inevitably
be a *rapprochement* with Japan and developing economic relations
for mutual advantage why then go on with the war? Why not just
negotiate? He could hardly have chosen a less suitable time to advance this ingenuous argument. He did not appear to have considered whether the Japanese, in their full flush of conquest, would fall
in calmly with such a sensible notion. And in a Western Australia
which undoubtedly felt itself likely to take the first force of an enemy
attack, expected any day, such propositions, however innocently
meant, were certain to be misinterpreted.

It is not proof of anything to note—as Richards did—that Bullock bothered to study Mosley's British Fascist paper *Action* in the
Perth Public Library, any more than it is necessarily suggestive to
record that Quicke and his wife borrowed *Mein Kampf*.

The remaining principals in the Western Australian affair
(Stephensen described them all as 'simpletons') were Williams, then
aged thirty, who met Bullock on his rounds at Manjimup, and Miss
Krakouer who was separated from her husband (Reginald Norman
Moss) and was a friend of Bullock, but had no political interests.
Williams was another English migrant who came out as a boy with
his father on the group settlement scheme. He suffered badly in the
Depression and his main political concern thereafter was to see that
nothing like it ever happened again.

Neither Bullock, Quicke, Williams nor Krakouer had any firm
affiliations with the *Publicist* group in Sydney. Bullock and Quicke
had written to them but that was all. Bullock received no encouragement of his suggestions that they get things moving in Western Australia. Williams and Krakouer had no interest in what was happening
in Sydney. In Sydney there was the minimum of interest in Perth.
One person from Burekup, and probably some other Western Australians, had responded by mail to Stephensen's call in the *Publicist*

John Kirtley, 1950

A. R. Mills, about 1944

Leslie Cahill, 1961

Mr Justice Clyne, 1955

Adela and Thomas Walsh
(*Japan as Viewed by Foreigners*, 1940)

in 1938 for readers' groups but nothing came of this. Miles could not have been in Western Australia after 1929 and Stephensen's last call had been on his way home from England in 1932 when he briefly met Katharine Susannah Prichard.

When Australia First propaganda and its riot-prone public meetings began to agitate Army Intelligence in Sydney, word filtered through to Richards in Perth. From his knowledge of potential activists he saw Mrs O'Loughlin and Bullock as likely starting-points for any investigations. At some stage their mail was intercepted and scanned before delivery. Both, in Richards's mind, had pro-German tendencies. When war with Japan heightened the threat to Western Australia's security a further investigation was clearly required.

Official word of Australia First activities in Sydney reached Perth in January 1942 in the form of a report compiled by two constables, Doyle and Walsh. But already the staff officer in charge of Army Intelligence in Western Command, Colonel H. D. Moseley, a chief stipendiary magistrate, had decided the time had come for action, so Richards sent one of his men to check. Had this man been a purely passive investigator nothing further may have been heard of the matter, although Bullock's talk of a peace with Japan would perhaps merely have brought restrictions on his activities had not Richards sent Frederick James Thomas as his agent.

Thomas had already tested a suitable *modus operandi*. He had earlier joined the Communist Party under instructions from Richards to find out something about that organization from within. He took part enthusiastically in its activities. Subsequently communists claimed he had planted subversive literature on their premises so that police could get evidence against them.

A rolling stone for most of his life, Thomas, born in Auckland, had gone to Western Australia in 1934 after stays in Queensland and New South Wales. He had convictions for 'jumping' trains in eastern States. After the outbreak of war he tried to enlist but had been rejected because he had only one good eye. He joined the police in 1941, Richards taking him on as an investigator at £5 a week. To tackle his Australia First assignment he adopted the name of 'Frederick Carl Hardt', a German from Sydney. 'Hardt' also happened to be the name of a Nazi Party leader in Sydney. He presented himself as 'Hardt' to Mrs O'Loughlin, saying he had come from eastern Australia on behalf of the Australia First movement, and that he had met Mrs Adela Pankhurst Walsh who had mentioned Mrs O'Loughlin's name. Mrs O'Loughlin suggested that Bullock would be interested and arranged for a message to be sent to him as he was in the country on Primary Producers' business. This message was passed on by Nancy Krakouer, who said that a man had come to see him on a special business and added that she would like to see him that coming weekend too. So Bullock made the train trip in from Bunbury on Friday 13 February to meet Miss Krakouer and 'Hardt' at the Perth station. 'Hardt' told him that he had come to Western Australia to form an Australia First branch. This interested Bullock but he felt a little put out as he had ideas of himself as the Australia First organizer.

What was subsequently said between 'Hardt' and Bullock and other conversations involving Quicke, Williams and Krakouer provided the subject of dispute at later court proceedings. Thus though the general outline of events in the succeeding three weeks is fairly clear there are disagreements about who said what at some vital points. Lacking independent third-party testimony, it is still difficult to establish the facts. It will be fairest first to present the 'Hardt' (Thomas) version, follow it with Bullock's story and then add what comments common sense seems to suggest.

'Hardt' said that on meeting Bullock he produced a Sydney Australia First pamphlet, one advertising an Adyar Hall meeting, as evidence of his involvement. 'Hardt' asked what the chances were of starting Australia First meetings in Perth, to be told that action was wanted as they were too slow in the East. Bullock said he obtained Nazi propaganda from Schreimer, the German propaganda chief for North America, and added: 'I'm an out-and-out National Socialist.' He complained that he had been raided by police in 1940 because two King Street printers called Jarvis had 'put him away' after he had explained his ideas to them. Richards and Baseley had made the raid; he intended to 'get' that swine Baseley. Bullock continued:

Singapore has fallen, Java won't last long; we can't hold Northern Australia and Darwin; we should negotiate a peace with Japan at once. Of course Curtin & Co. won't do this—they'll fight. I know the farming community of this State very well; I am certain if we could get control of the broadcasting stations they would be in favour of a negotiated peace with the Japanese. All the atrocity stories put out about the Japanese are all 'hooey' and 'propaganda'.

Miss Krakouer, according to 'Hardt' 's story, at this stage expressed a dislike of the Jews. (Miss Krakouer's paternal grandparents were Jewish.) The next day Bullock told him that he had held a highly successful meeting of Australia First supporters at Manjimup early in January. (No such meeting was held.) 'Hardt' showed Bullock a photograph album with pictures of Axis leaders. Bullock then praised Hitler for his choice of *Gauleiters* and fifth columnists and said that such men were the true patriots of their countries. He himself had a reliable *Gauleiter*—Quicke—in the south-west, and with 'half a dozen more like him' they would be set.

On 21 February Bullock and 'Hardt' met at the latter's and Bullock drove him towards South Perth. West of the causeway he pointed to the foreshore and said: 'This is where the Japanese and German aircraft will land.' They drove to Crawley where, opposite Matilda Bay, Bullock commented: 'This is where Japanese flying boats will land.' Later, in Bullock's room at the Rex Hotel, Quicke, introduced to 'Hardt', remarked: 'This is not like the Munich beer cellar.' Bullock said it was usual at such meetings to begin with a preamble and offered as a suitable statement: 'Quisling is the true patriot of Norway and we are the true patriots of Australia.' After a discussion of Quisling, Bullock said, 'I will now form an Australia First Party', and was nominated as leader by Quicke. Bullock suggested Miss Krakouer as secretary. Proposing the use of sabotage to assist the Japanese invaders, Bullock said the blowing up of the Midland Junction workshops would undermine the morale of the people. Other grandiose plans were laid. 'Hardt' was assigned to take care of the north-west of the State, Quicke the south-west and Bullock the Perth metropolitan area. Under Japanese occupation, they decided, the C.M.L. building in Perth would be their headquarters.

The day after this meeting Bullock brought Williams, regarded as an expert on fuses, to see 'Hardt'. Williams detailed technically how the Ford motor works at Cottesloe could be blown up.

An attempt by 'Hardt' to get corroboration for the story he was building up was frustrated by Bullock, perhaps unknowingly, on 27 February when 'Hardt' invited Bullock, Williams and Krakouer to his house, where two detectives were hidden. Bullock however did not enter the house, proposing instead that they go out to his car. There he read out a draft proclamation headed 'National Socialist Government of Australia', declaring it 'open for comment'. On a point dealing with Jews, Williams commented they should all be sterilized. Miss Krakouer wanted all Roman Catholic priests put on road-work and the church hierarchy shot. Bullock named people to be liquidated, including Richards, Baseley, Moseley, W. Mountjoy (a Labor M.H.R.) and the two King Street printers. All Communist Party members were to be handed to the Japanese to be shot. Bullock named twenty-one men who he said were his agents in various country centres, and mentioned two, one at North Dandalup and the other at Manjimup, who would have radio transmitters. It was an incredible performance. Somebody's imagination—either Bullock's or 'Hardt' 's—had been working overtime.

On 4 March 'Hardt' went to see Quicke at Balingup. (A police constable at nearby Greenbushes had earlier reported to Perth that Quicke was a strong National Socialist.) 'Hardt' told Quicke that Wyndham and Broome had been bombed—and this at least was fact, not fantasy. He asked Quicke if anyone locally wanted a negotiated peace and Quicke gave him five names. During lunch that day Mrs Quicke told 'Hardt': 'Ted and I used to take *Mein Kampf* to bed and read it chapter by chapter like the Bible.'

The next meeting on 8 March, involving 'Hardt', Bullock, Krakouer and Williams, was the last. There Bullock read another proclamation, this time headed 'Australia First Government'. It included a welcome for the Japanese and an expression of pleasure at being liberated from Jewish domination. Bullock arranged the following appointments for an Australian First National Socialist government to take over when the Japanese arrived: Bullock—Premier, Army, Treasury; Quicke—Police; Williams—Labour, Transport; Krakouer—all women's organizations.

As on 27 February a liquidation list was prepared but this time extra names were added, including Premier Willcock and Major-General Gordon Bennett, who was suggested by Miss Krakouer. (This was indeed strange. Bennett, until the announcement of his appointment as G.O.C. Western Command in April, had no special connection with Western Australia; in March the G.O.C. was Major-General E.C.P. Plant. Bennett did not arrive in Western Australia until 15 April.)

The East Perth power house, the Mundaring Weir and the Canning Dam were all marked down for demolition by the four plotters. A government policy draft of twenty points was prepared. Point 1 was a friendly foreign policy towards all anti-Jewish, anti-communistic and anti-democratic powers. The proclamation called on Australia to play its part in the Japanese Empire. On the way home from this meeting at the Rex Hotel, Williams told 'Hardt': 'If the Japanese invade the Eastern States, the Australia First Movement will take over there, so that we can take over the Commonwealth. I hope the Japanese invade here, so that we can take over the Commonwealth. We shall have to get more members for our government.'

That story of incredible plans for the reception of the Japanese in all its occasional strength and frequent weakness and implausibility was the plot as outlined by 'Hardt'. Presented before the Perth Police Court and later the Western Australian Supreme Court, it meant gaol for Bullock and Williams. Some corroboration for parts of 'Hardt' 's tale was available but in the hardest-to-believe and most important sections such as the proclamations and who was centrally responsible for them, it was just his word against that of others. The convictions of Bullock and Williams were based essentially on the unsupported evidence of an informer.

In court Bullock made a number of admissions. He had met 'Hardt', he had joined in several meetings and had typed several proclamations, but he had regarded the proclamations and the planning as a joke to amuse themselves. The final proclamation on 8 March had been read out on a morning when they were still affected by a night drinking party. All suggestions for action and the ideas in the proclamation had come from 'Hardt'. Most of the provocative remarks attributed to him had in fact been made by 'Hardt'. He had never said he was a National Socialist, or that he would 'get' Baseley or that Japanese atrocity stories were just 'hooey'. He did not know any King Street printers called Jarvis. He had never spoken of *Gauleiters*. 'Hardt' had given him two pages of ideas and from them, in a spirit of fun, he typed a proclamation and had commented to Williams: 'At least Hardt thinks we can govern the country for five minutes.' He had gradually begun to sense, but too late, that quietly but surely they were being pushed along a path quite different from the one they had intended to follow.

Bullock contended that the spirit of the meeting that approved the final proclamation and decided on 'liquidations' was never serious except when he composed a letter to be sent by Miss Krakouer to the Sydney office of the Australia First movement about founding an Australia First Party in Perth.

Bullock said he had been warned by Mrs O'Loughlin to be careful of 'Hardt'. Perhaps he for one did have some reservations while playing in fun 'Hardt' 's charade, but not all those present took everything in jest. Quicke swallowed whole some of the talk, if not all of it, as shown by evidence he gave in subsequent court proceedings. He told the prosecutor that he assumed the Japanese had only to land in Western Australia and the defences would crumble. He understood he was expected to inform the Japanese commander that the Perth nucleus of the Australia First Party approved a negotiated peace and then inform them of Australia First policy.

The prosecutor, who no doubt was having some difficulty with his emotions, succeeded in confirming the evidence of his ears by asking: 'Then I suppose they would have thanked you, paddled out to their warships and sailed away?'

Quicke: 'I don't know what they would have done.'

Chief Justice: 'What were you going to do with the invaders?'

Quicke: 'Present the Australia First policy to them, which I was assured they would agree with; then we would set up a government and the Japanese would withdraw.'

Chief Justice: 'You were going to arrange with them to go away?'

Quicke: 'Yes.'

While 'Hardt' was conducting his investigations he was reporting daily, sometimes twice daily, to Richards by telephone. It took him about a month to bring the four people together and get them to record treasonable intentions in writing. After the 8 March proclamation had been typewritten little more was needed by the police.

Very early on 9 March Richards, two constables and a policewoman called on Bullock and Miss Krakouer at Manly Flats, Terrace Drive, East Perth. A search uncovered the proclamation and in Miss Krakouer's room Richards said he found notes on Australian naval and military movements. A letter in the flat from 'Laurie' to 'Nancy' sent from Waroona contained this sentence: 'Enough of politics because Australia and Australians must now be educated by bombs or bayonets.'

Bullock and Krakouer were taken to the Roe Street lock-up and detained. Later two constables brought in Williams, who was questioned at the Special Bureau, and another two policemen went to Balingup for Quicke. Balingup is about 140 miles from Perth and Quicke did not reach Perth until about midday. Before Detective-Constable Alford, in charge of the arresting party, left on the return trip he rang Richards for instructions. He told Richards that Quicke, who had written to Sydney on 6 February about forming a branch of the movement in Western Australia and had received back details with advice that a branch there was not being considered, had mentioned P. R. Stephensen as being the leader or a leading member of the New South Wales movement.

Bullock, Krakouer, Williams and Quicke were taken to Fremantle gaol, being held under section 13 of the National Security Act, later under regulation 26 and finally charged with an offence under the Crimes Act. Mrs O'Loughlin, though visited by police on 10 March, was not detained or in any way restricted.

Richards consulted Colonel Moseley about the detentions, and together they decided to warn army commands elsewhere about their discoveries and what action they had taken. Moseley trustingly took Richards's word on the facts including Alford's reported reference to Stephensen; he had himself heard of Stephensen about a week earlier. Moseley prepared the following cipher telegram for Eastern Command, Sydney, and after showing it to Major-General Plant, despatched it at 11 a.m. (1.30 p.m. Sydney time):

Letter on this morning's air mail from Australia First movement being addressed 'Australia First Movement, Room 45, No. 25 O'Connell street, Sydney'. You should obtain this. Four principals in movement here, Laurence Frederick Bullock, Leonard Albert Williams, Edward Cunningham Quicke and Nancy Krakouer, detained this morning under section 13 National Security Act, had in their possession most incriminating document. Shows intention to make contact with Japanese Army at moment of invasion. Plan for sabotaging vulnerable points this command. Plan for death of head of army, police, democratic politicians, hierarchy of all denominations and businessmen. Proclamation with heading 'Australia First Government' for Australia-wide broadcast and signing of armistice with Japan contains the following: 'This expression of belief of Australian nation tribute to valiant effort of Japanese who have so successfully fought for liberation of our people from Jewish domination and danger of communism. We welcome to our country as liberator and friends military leaders and army.' The proclamation contains 20 points of policy and instructs AMF to lay down arms on penalty of death. P. R. Stephensen your command named by Quicke as leader of movement. Suggest urgent action. AHQ, and all commands and districts have been notified.

This alarming message was decoded at Eastern Command headquarters in Sydney by a Major McGowan and the deciphered version passed to Lieutenant-Colonel J. R. Powell, who that night was in charge of Intelligence, Eastern Command, about 11 o'clock. It is not known why it took so long to reach its final Sydney destination.

Colonel Powell acted in the spirit of the message and brought about the arrest in Sydney of thirteen men early on the morning of 10 March, another man just outside Sydney and a further two at military camps in northern New South Wales later the same day. These men were either members of the Australia First movement or friends of Stephensen or *Publicist* contributors. The homes of female members of the movement's executive were searched but the women were not arrested.

In Perth nothing was made public about the detentions of Bullock, Williams, Quicke and Krakouer. This may have been the result of a censorship order or, less likely, it may have been that the press simply did not discover what had happened. For whatever reason, no word of it can be discovered in Western Australian papers until early May, except for one reference in a statement by Kitson, the Chief Secretary, in the W.A. Legislative Council. Kitson on 10 April said that recent disclosures about an organization known as the 'Australia First Movement' were brought about as a result of the 'splendid work' of the Special Bureau of the W.A. police. The disclosures to which he referred must have been those by the Minister for the Army, Forde, in Canberra on 26 March which, though they mentioned the substance of the Perth allegations, did not include names or places.

The serious offence with which the four were charged—having conspired between 7 December 1941 and 9 March 1942 to assist within the Commonwealth a public enemy, to wit the armed forces of Japan—became public knowledge finally in the 7 May issue of the *West Australian,* which published a notice of that day's scheduled hearing of the charges in the Perth Police Court and the text of the proclamation the four would be accused of having compiled. This began: 'Men and women of Australia: Today a new Government assumes control of your destinies. Your Government brings with it an entirely new system based upon a negotiated peace with Japan.' After listing the twenty-point policy, which included £100 marriage loans, abolition of the White Australia policy and removal of Jews from all government positions, it added: 'The Australian nation is ordered to lay down its arms. The Japanese army of occupation will maintain law and order until such time as the Government feel that the new system has been safely established.'

Publication of this document before the hearing was not the result of a deliberate leak by Richards or the Crown. It came from the solicitor for Bullock and Williams, a man who was to inject a great deal of life into the proceedings, T. J. Hughes. That former associate of Bullock had started work as a telegraph boy and worked his way up in the public service to become audit inspector, at which stage he retired to enter Parliament. He studied law, graduating LL.B. at the age of thirty-six and was admitted to the Western Australian Bar in 1936. In and out of Parliament Hughes was always busy on the trail of political scandal, at times right on target with his tales of corruption, at other times extravagant in his accusations. It is easy to see why Bullock had been attracted to him. Some of Hughes's own wartime statements in Parliament were as incautious as those made by the man he was to defend. On 16 April 1942 he told the Western Australian Assembly:

> To hear people talking about Hitler having caused the war and singing hymns of hate, is to my mind all wrong. After all is said and done Hitler played a very small part in causing the present

war. In my opinion . . . three men were more responsible for the present war, namely Poincaré, Foch and Clemenceau . . .

This theory was defensible but the time was ill-judged to ventilate it. But like Bullock the impetuous Hughes did not worry about considerations like that.

The police court hearing was held before Mr Wallwork, S.M. A reporter described the defendants as 'Three young men of quiet, self-possessed demeanour and a young woman, neatly dressed and facing her ordeal with complete outward composure'. Fifteen prosecution witnesses were called, including eight policemen, all but one from the Special Bureau.

First and key witness was Thomas, who told of his investigations as 'Hardt'. A severe mauling in cross-examination, principally from Hughes, must have lessened the impact of his evidence. Not only did his interstate convictions come to light but his communist past suffered a sea change in the telling. An adjournment and consultation with Richards was needed before he would reveal that he had joined the Communist Party during earlier investigations under instructions from Richards.

The magistrate had little choice but to commit the defendants for trial at the June sittings of the Supreme Court, allowing each £500 bail plus two similar sureties.

The trial began on 3 June with the Chief Justice, Sir John Northmore, presiding. Their jury, according to one press report, was composed of 'middle-aged, hard-headed businessmen . . . who twice made their own comment'. Non-police witnesses were first called by the prosecution to tell of conversations they had had with Bullock. A Greenbushes dairyfarmer, Frederick Heywood, and his daughter, Clare Porter of Mosman Park, remembered Bullock discussing the weaknesses of Margaret River and Busselton defences on 11 February. An insurance inspector, Reginald Lewis Kempe, said he had reported to the police Bullock's remark to him on 4 March that Britain had let Australian down and Australia must sign a separate peace with Japan. (Bullock was not alone in feeling that Britain had let Australia down. In *You'll be Sorry,* published in 1944, Gilbert Mant, a war correspondent, said that after Singapore he heard misinformed criticism of Britain wherever he went in Australia. 'A wave of ill-feeling was sweeping across the country,' he recorded.)

A P.M.G. mechanic, Robert John Leggett, related Bullock's remark that if Australia was invaded by Japan it would be no worse off than Norway under German rule. Frederick Vincent Black of Yarloop had also passed on to the police a comment by Bullock, referring to an Australian party suing for a separate peace with Japan. The Waroona Hotel proprietor, Charlotte Hickey, said that in mid-February Bullock had told her there was no need to worry about what would happen if Japan invaded Australia. A company inspector, Edward Rawlinson Fletcher, told the court he heard Bullock on 4 March say the Japanese would be at Fremantle in a fortnight and it would be best to sue for peace. Australia had been practically ruled from Bradford but after the Japanese arrived we would get a better deal.

Evidence like this must have tended to make the jury more receptive to some of the wild things 'Hardt' claimed Bullock had said. There was little doubt that Bullock had been doing some wild talking and had been incited by the prevailing hysteria. All this, nevertheless, had no bearing on the central claim of the defence, put in a nutshell by Hughes: 'No Thomas, no conspiracy.' Thomas was now far more vulnerable as, after the lower court hearing, Hughes knew more about his weaknesses. During his three and a half days in the witness box Thomas faced a stern questioning, with Hughes insisting that Thomas had not discovered a conspiracy, but had created one. Hughes made Thomas admit that he was 'a master of terminological inexactitude' though there was the qualification that he had acquired and practised this mastery 'only in his country's interests'. Thomas maintained that the accused were not simple and unsophisticated; on the contrary, they were cold and callous.

Bullock's cross-examination by the prosecutor, G. B. D'Arcy (for the Commonwealth Crown Solicitor), did not materially affect the case but several shrewd blows were landed. Bullock might, he admitted, have written to Miles in December 1939 about the Australia First movement but no, he could not recollect having written to Miles that he believed in Germany's struggle and wanted to see her win the war. Yes, he did possess certain anti-Semitic literature but was not responsible for marking some passages. He did not report 'Hardt' to the police when 'Hardt' showed him a scrapbook with Axis leaders' pictures because 'he did not attach much importance to the matter'. To Hughes, Bullock said that international financiers made and unmade wars.

Chief Justice: 'I wish they would unmake this one.'

Hughes: 'Perhaps they will when it suits them.'

After a fourteen-day sitting the court heard Hughes in his final address suggest that the proceedings were 'a vast comedy, a poor comedy and a very expensive comedy staged by the Commonwealth Government.' Even if Thomas's allegations were taken at their face value—and they should not be—allegedly conspiratorial utterances should be regarded as nothing more than 'the ravings of a bunch of lunatics'.

D'Arcy reminded the jury that the conspiracy offence lay not in the doing of illegal acts, but in making an agreement to do them.

Hughes opened the defence with a claim that it was all a police frame-up. Williams's lawyer, Howard Bath, dissociated himself from this, limiting his complaint to a suggestion that Williams had been framed by Thomas. He had an open mind about the rest of the police.

On the sixteenth day of the trial the Chief Justice, summing up, said the sole question was whether the accused had entered into an agreement to assist the Japanese Empire.

The jury found against Bullock and Williams and acquitted Quicke and Miss Krakouer.

Bullock, 'undoubtedly the ringleader', was sentenced to three years' gaol with hard labour. Williams, the jury having recommended mercy, received only two years. The Chief Justice told the two men that assisting a public enemy was a treason, and punishable by death —'so you are fortunate that actually you have not done any act to implement the conspiracy.'

Though acquitted, Quicke and Krakouer were remanded to their former custody under National Security regulations. Their lawyers, Howard Bath and L. D. Seaton, sent telegrams to Forde in Canberra seeking cancellation of the internment orders, but without success. Hughes appealed to the Western Australian Court of Criminal Appeal on ingenious grounds, pointing out that the judge had stated that if there was an agreement, it was at the meeting of 21 February. As Quicke and Krakouer were acquitted and they were at this meeting while Williams was absent, there was therefore nobody present with whom Bullock could have made an agreement. Leave to appeal was denied by the Appeal Bench presided over by the Chief Justice, who stated his opinion that on the evidence all four should have been convicted.

Later interest in what happened at the trial brought to light the remarkable fact that no shorthand notes had been taken in the Supreme Court. Newspaper cuttings provided the sole record.

Richards considered that the arrest of the four Western Australians had cleaned up the 'quisling plot' and sent an official report to Sydney saying so. This report, dated 20 March 1942, suggested that it was time to give some publicity to the detentions, as word of the successful exposure of would-be quislings, if handled properly, could be nothing but beneficial. Foreseeing later criticism, he predicted there would be attempts to brand Thomas as an *agent provocateur* but thought that such attempts 'would meet with little sympathy'. The key section of Richards's report stated that there was no evidence that the Sydney section of the movement had any knowledge of Bullock's activities.

The only other police report from Western Australia publicly known to have any bearing on Sydney events was one dated 6 July 1942, approved by Colonel Moseley though not compiled by him, which contained a recommendation that Quicke and Krakouer should not be released from internment, as to set them free would strengthen the position of the eastern States internees.

The National Security advisory tribunal in Western Australia, presided over by the Chief Justice, refused Quicke and Krakouer leave to appeal against their detention. Quicke and Krakouer later appeared before the South Australian advisory committee in Adelaide in March 1943. Mr Justice Reed (later to become Commonwealth Director-General of Security) was chairman of this tribunal which advised against release. Afterwards Quicke claimed the committee was confused, as its recommendation stated that 'Hardt' was one of those convicted of conspiracy.

When the gaol terms of Bullock and Williams (which they spent in a compound in the hills near Perth) expired, they too were re-interned. Bullock served two years and three months in gaol, having earned the full remission for good behaviour. While in gaol Bullock, originally a Protestant, served Mass on the altar for the gaol priest, Father Moore, and was pursued as a possible convert by a Jehovah's Witness minister, Ivan Smith. He does not now believe in any organized religion and is a member of the South Australian Humanist Society.

In the final weeks before the Perth arrests only three letters are known to have bridged the gap between the Australia First movement in Sydney and Bullock's friends. Bullock wrote on 20 February to Stephensen asking if he could become the movement's representative in Western Australia. There is no record of any reply. A few days later Quicke wrote to Mrs Rice seeking literature, which she sent. Then on 8 March Miss Krakouer sent an airmail report on the formation of the new party and seeking affiliation. This letter, which was not received at the other end, was apparently intercepted by censorship officials.

Bullock met Stephensen for the first time in Loveday internment camp, South Australia.

9

Round-up

MILITARY POLICE INTELLIGENCE had been busy in Sydney and elsewhere in Australia since the start of the war rounding up enemy
aliens. There was more urgency about their task than in World War I
because in 1939 Fascist organizations existed among some Queensland Italians, and there were Nazi groups in Victoria, South Australia
and New South Wales.

Procedures laid down in the Defence Department's Commonwealth War Book, a compilation of plans for the change from a
peace-time to war-time administration, left intelligence and security
to Army Intelligence. One section of Army Intelligence was concerned with enemies overseas and the other with enemies, agents and
suspects within Australia. As this latter task grew bigger the army
enlisted the aid of some civil police who became known as Military
Police Intelligence. It took some years before a nationally organized
security service was developed. Had there been such a service run
along the relatively sophisticated lines of the Australian Security
Intelligence Organization, set up in 1949 with Mr Justice Reed as
Director-General, official action against the Australia First movement might well have been less arbitrary and ham-handed. War-time
intelligence activities remain 'classified' information but in one way
or another enough has been divulged to show that in this instance at
least the job was too big for most of those concerned. Some Intelligence officers can be thankful the official screen has been kept in
place.

In peace-time surveillance of subversive people, whether enemy
agents or not, had largely been the concern of special branches of
State police forces, such as that operated in Perth by Detective-Sergeant Richards. The Commonwealth had several small organizations

dealing with national security, apart from its Peace Officer force,[1] the main one being the Commonwealth Investigation Branch for which funds were first voted in 1919. This followed the Counter-Espionage Bureau, established in 1916, which employed the services of a number of State detectives. Behind the formation of the Commonwealth Investigation Branch was the idea of forming a body of trained investigators to keep watch on anti-constitutional groups.

In World War II the first Menzies government found the unhelpful (to put it mildly) attitude of the Australian communists to the war particularly trying and verging on the subversive. This was undoubtedly a busy time for the Commonwealth Investigation Branch. The communists, a sizeable minority (there were about 4,000 party members) with strong industrial ties, were a major headache. In the event the solution came not with the banning of the party in June 1940 but with Russia's entry into the war on 22 June 1941.

In January 1940 the federal cabinet called a conference of intelligence officers of the army, navy and air force, the Commonwealth Investigation Branch, police and censors to consider action against local subversion. Out of this the Attorney-General, W. M. Hughes, then aged seventy-six, managed to get approval for a counter-propaganda bureau run on an annual budget of £3,000. This was sufficient to finance what was known as the Australian Democratic Front, an organization with a president, a secretary and a policy of printing leaflets containing speeches by Hughes. The front, which showed no interest in watching Fascist activities, did not outlast the advent of the Curtin government in October 1941. It became the subject of a Royal Commission.

The Commonwealth Investigation Branch, not to be compared in stature with Hughes's fly-by-night opportunist venture, had shown interest in right- as well as left-wing activities, although rapid shuffling of officials as the war emergency worsened did not allow it to become fully efficient. Intelligence and Security, like so many other service organizations, of necessity had a makeshift structure in the early war years. There was also rivalry and lack of co-operation between different organizations concerned with security. The Commonwealth Investigation Branch did not, for example, work in harmony with the Military Police Intelligence. Once the branch asked Military Intelligence, Military Police Intelligence and the police for help in a search of Japanese quarters at Point Piper authorized by W. M. Hughes, to meet three refusals.

In November 1941 came a move to establish some co-ordinated national organization. A skeleton security service was set up consisting in the main of one security officer (a military man) in each State. These officers had no power other than to advise the Military Police Intelligence. A proper federal security service was not established until May 1942 when the New South Wales Police Commissioner, W. J. MacKay, was appointed first Director-General of Security, to be succeeded in September by Brigadier W. B. Simpson.

When Colonel Moseley's urgent warning arrived from Perth in March 1942 three organizations were therefore involved in security in New South Wales—Army Intelligence, the N.S.W. police and the infant Security Service in the person of Major Beauchamp Tyrell. Tyrell reported to the Commonwealth Security Service director in Canberra, Lieutenant-Colonel E. E. Longfield Lloyd, who later (1945-9) became Director-General of Security.

Until this time most police energies had been taken up with aliens. For example, as late as February 1942 a party of eleven Sydney police under Detective-Sergeant Swasbrick joined a large squad of local police to take twenty-six unnaturalized aliens from Griffith for internment. Internment camps had been set up at Liverpool near Sydney, Hay (N.S.W.), Tatura (Victoria), and Loveday (S.A.). Inevitably mistakes were made, with anti-Fascist as well as Fascist Italians and Germans being put behind barbed wire. One of the worst instances was that of the 2,400 internees, many of whom were intellectuals and dedicated anti-Fascists, brought out from Britain in the liner *Dunera* with some German and Italian prisoners of war. Very many of them remained in Australia after the war, to this country's benefit. It is doubtful if any other single vessel ever brought such a cargo of concentrated intellect.

When they were described in federal Parliament as 'friendly aliens', Archie Cameron, a Country Party M.H.R. (who had been an Intelligence officer in World War I), objected in these terms: 'If he is friendly to this country, then he must be a traitor to his own, and I do not think it is our part to encourage treason.'

There are stories of others, living in Australia, who were wrongly detained, and in some cases the truth is difficult to establish. Senator J. I. Armstrong told Parliament in 1950:

We know how the security service worked in North Queensland. My opinion is that a list of Italian canegrowers was compiled and almost every second man named on it was interned. In another instance, a man who was overheard to make a certain remark when drinking freely in a hotel in Riverina was grabbed and thrown into a concentration camp for a number of years.

An Australian-born commercial apiarist, Charles Willyan of Murchison, Victoria, was interned for fourteen weeks in 1942 at the nearby Tatura camp. After the war he wrote an account, *Behind Barbed Wire in Australia*, in which no hint can be found of any reason for his detention apart from the ill-will of a district landholder who appeared to have gained the official ear. (In 1959 a pamphlet by Willyan, *We of the White Race*, was noted in the ultra-Right American periodical *Right* with the information that it was available for $3—from P. R. Stephensen in Sydney. This issue of *Right* also included an article by A. R. Mills.)

Another instance of internment came to light when a pastoralist, Robert Clince Little, sued the Commonwealth for £10,000 for false imprisonment. Little, born in New Zealand of British parents, was interned at Gaythorne (Queensland) and Loveday (S.A.) camps in 1942. It is not clear why Little, who had been living on Townshend Island, 95 miles north of Rockhampton, where he was running a few head of stock, was detained. The court proceedings (in which he was unsuccessful) suggested only that he appeared to have been the victim of gossip due to some local enmity he had incurred.

Civil police had the authority to enter premises without search warrants and arrest enemy nationals on behalf of the military authorities. Military Intelligence made the decisions for detention, restrictions or internment. Its recommendations went for approval to the Minister for the Army. Occasionally advice was sought from the Attorney-General's Department. In 1956 Dr Evatt recalled that some of the army recommendations were 'completely outrageous'. No fewer than 7,500 people were detained in 1942 on the advice of Military Intelligence. When MacKay's new security organization came into being, jurisdiction over internment passed to it. Then a government committee headed by A. A. Calwell and including Jessie Street investigated these internments and reduced the number held to about 500.[2]

On one man in Military Intelligence in Sydney rested the central responsibility for the detentions of the sixteen people there who were members of the Australia First movement or were friends of Stephensen. This man was Lieutenant-Colonel Reginald Powell, in civil life an advertising agent, who within a week or two of having been called up on the outbreak of war was put in charge of the IB section of Eastern Command Intelligence, which dealt with internal security. In 1940 Powell was promoted from major to lieutenant-colonel and made chief staff officer in charge of Eastern Command Intelligence. He was the officer to whom the newly decoded message from Perth

Nancy Krakouer, 1942   Laurence Bullock, 1942

E. C. Quicke, 1942   P. R. Stephensen, 1959

THE SUN

No. 10051 SYDNEY: THURSDAY, MARCH 26, 1942 (Phone: BO333) PRICE 2d.

PINEAPP
BACON HA
SAUSAGES

PY MURDER PLOT ALLEGED
ang Of 20 Caught, Says Ford

LANS FOR NVASION

FROM OUR SPECIAL REPRESENTATIVE

CANBERRA, Thursday.

ions that 20 persons—19 men
one woman — had formed an
d spy ring in Australia to help
apanese in the e v e n t of an
y invasion were made today
e House of Representatives by
Minister for the A r m y (Mr.
).

The broad sweep of Markham Valley, New Guinea. The Japanese recently penetrated
some miles along the valley from Lae.

2 Jap Bases Smashed; U.S. Fleet Raids

From Our Own Correspondent and
Associated Press

WASHINGTON, Wednesday.

Devastating attacks by US warships and
planes on two Japanese bases in the Pacific —
captured Wake Island and Marcus Island — are
described fully in a Navy communique issued in
Washington today.

MACARTHUR

Grim Mood In Britain

From Our Own Correspondent

LONDON, Thursday.

Japanese Raid On Katherine Damage Slig.

FROM OUR SPECIAL REPRESENTATIVE

KATHERINE, Thursday.

Flying in perfect formation in three flights,
Japanese bombers dropped more than 20 bomb
Katherine River, killing one aboriginal and
wounding two American soldiers.

No material damage was caused, and from a military
view it was a shockingly bad job.

The bombers flew at 20,000 feet. No one lost any time in
cover.

Outposts Stand Rec

Mr Forde's announcements headlined on the front pages of the
Sydney *Sun,* 26 March (above) and 27 March 1942

THE SUN

No. 10055 SYDNEY: FRIDAY, MARCH 27, 1942 (Phone: BO333) PRICE 2s.

NAVY BLUES

VIL TRIAL ORDERED IN PY RING ALLEGATION

rima Facie se"—Curtin

FROM OUR SPECIAL REPRESENTATIVE

CANBERRA, Friday.

uthorities w ill be directed to
ulate charges against the 20
ed members of the Australia
Movement, who were alleged
e Army Minister (Mr. Forde)
rday to be concerned in an
nage plot.

ouncement was made in the House of
ntatives today by the Prime Minister
urtin), who said there was a prima facie
gainst the arrested people—19 men and
man.

nt followed a demand by the Opposition leader
dden) for trial of the arrested people on a charge

ternment Refused

Poles Honor MacArthur

WASHINGTON, Thursday.

US Oil Company Is Accused

Rubber Formula Given To Nazis

WASHINGTON, Thursday.

New formula for syn-
thetic rubber, which
produced more and better
rubber at less cost than
the method used by the
Nazis was transferred to
the German Dye Trust by
the Standard Oil Co. of
New Jersey before the US
entered the war.

Gesture.— General
MacArthur, Supreme Com-
mander-in-Chief of the
Allied forces in the South-
West Pacific, set with the
War Council in Canberra
yesterday. Here he is seen in
earnest discussion with the
Prime Minister.

STUKAS SMASHED OVER MALTA

LONDON, Friday.
Spitfires and Hurri-

Getting Together.— General MacArthur and Mr.

Japs Driv 27 Miles In N.Guine

From F. C. POLKARD, The Sun's War Correspo
in New Guinea.

Japanese forces in the Mark
Valley have penetrated 27 miles u
river from Lae to Mabrak, where
flat country around the mission stret
is suitable for a dozen aerodromes
they have not tried to go further.

[Our special correspondent in B
suggests that similar Jap hesitancy in
may be due to their doubts of Allied str
He puts forward one view that the Ja
calculate on being free to concentrate on
Australia by the end of March.]

Raid On Koep

CANBERRA

was first handed on the night of 9 March 1942 between 11 p.m. and midnight. The officer who normally would have been in charge and handled the situation was Lieutenant-Colonel J. M. Prentice, the senior Intelligence officer at Eastern Command's Rear Headquarters. Prentice, who had been a popular commentator on foreign affairs on radio 2UW in Sydney and later also in *Man* magazine when it began in 1937, was strongly anti-communist and pro-appeasement. He refused to believe that there would be war in 1939. An issue of *Man* had to be recast in September of that year when events in Poland made it necessary for the editor, Frank Greenop, to remove Prentice's regular commentary which explained why Germany would not go to war.

Powell's first response to the Perth message was to send for Major Tyrell, Captain G. H. M. Newman (then in charge of IB sub-section) and Inspector W. C. Watkins, who had charge of the police side of Military Police Intelligence. Unsuccessful efforts were made to reach Captain F. B. Blood, who for eighteen months had been closely concerned with IB investigations into Australia First and had been in favour of interning members, and he did not arrive until next morning. One of the policemen who came with Inspector Watkins to police headquarters where the conference with Colonel Powell was held was Detective-Sergeant Swasbrick who had been with Military Police Intelligence since April 1939.

After the military officers had conferred about the Perth message and the decision was made to intern some Australia First movement members in Sydney, Inspector Watkins obtained authority from the deputy Police Commissioner—MacKay was absent on leave—to act on behalf of the military. Watkins had forty men ready for duty and in an emergency could have mustered one hundred.

Swasbrick went with Tyrell to the Intelligence index which listed sixty names of movement members and sympathizers. Tyrell chose twenty names including those of P. R. Stephensen, his brother Eric, E. J. Arnold, K. P. Bath, Valentine Crowley, his brother Clarence, S. B. Hooper, J. T. Kirtley, Harley Matthews, E. C. Masey, G. T. Rice, C. W. Salier, W. F. Tinker-Giles and M. F. Watts. Swasbrick took down the names and had a list typed.

The list also had on it names of female members of the movement executive and also that of Malcolm Smith. Somebody, probably Colonel Powell, crossed off the names of the women. It was not government policy, he understood, to intern women. Perhaps it wasn't but this did not save Adela Pankhurst Walsh. Somebody also crossed off Smith's name on the ground of insufficient evidence for detention.[3] Apparently no doubts were held about the sufficiency in all other cases. It is not known if the list included Ian Mudie, an executive member who shortly before had left Sydney for his home city of Adelaide, outside the jurisdiction of Eastern Command. The possibility of including Richard Ludowici, who had frequently attended the Yabber Club and subscribed to the *Publicist*, was probably discussed.

Dossiers on the movement, its members and their activities plus files of the *Publicist* were available to the officers at this late night-early morning conference. Compilation of these files had largely been in the hands of the absent Captain Blood. When he finally did arrive in the morning (10 March) his only suggestion was that another two suspects be interned, both of them soldiers then in N.S.W. camps, Trooper C. K. Downe and Private L. K. Cahill. Powell accepted this advice and later that day police went out to bring them in. (In Britain some members of the British Union of Fascists had been able in 1940 to escape arrest by enlisting.)

Memories of those who attended the conference at police headquarters conflict on the point whether it was decided to detain all those left on the list (fourteen or fifteen) or first search their premises and then telephone the results of the search before any decision on detentions was made. At all events, Ludowici was visited by police, searched, made to sign an undertaking not to have anything more to do with the movement, but not detained. And although the women's names had been struck from the list an official report states that their homes were searched on the morning of 10 March.

Although the immediate cause of the night Intelligence conference and its decision to arrest the Sydney men was the message from Perth, the notion of arrests was not new. It had been suggested, and rejected by higher authority, before. The general predisposition of the Military Intelligence staff to Australia First was such that very little extra was needed to get them to act.

The Commonwealth Investigation Branch, probably the most professional of Australia's intelligence organizations, despite the extreme difficulties under which it worked, did not feel the same way. Its agents could find nothing objectionable in Australia First activities. But the branch was not involved in the arrests. It was, in fact, surprised the next morning to learn of the action and lodged a protest with Eastern Command and the Canberra authorities.

Mid-March 1942 saw Australia facing the most dangerous external threat in its entire history. The seemingly invincible Japanese were pressing forever southwards, and although they were at that time nearing the end of their logistical tether, it was hardly a time in Australia for risk-taking with any individual or organization thought to be a danger to the country's security. This plea, and there was considerable justification for it, was subsequently to be raised every time the action taken by Intelligence was questioned. Powell saw it as his job to disband a movement that was, according to the weight of evidence he had seen, anti-British in character. Much of the evidence came from the files which included one report describing Harley Matthews as 'pro-Nazi' in outlook. Another had Stephensen down as a son-in-law of Miles—Blood still thought this was so in 1944.

It was partly on the basis of inaccurate evidence like this that Matthews and others were detained. Blood's view was that to deal with subversive organizations it was vital to break them up by taking into custody those most closely associated with them, and one should not be distracted too much by individual cases. He had discussed this viewpoint with Powell and Captain Newman in the months leading up to March 1942. Though we can never be certain what motives guided Powell, Tyrell and Blood, the decision to detain was eventually made, and, with varying soothing explanations or with none, the thirteen men were woken up in the small hours and brought in. All 'went quietly', some expecting to be back home within hours. As a consequence there was little drama and nobody made claims of violence as did Bullock in Perth who alleged that Richards climbed in through his flat window and hit him in the face with a revolver.

A bus collected the thirteen men (Kirtley was brought in later from Woy Woy) from various police stations throughout metropolitan Sydney and took them to the internment camp at Liverpool, otherwise known as the Anzac Rifle Range. It had all been done with the authority of section 13 of the National Security Act as had the initial apprehension of the four Western Australians the day before. Section 13 empowered any constable or Commonwealth officer or anyone authorized by the Minister for Defence to arrest without warrant anyone found committing an offence against the Act. Clause 2(a) provided for the release of the suspected person within ten days of arrest if no charge was laid. In the Bill originally introduced by W. M. Hughes as Attorney-General in 1939 there was no ten-day holding limit, only provision for release 'within reasonable time'. With good cause, thinking back to parallel legislation brought in by Hughes in 1914 in the form of the War Precautions Act, several Labor M.P.s questioned the wisdom of this vague provision. P. C. Spender (a Minister without portfolio assisting the Treasurer), who was seeing the second reading through the House of Representatives, told J. S. Rosevear that it would be for the court to determine, on a habeas corpus application, what was 'reasonable'. This was not good enough for Rosevear who persisted with his objection. After another three Labor M.P.s, H. C. Barnard, G. W. Martens and R. James, also worried the same point, Spender said he did not mind a specific time limit and suggested ten days. Such an amendment was agreed to on 8 September. Martens pointed out that the Act was similar to the notorious Queensland Peace Preservation Act of 1894, passed after a bout of woolshed burning in the shearers' strike. He knew something of the operation of that Act as he himself had been arrested for an alleged contravention of it in 1911.

Australian national security legislation was one with Britain's 1914 Defence of the Realm Acts (DORA), legislation not framed with special concern for civil liberties. As F. M. Forde, then an Opposition M.P., pointed out in 1939, unlimited power of this kind is invariably abused. (In 1916 Frank Brennan complained in Parliament of Hughes's War Precautions regulation under which men were being seized and interned without knowledge or means of knowing the crime for which they were imprisoned. But in the atmosphere of that time his mild complaint drew the response from W. Elliot Johnson that Brennan must be referring to enemy subjects.

Brennan: 'British subjects, naturalised subjects, suspected persons. I am not making any charge that is not capable of being sustained.'

Sir John Forrest: 'I think you must be pro-German.')

Section 13, as amended, and clause 2(a) allowed the Curtin government, on whose behalf Colonel Powell had acted, ten days to do something about the sixteen internees, either to charge them or let them go. There was no public pressure one way or the other. The detentions had been carried out in secret. Even so, if legality was to be preserved, some decision had to be made by 20 March. Although the regulations were at this time administered by the Defence Department there was provision in section 13 for a report of a person's detention and its circumstances to be made forthwith to the Attorney-General. As the Attorney-General, Dr Evatt, had just left for the United States and Britain on an urgent supply mission this department was in the hands of J. A. Beasley, who was not advised of the arrests.

What decided the next official step was a report from Military Intelligence compiled by Captain Blood and approved by Colonel Powell. This report, dated 13 March, based largely on the same

information on which the decisions to arrest were made, offered a prima facie case for the internment of the sixteen detained persons under regulation 26 of the National Security regulations. Blood stated that the group had been under observation before the outbreak of war because of its German and Japanese associations and the pro-Nazi and pro-Japanese writings of those preparing material for the *Publicist*. The policy of the *Publicist*, he went on, was shown in a short form in its fifty points, which he reproduced. Among the points were:

3. For self-dependence; against colonial status.
6. For national socialism; against international communism.
13. For peace in the Pacific; against war-seeking.
16. For Aryanism; against semitism.
18. For monarchy; against republicanism.

Blood referred to an earlier report to army headquarters dated 28 January 1942 calling for the prohibition of publication of the *Publicist* and a search of the premises of those associated with it in Eastern, Southern and Western Commands. That earlier report had contained evidence, he said, of liaison between the paper and the Anglo-German Link. Then there was the Yabber Club at which anti-British and pro-Axis sentiments were aired. He went on to note that there was no apparent explanation for the sudden formation of the movement in 1941 apart from the desire of Stephensen and his close associates to spread the subversive doctrines of their organization. After mentioning Thomas Potts Graham's subversive pamphlets, the public disturbance on 19 February at Adyar Hall and the cipher message from Perth, Blood appended to his report short personal details of those detained. Keith Bath was noted as 'verging on the fanatical in his beliefs in the policy of the movement', according to 'information from reliable contacts'. One of these contacts may well have been a Manly businessman who had reacted with antagonism when Bath offered him a dodger advertising the projected Manly meeting, and threatened to report him to the authorities. Another 'contact' could have been a Sydney radio announcer who in January 1942 warned Bath not to have anything to do with Stephensen. Kirtley, according to Blood, had written letters which showed he was almost intensely anti-British and anti-Australian and 'in consequence, guilty of subversive activities'.

An attachment to the report contained a stilted discussion, signed by Major Tyrell, about the connection between A. R. Mills's cult of Odinism and the Australia First movement. This was based largely on a letter from Cahill to Mills which suggested that Cahill was trying to convert Stephensen to accept Odinism. Tyrell's appendix ended: 'It is not suggested that all associated with the movement are intentionally subversive, but they are more or less at the mercy of rather clever propagandists, whose inclinations are pro-Axis.' Tyrell presented a translation from a treatise in the *Revue de deux mondes*, found in the Fisher Library, on the subject of German myths and legends, an account of a sort surely rare in police files.

Blood's report, which turned out to be of key importance, was signed by the Eastern Command base commandant, Major-General Fewtrell. Everything goes to suggest that it was upon this document, which urged 'extreme urgency' in the execution of warrants issued under regulation 26, that Forde, the Minister for the Army, relied in ordering the internments. Although the report stated that the immediate action taken on the night of 9–10 March against the Sydney members arose from the message from Western Command it should have been fairly clear, though Blood did not mention it, that there was no real connection between the two groups of people. Thus there was no justification for saddling Stephensen and his colleagues with the wild plans of 'Hardt' and/or Bullock. Detective-Sergeant Richards had sent a report from Perth on 20 March stating he could see no link between the groups but this either came too late and was not considered, or was noted and disregarded.

What happened in the war cabinet if and when Blood's recommendation or some condensed version of it reached those heights is not known. One would suppose that the internment of sixteen Australian citizens would call at some stage for cabinet approval or discussion. Labor Party caucus minutes, which are available for perusal, give no clue. The few sources available indicate that when cabinet considered Australia First Forde did not take a strong line. It seems likely that the internments were ordered by the Minister alone, and that cabinet may later have discussed what would be done with the internees.

The immense power given by regulation 26 had potential dangers which had not gone unnoticed. It allowed the Minister to detain or restrict the activities of anyone to prevent them 'acting in any manner prejudicial to the public safety or the defence of the Commonwealth'. It was not necessary, as subsequent court applications showed, for the Minister to base his opinions on evidence admissible in a court of law. And once detention was ordered under regulation 26 there was no limit to its duration while the Act remained in force.

In federal Parliament on 8 September 1939 E. J. Ward asked the

Minister for Defence, Brigadier G. A. Street, what redress there was for persons wrongfully held. He was told that regulation 26 provided for an appeal to an advisory committee presided over by a judge. Beyond that, British subjects had their rights under civil law. Both the Australian Council for Civil Liberties, in a published survey of the war and civil rights, and the Council's president, Maurice Blackburn, in a parliamentary comment, noted that the regulation took away the rights of habeas corpus altogether. The Minister for Defence could commit anybody to custody without any charge being preferred and that was an end to it. There was no legal redress. The A.C.C.L. survey noted that to December 1940 there had been only one case of detention under regulation 26, that of Paino in Western Australia. This case, it said, 'shows that the 1914–18 wind is again blowing chill on our liberties. As long as regulation 26 remains unrepealed, every outspoken citizen, Australian-born or not, is liable to precisely what happened to Tom Barker, to Wallach, to Asmus in 1916–18.' Prophetically, the survey added: 'It cannot be ignored that a possible outcome . . . in a future perhaps not far distant is the active use in Australia of regulation 26 of 25 August 1939 to imprison without trial Australian-born critics of the Government'.

Regulation 26 was used on 26 May 1941 against an Australian-born Gallipoli veteran, Horace Ratliff, aged forty-six, and Max Thomas, twenty-nine, born in New Zealand, both communist critics of the government. Ratliff and Thomas had been sentenced to serve six months' imprisonment in December 1940 on charges of having possession of articles with the object of influencing public opinion in a manner likely to prejudice the efficient prosecution of the war. They had been preparing printed propaganda at a time when the Communist Party was banned and its publications proscribed. After their release from gaol in May 1941 they were rearrested within about three weeks, under regulation 26, and interned at Liverpool on the order of Spender, the Minister for the Army. When Germany attacked Russia they were still interned though the justification for their detention had virtually disappeared. This reasoning was put before the regulation 26 advisory committee, under a retired Land Valuation Court judge, Mr Justice Pike, before which they appeared in July 1941. The committee was not convinced. It took a change of government, the advent of the first Curtin administration, to get the men released. Considerable pressure was applied by trade unions, the left wing in general and the civil libertarians over the use of regulation 26 in this case. Dr Evatt, soon to become Attorney-

General under Curtin, was prominent in the agitation for the freeing of Ratliff and Thomas. He said they were being punished twice for one offence; in such cases Australian citizens should be charged and tried in open court. On their release Evatt said the government's view was that national security was not dependent upon the detention of the men without charge or trial. Later critics of Evatt, notably the *Bulletin*, were gleefully to resurrect this opinion.

Regulation 26 orders, dated 20 March, were applied to the Australia First detainees at the Liverpool internment camp on 25 March 1942, five days after the legal limit for their detention under section 13 had expired. To them it made no practical difference. Before, they were detained; after, they were interned. Either way, they were behind barbed wire.

Stephensen was taken into custody by four police at his home in New South Head Road, Rose Bay, about 4.30 a.m. on 10 March. He recognized one of the four, Detective-Sergeant P. J. Byrne. Detective-Sergeant A. L. Nye, who led the police, told Stephensen that they had come to search for documents. This they did, and two hours later left with a bundle of papers and Stephensen. Accounts by Nye and Stephensen of the event differ in several particulars, the most important being Nye's insistence and Stephensen's denial that he was told he was going to be detained under National Security regulations. None of the detainees were told by police where they were going. Stephensen was taken to the *Publicist* office to find it already occupied by police. Another two-hour search of papers was made and a large pile, including many of Miles's effects, were removed. At about 9 a.m. Stephensen was driven first to Sydney police headquarters, where one policeman got out and ran inside, returning five minutes later. The car moved on to Central Police Station where Stephensen was searched and locked in a cell. 'Am I under arrest?' he asked, to be told: 'This is a matter for the military. It has nothing to do with the police.' When he asked for his solicitor, Herman Faull, he was told there was no need for that as he would not be there long, and after an hour or so in the cell he was taken out to find his brother Eric and Gordon Rice in the corridor. They were escorted to a bus driven by an armed soldier. Already on the bus were Bath, Valentine Crowley, Masey and Salier, who had been taken on at North Sydney police station, Valentine Crowley's brother Clarence, taken on at Paddington, and Hooper and Edmund Arnold, taken on at Darlinghurst. On the way to the internment camp the bus picked up the movement's former treasurer, Tinker-Giles, at Newtown and finally the two World War I men, Harley Matthews and Martin Watts, then a peace officer at the St Mary's explosives factory, at Liverpool. Hooper was the only one who had packed a bag and brought it along. On the way Stephensen told the others it was all a mistake and it would not be long before they were free again. Later that day in camp at Liverpool the commandant, Major Bass, told them they had been interned for ten days under section 13 of the National Security Act. They were neither interrogated nor told what offences they were accused of having committed.

John Kirtley, who lived at Ettalong Beach, Woy Woy, did not reach Liverpool until the next day. After searching his house police took him first to Phillip Street, then to Victoria Barracks for the night of 10 March. The next day he joined the others at Liverpool. Kirtley was not told why he had been detained but he was not particularly surprised. Fatalistically, he felt something was likely to follow the complaints made in parliament by Falstein and Landa about the Australia First movement. He thought the projected Manly meeting had been foolhardy, just inviting counter-action.

Harley Matthews, however, was taken completely by surprise. One of the two detectives who called at his vineyard home near Liverpool asked him, among other things, what he thought of the Labor Party. Matthews replied that he had always voted Labor but if they were coming into his house at such a time to ask about his political beliefs he was not answering. He said he was not a member of the Australia First movement—this was a fact—but the detectives took him to Liverpool police station, ostensibly to see an Intelligence officer, but as one was not there he was added to the bus-load. There he joined some friends and many strangers. To these fourteen internees was added Trooper Downe, a movement member, on 13 March. Downe was taken from Tamworth, where he had been serving with the 11th Australian Armoured Car Regiment, to Sydney on 12 March. At Tamworth police station he was told he was being held under section 13 and would be taken to Sydney for questioning. The remaining internee was Cahill, who had enlisted on 6 January and was serving as a private with the 20th Garrison Battalion at Fort Scratchley, Newcastle. He was taken to the city police station by two policemen, and thence to Victoria Barracks, Sydney. The next morning he was moved out to Liverpool on the same truck as Kirtley. They did not know each other and each thought the other a government agent.

One other member of the movement and an ex-member were later arrested but the authorities said their detentions were not exclusively due to their connection with the movement. The ex-member was

Adela Pankhurst Walsh, taken into custody in Sydney on 20 March, and the member was Alexander Rud Mills, detained in Melbourne on 7 May. For Mrs Walsh it was not the first time. She had been in gaol before for her beliefs, first as a suffragette and later as an anti-conscriptionist. This time she was detained until mid-October 1942. Her detention was largely due to her close association with Japanese officials in Sydney. She had foolishly attempted to pass on to a Japanese company, Mitsui Ltd, an official N.S.W. censorship order forbidding reference to the proposed visit by a U.S. general from the Philippines. On 3 November 1941 she had written to an official of the Japanese Chamber of Commerce that 'the Australia First Movement which is now being organised will certainly be most friendly to Japan.' According to Captain Blood, she was lucky not to have been interned earlier.

Rud Mills was arrested mainly because security officers thought he had Nazi sympathies. He had done little if anything in the Australia First movement other than send by post a subscription fee to Cahill and write for the *Publicist*. His association with the Nazi movement in Germany in the early thirties counted heavily against him. Major Ted Hattam of Military Intelligence and Sub-Inspector Birch of the Victorian CIB Special Branch visited Mills on 10 March. They already knew about his past and his odd philosophic ventures into the Nordic twilight. When searching his premises they found little new except a photograph of the infamous Julius Streicher. He managed to convince the officers he was not the Melbourne agent of the movement, and another eight weeks were to pass before he was taken into custody. Mills himself believed the only additional factor involved during this time, and thus to be suspected as the cause of internment, was a letter he wrote to Stephensen at Liverpool offering him legal advice. Three policemen called for Mills at his flat in suburban Canterbury and took him to a place in Flinders Street, then to offices at the Exhibition Buildings and finally under armed guard, with two Italian prisoners, to Broadmeadows camp. From there he was sent to Loveday in South Australia.

Members of the almost dormant Australia First group in Melbourne were visited by police during the 10 March scare. Some searches were made and questions asked of R. D. Collins, a man called Knight and several others, but nobody was interned. The undergraduates who had been toying with Stephensenian nationalism and cultural friendship with the Japanese were not regarded as serious dangers. In Adelaide, the day after the Sydney arrests, Ian

Mudie was questioned by a Commonwealth Security officer and a State police detective. They put it to him that he had spent Saturdays and Sundays at Port Adelaide talking to Japanese sailors,[4] but Mudie, South Australian born, had not long returned from Sydney. After lengthy haggling the pair decided against taking him in. Later in 1942 he joined the army but kept in touch with the internees with whom he felt continued kinship. In a letter to fellow-poet Rex Ingamells, who had also been questioned by police over his Australia First connections, Mudie wrote: 'Well, if P.R. and the rest were guilty, so was I. If they were innocent—and that I know for a fact, despite all the justices—then I was equally so.'

W. D. Cookes, the wealthy shoe manufacturer, although the subject of at least one recommendation for internment (signed on 25 July 1942 by Colonel S. T. Whittington, the Victorian Deputy Director of Security), escaped detention. He was almost certainly not a member of the movement, but equally certainly was in sympathy with its ideas and ready to help financially and in other ways. In October 1942 the Director-General of Security, Brigadier Simpson, himself went to interrogate Cookes. On the face of it, grounds for his internment appeared as strong as those for any of the Sydney internees. But perhaps his ill-health, his isolated situation (like Mudie) or his assurances given to officers, or all three, kept him free.

At the time the detentions were made in Sydney federal Parliament was in recess. Several days before, on 6 March, Senator Ashley, representing the Attorney-General in the Senate, had answered Senator Collett's question seeking information about the movement. A factual reply, it listed names of office bearers, date and place of the first public meeting and the subject matter of manifestos issued. Appropriate action, the reply concluded, would be taken against anyone threatening national security.

About 10.30 p.m. on 25 March, more than a fortnight after the internees had been detained and on the day regulation 26 had been read to them, federal Parliament was at last told what had happened. Maurice Blackburn, speaking in an adjournment debate, said that before the recent recess (6 March to 25 March) he had written to the Attorney-General, Dr Evatt, about the Australia First movement being prevented from holding public meetings. He said he had now been told that after the House had risen fifteen members of the movement, all Australian-born, had been interned at Liverpool. He did not believe, although Dr Evatt had made some such suggestion, that the internees were in any way in sympathy with the Japanese. Blackburn continued:

I have consistently taken the position . . . that persons, particularly those who are Australian-born, should not be imprisoned without trial or on mere suspicion that they have committed offences. I have also taken the position very strongly that the agent of a foreign enemy, or spy, in Australia is not likely to be a person engaging in addressing public meetings, and openly opposing Government policy. Spies are not likely to be found among persons constituting minority groups.

C. A. A. Morgan, the Labor member for Reid, asked whether one of the men was a Rhodes scholar. Blackburn responded:

I do not think that Mr. Stephensen was among the persons interned. I strongly disagree with certain views held by Mr. Stephensen, but he is a man of great ability, energy and courage, for whom I have considerable admiration. Although he has expressed unpopular opinions, I do not believe that he is the kind of man who would be an enemy agent.

Blackburn urged, as had Evatt in the Ratliff and Thomas case only a few months before, that the fifteen persons interned should be brought swiftly to trial. S. M. Falstein interjected that they had a right to apply for a hearing. Blackburn answered: 'We know how much that means', and asked Beasley, as acting Attorney-General, to consider either having the men brought to trial or set free.

Blackburn's reference to internments was made too late at night for dramatic treatment by the next day's morning papers and perhaps censors had a hand in the matter too. The *Sydney Morning Herald* gave it five inches of single-column space on page 5.

Forde's statement of 26 March may well have come as a reply to Blackburn's remarks, or it may have been a consequence of the suggestion made by Detective-Sergeant Richards in his report of 20 March, that it was time for publicity. At some time between 2.30 and 3 p.m. the member for Newcastle, D. O. Watkins, rose at question time to put this 'Dorothy Dix' to Forde: 'Was it true that some members of the Australia First Movement had been interned?' Forde's reply created what one critic, Herman Homburg, has fairly called 'the greatest sensation of the war'.[5]

I wish to state that 20 persons, 19 men and one woman, who were believed to have been associated with the so-called Australia First Movement have been arrested and interned. Documents and papers which have been seized purport to show that certain people in Australia intended to make contact with the Japanese Army at the moment of an invasion of Australia. The documents set out elaborate plans for sabotage at vulnerable points in this country, and describe methods calculated to make resistance to the Japanese impossible. Plans for the assassination of prominent people are set out. One document purports to be a proclamation with the heading 'Australia First Government' and welcomes to this country as friends and liberators the Japanese leaders and army. The documents indicate a fifth column activity of the worst kind by a very small band of people. The Military authorities have been investigating the activities of the so-called Australia First Movement for a considerable time, and arrests took place as a result of these inquiries. In view of the foregoing I wish to warn people that, before associating themselves with any movement, they should assure themselves that it is a bona fide and not an organisation which, under the cloak of a pleasing name, is engaged in subversive activities. We shall stand no Quislings, whether they come from the highest or the lowest.

In this, the first official statement about the Perth and Sydney internments (though no place names were given), the proclamation devised in Perth was thus in effect foisted on to the Sydney movement. (As has been noted, the Richards report of 20 March concluded that there was no connection between the two.) Asked to comment on Forde's startling statement and to offer some expansion, Military Police Intelligence refused, 'due to the delicate nature of the whole affair'.[6] A. W. Fadden, the Leader of the Opposition, briefly supported Forde. People who were ready to organize themselves against the well-being of their fellow citizens should, he said, be immediately confined to places where they could do no harm. There the matter lay, as far as Parliament was concerned, until the next day.

Sydney's afternoon papers of 26 March, some copies of which appeared at Liverpool camp, gave the internees and their guards some idea what was being held against them. 'SPY MURDER PLOT ALLEGED' was the banner headline in the *Sun* over a report which referred prominently to 'Treason at its worst' and 'Gang of 20 caught'. With no names yet mentioned, speculation spread in Sydney. According to the defence correspondent of the *Sydney Morning Herald*, newsboys whispered names to their customers, names of leading businessmen; poster boards proclaimed, without any justification, that twenty businessmen had been arrested. This 'businessmen' slant was probably a deduction based on Forde's reference to 'the highest or the lowest'. Of the internees only Tinker-Giles (a shoe retailer) and Bath (an estate agent) could be classed as businessmen.

The sensational report in the *Sun* (most other Australian newspapers were almost as breathless) was later the subject of a libel

action, known to be hopeless before it was begun, by Harley
Matthews. He sought damages against the newspaper as one way of
publicly clearing his name. The jury accepted the defence put forward by Barwick K.C. that the report was a true account of parliamentary proceedings and that a leading article in the next day's
issue denouncing the activity of the internees was fair comment on
Forde's statement. It was revealed that the editor of the *Sun,* Howard
Ashton, had not known at the time the leader was written that
Matthews, once a *Sun* journalist, was one of the internees. Mr Justice
Street said he agreed with the jury's verdict but added that this was
no reflection on Matthews.

On 27 March the *Sun* kept Australia First on its front page with
the headline 'CIVIL TRIAL ORDERED IN SPY RING ALLEGATION'. This
was not firmly based on fact. Curtin and Forde had mentioned in
debate that the matter was in the hands of the Solicitor-General, Sir
George Knowles. Curtin said that the military authorities were carrying out investigations and the civil authorities would be directed to
formulate charges on the evidence available. It was quite some time,
however, before it became apparent that the government would,
except in the case of the four Western Australians, prefer no charges.

When federal Parliament resumed on 27 March, members, some
well briefed, others bursting with misinformation, were given the
chance to canvass the matter at length. C. A. A. Morgan, a Sydney
solicitor, wanted to know what action would be taken against these
people said to be guilty of conduct tantamount to high treason.
Forde replied that internment was a first step, and what followed
was something that was being looked into. Fadden sought, and was
allowed, an adjournment debate to deal with Forde's disclosures.
Members gradually became aware how serious the matter was. True,
the continuing threat from the Japanese pushed most other events
into the background but this was part of the threat—a set of disloyal
Australians willing to sell us to the invader!

Opening the debate, Fadden saw Forde's charges as being without
parallel in Australian history, and in British history at least since
the Guy Fawkes plot. Later an historian-M.P., Dr Grenfell Price,
saw the accusations as the most serious in Australian history. Indeed,
had the accusations matched reality they would assuredly have
quickly been given a prominent place in our modern history text
books. Carried away, Fadden called for the internment of all enemy
aliens, to be reminded by the vigilant Maurice Blackburn that there
had been no charge of treasonable practices by aliens. Predictably,
Fadden called for a greater degree of vigilance over left-wing organ-

izations such as the Legal Rights Committee of New South Wales.
Eric Harrison, after disparaging the movement as 'traitorous', com-
plained that the cause of the internees had been prejudiced by the
Minister's statement.

Curtin told the House that the first obligation of the government
when evidence was submitted by its Intelligence departments was
not to judge on the facts or to decide if the persons concerned were
guilty. The government had to take the elementary precaution of
removing them from any possibility of carrying on their activities
until the evidence could be examined. Investigations then being
carried out had been put into the hands of the New South Wales
Police Commissioner. Calwell interjected that the Commissioner,
MacKay, was Fascist-minded. After a brief exchange about Mac-
Kay's past, Curtin said he had never met the man but he had been
recommended as highly qualified for the task.

W. M. Hughes demanded to know why the men who started the
Australia First movement in New South Wales 'still walked the
streets'. Forde replied that they did not. Hughes then asked whether
Stephensen had been interned, to be told that Forde was not giving
any names. Frank Brennan, who, like Maurice Blackburn, really
cared about civil liberties, said he declined absolutely to accept an
ex parte statement about the men's guilt, even from Forde. J. A.
Beasley said Forde had made his original statement 'upon reports
submitted to him'—already a wary note of justification was creeping
into statements from the government side. Beasley added:

> The Department of Army is now dealing with this matter and it
> has not yet been referred to me for final action by the Attorney-
> General's Department. I am unable to give details as to how the
> report upon which the minister made his statement was arrived at,
> but he received it only a few days ago. He took immediate steps to
> place certain members of this organisation where they can no
> longer do what it is alleged they were doing or attempting to do.
> In the meantime he has taken the necessary steps to prepare
> evidence to lay the necessary charge.

Beasley added an intriguing footnote: 'I am unable to advance any
reasons why the Minister made the statement. It may be interesting
to honourable members to know that, when he made it, it was the
first I had heard of it.'

Parliament turned to other matters until 30 April, when Calwell
asked when the internees were either to be brought to trial or set
free. This plea was raised again in the months ahead by Calwell and
others such as J. S. Rosevear and Sir Frederick Stewart. Calwell

persisted in his critical attitude to the government's action even after he himself joined the Curtin ministry in 1943. When questioners in May and June 1942 asked when the internees were to be tried or freed, government spokesmen parried with references to the trial of four people in Perth as if that were answer enough for the whole twenty. Finally, on 2 June, Forde admitted that the government, on the advice of Knowles, had decided not to take court action against movement members in New South Wales.

While parliamentarians were talking, political commentators were as busy as newsprint and censorship allowed. For the right wing, the *Bulletin*, and for the (illegal) left, the *Tribune*, were two papers which could always find space to accommodate selected opinions. *Tribune* bothered no more about censorship than about its own illegality.

Four censorship orders had been directed to newspapers in the fortnight after Forde's statement. Two requested that everything dealing with the internments had to be submitted for censorship, one that nothing at all was to be published about the internments and one that only ministerial statements were to be printed. Perhaps because it was printed illegally, operating from no stated address, *Tribune* did not receive censorship instructions. On 29 April it published fifteen names of Australia First members interned under the heading 'These Are the Spies'. It was the only paper to publish names, which had already been mentioned from the communist platform in the Domain. Only J. T. Kirtley was missing from a list that was more or less accurate, allowing for several misspellings. Any close and intelligent observer of the Australia First movement with a *Publicist* file, assisted perhaps by a friendly policeman or a Liverpool camp guard, could without too much difficulty have compiled such a list. More importantly, waterside workers had taken the membership receipt book at the 'Battle' of Adyar Hall.

The publication of names by *Tribune* provided right-wing M.P.s and publicists with ammunition for their recurring charge that the internments were made at the direct behest of communists. Without doubt the Left had consistently called for internment and communists had boasted about their part after the internments had been carried out but no connection has been proven or seems capable of proof between the communists and the man who finally determined the Sydney detentions, Lieutenant-Colonel Powell. Indeed when Powell came under parliamentary notice after he left the army he was in the employ of the right-wing Sane Democracy League canvassing donations from industry.

The *Bulletin* began its extensive commentary on the internments with a thoughtful note. This was a leader on 1 April headed 'Case of the 20', which suggested that on the face of it the Australia First programme was harmless enough. There was nothing seditious about its ten points. But what the *Bulletin* took as the movement's ten-point policy were the points outlined in the circular Stephensen sent to M.P.s to show what he intended to tell the Manly meeting. Even so, serious objection could hardly be taken to either set of policy points. Later the journal's tone grew more shrill, as in Frank Forde's 'Folly' (2 September) when it was seen as a good opportunity to attack the Labor administration.

By 8 April the *Bulletin* had discovered that one of the twenty persons 'lying in the shadow of the dreadful charges' was an 'Old Digger'. Few objects were more sacred to the *Bulletin* (or to its larrikin contemporary *Smith's Weekly*) than an 'Old Digger'. The journal also suggested that Fadden had been astray in his analogy to Guy Fawkes, adding that the Cato Street Conspiracy was more to the point. This exceedingly apt parallel had already been noted on 29 March by the *Sunday Telegraph*. The first that many servicemen learned of the plot to aid the Japanese (as told by Forde) was in their army paper *Salt* on 6 April, which admitted to no doubts about the allegations, stating them firmly as facts and labelling Australia First members as quislings.

Captain Blood had succeeded in his objective of breaking up the movement by removing its main officials. In the process, of course, others who had little or nothing to do with the running of the movement had been gathered in. Strangely, the *Publicist* was not banned and the movement was not officially proscribed. However, when Stephensen, Crowley and Hooper, the *Publicist* management, had gone there was nobody left with the desire or knowledge or finance to keep the paper going. For any of the men not interned there could have been nothing but discouragement, and the likelihood of a quick bus trip to Liverpool, had they ventured to take over. In any case, few of the active male members were left free. Mudie was in Adelaide, soon to join the army, and in Sydney there were only Richard Ludowici, P. C. Lang (who had resigned from the movement the morning after he heard of the internments) and Malcolm Smith.

After the internments the women on the executive of the movement did not carry it on. Clearly this would have been most unwise even if it had proved possible. They did not desert their menfolk when they heard of the arrests. Some found out what had happened at a movement speakers' and study class on the night of 10 March, conducted by Lang in the unexplained absence of Masey. At the end of the class Miss Walton announced the detentions. On 26 March, following Forde's statement, the women told *Sydney Morning Herald* reporters that the Minister's allegations had astounded them, as indeed items like the 'Hardt'-Bullock proclamation might. Mrs Sheila Rice, the secretary, said:

> I was absolutely horrified when I read of the minister's allegations. It all seems too preposterous. I have been the honorary secretary of the Australia First Movement since it was formed last October, and never in any shape or form has anything against Australia been discussed at our meetings.

Neither Mrs Parkinson nor Miss Walton had heard anything subversive.

Subversive or not, however the word is defined, the Australia First movement was finished. It has never been revived.

10

Internment

Why am I in this narrow yard?
You ask. Well, I will tell you why.
Outside some say that I should die.
So here they brought me, stood the guard.
There, shut the gate, made the barbed wire high,
And all because so far as I can see,
I loved my country and they hated me.

HARLEY MATTHEWS, Anzac Internment Camp,
1 April 1942.

MOST AUSTRALIANS know far more about German war-time Stalags
and Japanese 'horror' camps in Malaya than about the camps established in their own country for prisoners of war and enemy aliens.
With one exception, almost nothing has been published on the subject, while the literature about Axis camps must run into hundreds
of volumes. To be penned inside an Australian internment compound
was relatively unexciting. With the nearest 'friendly' territory so
many thousands of miles away there was little future in attempting to
escape, and thus this dramatic incentive, which provided the theme
for so many overseas best-sellers and popular films, was almost
entirely lacking. The mass break-out in August 1944 of Japanese
prisoners from Cowra, prisoners who felt that their capture dis-
honoured them and that they had nothing to live for, involved too
many people outside the camp itself to be kept permanently embar-
goed. This spectacular incident has provided material for two books,
one a novel and the other a factual account, *Breakout!* by Hugh
Clarke (1965). The fictional work, by the late Seaforth Mackenzie,
entitled *Dead Men Rising* (1951) has, however, still not been released
in Australia, apparently through fear of libel. Mackenzie, an orderly
room corporal at Cowra who witnessed the break-out, described it

as 'the greatest prisoner-of-war mass-escape in Christian history'.

War histories shy away from the camps, and the whole process of internment has for some reason been kept in the shadows.[1] Occasional articles in journals such as *Nation* and *Twentieth Century* have discussed the fate of that exceptional band who were forced to migrate on the *Dunera,* but little else has been committed to print. Yet in September 1942 an official count revealed that there were 6,780 people, mainly enemy aliens, in our internment camps, most of whom were Italians, many interned under omnibus warrants. Their numbers were quickly whittled down by the Aliens Classification and Advisory Committee, chaired by Arthur Calwell, which began work in 1942; on the file handed to Calwell when he began this task was this note from Forde: 'I hope these people will be given an opportunity to establish their innocence at an early date.' Also behind wire at this time were 1,036 Japanese prisoners of war (the most feared because the least understood) and 1,029 Germans. Australia had had some experience of caring for prisoners and mistrusted aliens. At the start of World War I internments were carried out in each military district. In 1915 most internees were transferred to the one camp at Liverpool.

In 1939 the first camp to be established in New South Wales was at the Anzac Rifle Range at Moorebank, Liverpool, two miles from Harley Matthews's vineyard. Later, larger camps were set up at Orange, further west at Hay (where the dusty, desiccated atmosphere so upset the Central Europeans from the *Dunera*) and at Cowra. There were also camps at Tatura (Victoria), Loveday (South Australia) and in Queensland and Western Australia. Loveday grew to be a major holding centre: originally planned to accommodate 1,000 prisoners, the entry of the Japanese into the war doubled its size. Guard strength went up proportionately, for the Japanese were to have four times the number of garrison battalion troops to guard them as had the Italians who were held there in 1941. In March 1942 Loveday held 3,951 prisoners; this rose to 4,997 by January 1943. Some were Japanese, some Italians and some internees sent from Britain. Australia First internees from Sydney were all, as we have seen, sent to Liverpool. As 1942 wore on most of them were released. Stephensen, Cahill and Kirtley alone were held in custody. They were sent to Loveday in September. Stephensen was kept there for five months before being transferred to Tatura in February 1943. Cahill and Kirtley stayed at Loveday until their release in 1944.

As the war progressed large numbers of aliens appeared before tribunals seeking release and many were set free. At one stage there

Notice to the Public

Memorandum to subscribers of "THE PUBLICIST"

Subscribers to "THE PUBLICIST" are hereby notified that this monthly newspaper, which is registered under the Newspapers Act, has temporarily suspended publication since 1st March, 1942. Its three proprietors, including the Editor, were interned on 10th March, 1942, by order of the Minister for the Army. They were interned in company with thirteen other Australian-born men, all residents of New South Wales, among whom are several writers who have regularly or occasionally contributed articles to "THE PUBLICIST". In these circumstances normal monthly publication could not be maintained. Arrangements will be made in due course, either to resume publication, or to refund unused subscriptions.

Since it was established in July, 1936, "THE PUBLICIST" has strictly conformed with requirements of the law. All its contents since May, 1940, have been submitted to, and passed by, the Official Censor appointed by the Commonwealth Government. No charge has been preferred against its proprietors, or against any of the sixteen men interned in New South Wales. None of these sixteen men has had any association with four persons in Western Australia who have been charged with conspiracy to assist the enemy. These four accused persons were not at any time members of, or connected in any way with the organisation, established in Sydney in October, 1941, which was named "THE AUSTRALIA-FIRST MOVEMENT".

Relying on justice, and seeking release and exoneration, the proprietors of "THE PUBLICIST" request you to communicate immediately, by telegram, letter, and personal interview with Ministers of the Crown, Members of Parliament, and editors of newspapers, to call for a full inquiry into the internment of these sixteen men in New South Wales; to press for their release and exoneration; and to ask for a lifting of the censorship instruction which has preverted their side of the case from being stated in newspapers.

Interned now for almost three months without trial, despite allegations of the most serious nature which were made against them in Parliament on 26th March, these sixteen men of "THE PUBLICIST" and of "THE AUSTRALIA-FIRST MOVEMENT" in New South Wales declare that they are entirely innocent of any conspiracy or illegal activity whatsoever. They rely now on an awakened public opinion to protect their rights as Australian-born citizens to a fair and speedy trial, or to release and exculpation by proper processes of law.

Issued by

"AUSTRALIA-FIRST MOVEMENT", Room 45, Fourth Floor, 26 O'Connell, Street, Sydney.

27th May, 1942.

were men of twenty-nine different nationalities held at Liverpool; being close to Sydney the camp was invariably polyglot. When the Australia Firsters arrived they were at first put into a separate compound. Bath, one of the more impressionable, recorded: 'I was very disturbed to see a motley group of about 200 men, dressed in all sorts of garb, peering at us through the barbed wire. It was a sight I shall never forget and the thought of being put with them frightened me.' After a month their segregation ended and they were able to mingle with the others. This new freedom irked some of them when they found it involved washing the dishes of Javanese sailors.

The two-roomed hut with surrounding verandah accommodating the Australia First internees quickly became 'Australia House', and in it a tight communal life was organized. Almost from the very start, from 11 March, the internees gathered nightly for lectures given by one of their number. These lasted until 4 June, with a total of sixty-five talks being given. Harley Matthews spoke of Gallipoli; Kirtley, who had once been a stockbroker's clerk, told of the Stock Exchange; Stephensen lectured on 'Bygone Biggenden' and Salier on John Dunmore Lang. Hardly surprisingly, this most unusual adult education venture mainly covered Australian subjects.

The internees found themselves treated exactly like prisoners of war; there is little evidence of regulations being eased on their behalf because of their nationality. They were allowed visitors only at weekends for half an hour, when conversations could be held through a wire-netting fence with an armed guard standing by; visitors were not allowed to take notes. Each week they were allowed to write two letters, of twenty-two lines, on special camp paper. Later some did manage to write longer letters to the Attorney-General, but then the twenty-two-line limit was reimposed. In August 1942 Bath wrote to Forde:

> I know you have the power to keep me here for years, but there is one thing you cannot keep from me i.e. the truth of my case. If you want your name to be written in Australian history as a strong administrator admit your mistake, Sir. Admit that you were misinformed...

Mothers of two of the internees died during the period of detention and neither, Harley Matthews nor J. T. Kirtley, was allowed finally to leave camp alone on parole to attend the funerals. Matthews went with one officer as escort. The more touchy Kirtley refused to go when told there had to be an escort.

At first there was no marked animosity among the camp guards towards these native-born prisoners. This was probably because nobody quite knew why they were there. Major Bass told Matthews on his arrival that all he knew was that he had orders to prepare the camp for 'the most dangerous gang that ever came out of Sydney'. After the newspapers' reference to 'quislings' on 26 March a change rapidly became apparent. The guards then saw them as men who had been prepared to sell out to the Japanese, and muttered threats about 'a dirty lot of Jap. spies' became common.

The internees attempted to have their case advertised in the press, engaging a barrister, Carl Shannon, briefed by a Liverpool solicitor, but he found censorship an obstacle. They smuggled out the text of a 'Notice to the Public', which was published by their usual printer, dated 27 May 1942, calling for release of the internees and a lifting of the censorship screen. But apart from telling wives and other weekend visitors to lobby M.P.s about their plight, they had only one means of working for their release—appeal to an internment tribunal. This was provided for by sub-section (d) of regulation 26 and Major Bass informed them of this soon after their arrival, but they did not know how the tribunal worked. On 25 March when regulation 26 was read to them, they were advised that if they wished to object to their detention they should apply to be heard. Most did so; some the next day and others later.

When the nature of the hearing before the tribunal became known (hearings were *in camera*, no charges were laid and the normal rules of evidence did not apply) seven internees withdrew appeals and a further two withdrew during tribunal proceedings in protest at the method of questioning and the attitude of the tribunal (Mr Justice Pike, Andrew Watt K.C., and a retired solicitor, S. McHutchinson). Those who persisted with appeals felt aggrieved over what they considered were deliberate or unnecessary delays in hearing their cases. People who had been arrested after they were appeared earlier before the tribunal. In particular they resented the priority given to Nash and Schaffer, two Romanians, believed to be Jews, whose solicitor was Abram Landa, M.L.A. The official explanation of their priority was that it had been found possible to fit them in as individuals before the tribunal went on a three-week recess from 8 June. The mass of documentation involved in the Australia First cases meant that these internees had to wait until the tribunal resumed on 22 June. This incident helped to feed the feeling of persecution and fear of conspiracy, only too easily linked with Jews, that developed in some of the internees. (Delay may have been frustrating, but the case of another internee showed it was not unlawful.

In Adelaide, P——, an internee who was a naturalized British subject of German origin, applied to the South Australian Supreme Court in 1941 for a habeas corpus writ on the ground of unreasonable delay in being heard by an advisory committee or tribunal. Arrested in November 1940 at Millicent, his appeal had not been heard by the following March largely because of various mishaps to members of the tribunal. Mr Justice Murray ruled against P——, holding that delay did not turn a lawful detention into an unlawful one.)

When the newspapers began to report proceedings against Bullock, Quicke, Williams and Krakouer in the Perth lower court Stephensen requested the Liverpool commandant, Major Thomas Miles, to ask the authorities to allow him to appear there as a Crown witness. Miles told Stephensen that his request could not be granted as it was considered that no evidence he could give would be of material value.

Far from being an average cross-section of the community, the internees were almost all literate individuals with a highly developed concern for their rights; not the sort to give in easily. Neither the disapproval of their guards nor the social ostracism their wives reported having encountered weakened their resolve. A few consented to abide by the rules of the game played by the government only so far as to leave their applications before the tribunal. The desire of this small group to get out of Liverpool was stronger than their dislike or mistrust of the tribunal. Those who managed to convince the tribunal, which was only an advisory body, that they could be set free without endangering national security were Watts, Tinker-Giles, Salier, Bath and Clarence Crowley. They were released on 22 August on the condition that they did not associate with other Australia Firsters.

Watts, who had to promise that neither he nor his wife Dora would write for publication, described himself as 'no more than a prisoner at large'. He found his former job at the munitions factory gone, as was his travel concession as a partially incapacitated returned soldier. His health, never good, had not been improved by his stay at Liverpool. In June 1944 he was admitted to a military hospital where he died about three weeks later from bronchial pneumonia, aged forty-nine.

The tribunal noted that Salier had, in their opinion, been led astray by Stephensen's 'word-spinning'. Salier had, however, often criticized Stephensen, and had offered Miles a critical contribution, 'The Pontifications of Percy on Poetry', which had not been published.

Bath was set free to find his world in ruins. One month after his arrest his prosperous real estate partnership, Coleman and Bath, was dissolved; then his home had to be sold at a loss to meet his debts. When he returned to 'ordinary' life he found that he had been struck off the electoral roll and his motor licence was cancelled; called up by the army he was rejected when doctors found he had diabetes. A Civil Construction Corps call-up followed and for a short time he worked as a labourer on the Captain Cook graving dock in Sydney. Until December 1943 all efforts to find a job more suited to his health and particular skills were unsuccessful. For nine months he worked as a machinist in a munitions annexe. Then on 26 December 1943 he became a chief clerk with the U.S. army in Sydney after passing a rigorous security check; although the Americans knew all about his internment they took him on their payroll and there he stayed for the rest of the war. This appointment proved ideal for the sustained correspondence he carried on to have an enquiry set up, his name cleared and compensation paid.

The Americans decided to use Bath as an agent of sorts in their own security service. He was asked to compile a detailed dossier at short notice on the Ironworkers' Union leader, Ernest Thornton, a prominent communist. A U.S. army colonel gave Bath two and a half hours to get the facts. He went straight to Malcolm Ellis of the *Bulletin,* a journalist-historian whose painstaking researches into the earliest days of Australian settlement were combined with probing of a hastier kind into the contemporary affairs of the Communist Party of Australia. Ellis agreed to help, and three hours after the colonel made his request a dossier on Thornton was in his hands. A day or two after this incident (in which the Americans had Bath trailed) the Sydney press reported that Thornton had been denied a visa to pass through the United States on his way to an international trade-union meeting in Paris.

Bath returned to the real estate business in January 1946, having lost since March 1942 an estimated £32,000 over his brief association with Stephensen and the Australia First movement.

W. F. Tinker-Giles was another of those released in August by the Pike tribunal.* He had never taken an enthusiastic part in the Australia First movement, except perhaps at the start. When the movement was formed he reluctantly agreed when Stephensen asked him to become treasurer, and it was as treasurer that Captain Blood saw him as one who should be interned.

* His mother married twice: first William Giles, then A. H. Tinker. Tinker-Giles sometimes called himself Tinker, sometimes Giles; the Intelligence officers saw this as sinister.

The oldest internee, S. B. Hooper (aged seventy-three in 1942), was first to appear before the tribunal (22 June) but he withdrew on the second day of the hearing in protest against the way it was being conducted. His account of proceedings influenced Valentine Crowley, who also withdrew his appeal. Hooper's counsel handed a statement to the tribunal which noted, *inter alia*, that there was a great divergence between the committee's view of patriotism and Hooper's; whether he was patriotic should be determined only by a public trial. He regarded questions put to him by the tribunal and H. J. H. Henchman, representing Army Intelligence, as irrelevant. No official record is available of the proceedings but Hooper by some means obtained or had recorded in some detail the questions he was asked.* These help to explain the attitude of the tribunal. The questions were:

When did you join the Australia First Movement?
Why did you join the Australia First Movement?
Did you confer with Mr. Stephensen and Mr. Crowley about the constitution and rules? [On replying 'No', Hooper was pressed on this question.]
How could you join without knowing the rules?
Did you help draw up the manifestos issued by the Movement?
What do you mean by Australia First?
Do you not think it selfish to put Australia's interests before those of other countries?
Is not putting Australia's interests first subversive to England and the Empire? [Hooper's notes suggest that the bench insisted that England did not put her own interests first.]
What do you mean by independence?
Why do you want more independence?
Have we not sufficient independence?
Did you approve the Government's action in recalling the AIF from the Middle East?
Is not Australia's frontier on the Rhine? Or in Syria? If not, where is it?
Do you think it proper to desire the presence of the AIF in Australia?
When did you first meet Mr. Stephensen?
When did you first meet Mr. Crowley? Are they friends of yours?
Have you ever heard Mr. Stephensen say . . .?
Have you ever heard Mr. Crowley say . . .?
Did you know the late Mr. W. J. Miles?

* A typed record of the questions is held by the author.

Are you a reader of *The Publicist*?
Do you agree with what you read in it?
Do you approve of . . . [extracts frcm a contribution by Stephensen to the *Publicist*]?
Are you anti-semitic?
Are you in favour of a republic for Australia?
Are you in favour of Nazism? Fascism? Have you any correspondents in Germany or Italy?
What did you drink at the Yabber Club?

Harley Matthews, never a man to knuckle under easily, refused to appear before the tribunal because he found its secrecy repugnant. P. R. and Eric Stephensen, Downe, Valentine Crowley and Cahill made the first step of applying to be heard but later withdrew their applications. Downe did not withdraw until the last minute; when brought before the tribunal he asked for a court martial. Neither Arnold or Kirtley was interested in any appeal.

Masey and Rice appealed but without success. Masey considered that he failed to get a fair deal. He complained that tribunal members took the inflexible attitude that the movement was subversive; they appeared to judge an applicant's unreliability by the amount of contact he had with Stephensen, taking it for granted that Stephensen was a villain. Masey also thought the bench had not considered for themselves on what grounds a man should be interned, and that the tribunal, which was not particularly well informed, spent almost all its time examining the political, social and philosophical views of the applicants.

Few of the internees were as thorough as Masey in documenting the weaknesses of the Crown material used against them. Gordon Rice, the eldest of a family of ten children, a man with a much more limited education than Masey, thought the tribunal had made up its mind in advance. He observed the members of the bench passing some book among them and also some documents, but had no chance to see them. It was only from a newspaper report published two years later that he learned that the tribunal had decided to maintain his internment because of his temperament and 'sardonic sense of humour'.

While these cases were being argued before the tribunal, Stephensen, following the example of Mrs Walsh, had taken the matter before a higher court. He applied to the Supreme Court of New South Wales in July 1942 for a writ of habeas corpus for his release and, like Mrs Walsh, was refused.

Mrs Walsh applied on 12 May on the ground that regulation 26, under which she was interned on 20 March, was not authorized by section 5 of the National Security Act. A bench consisting of Jordan C.J., Davidson and Street JJ., found that the general words of section 5 of the National Security Act—'The Governor-General may make regulations for securing the public safety and the defence of the Commonwealth and the territories of the Commonwealth'—did authorize the regulation. The Chief Justice, Sir Frederick Jordan, looked back to the case of *Lloyd* v. *Wallach* in the High Court in September 1915 and *R.* v. *Halliday* before the House of Lords in 1917. Both cases had decided that the phrase 'for the securing the public safety' was sufficient authorization. But Sir Frederick's judgment did more than refuse the motion for a writ of habeas corpus. Courageously, it canvassed the wider issue of the intention of the legislature. Judicial surprise was expressed at the drastic powers conferred on the Minister spelled out 'by construction from an apparently innocuous generality—for securing the public safety—in a section which appears to be directed to matters of quite secondary importance.' Sir Frederick continued:

I venture to think that most members of Federal Parliament must have felt considerable astonishment when it was explained to them, as I assume it was, that harmless looking general words in a section which seemed to be mainly concerned with property in general and the property of aliens in particular were intended to authorise the executive Government to confer on a Minister arbitrary powers over the life and liberty of every Australian citizen, themselves included.

During debates on the regulations Blackburn, Brennan and other members had pointed out that regulation 26 took away the rights of habeas corpus altogether. Sir Frederick, discussing the cases decided during World War I, noted that the Wallach decision was unanimously decided. However 'the legislature evidently apprehending the possibility that a contrary view might be taken, had hastened to indicate by enactment that it desired to confer a power of internment.' This referred to Hughes's amendment of 13 September 1915, which was introduced following a decision in the Victorian Supreme Court in Wallach's favour. This decision was soon (17 September 1915) to be reversed by the High Court of Australia. Hughes wanted to be sure of the Minister's power to arrest and to intern suspects. E. S. Carr, the member for Macquarie, saw the amendment as a virtual suspension of habeas corpus. Hughes replied that the safety of the country was 'infinitely more precious than empty talk about habeas corpus'. Another of the Supreme Court bench in the Walsh case in 1942, Davidson J., commented on regulation 26:

> Under the regulations a man can be interned on baseless charges made by unidentified persons and become liable for cross-examination before the committee on accusations, the nature of which is unknown to himself while having no power to subpoena his anonymous traducers or to compel them to substantiate their charges. In effect the onus is on the internee to show that his liberty would not be prejudicial to the Commonwealth.[2]

Mrs Walsh was refused special leave by the Full High Court to appeal from the Supreme Court rejection of her application. The bench agreed that *Lloyd* v. *Wallach* was binding.

Stephensen tried a different tack. He claimed that the Minister for the Army could not have been satisfied at the time of ordering the detention, as he had no evidence supportable in a court of law about the allegations made in Parliament. Stephensen put before the court a six thousand-word affidavit summing up his part in the *Publicist* and the Australia First movement, detailing also how the military authorities had acted and how the government had used its powers. Refusing his application, Sir Frederick said that none of the matters in the affidavit were examinable in a court for the purpose of questioning the validity of the ministerial detention order. The regulation made the Minister and not the court the authority for determining whether or not he was satisfied a person should be arrested. The Minister was not bound to restrict himself to material admissible in a court. (A similar decision was reached concurrently in England in a case concerning the parallel 18B regulation of the Defence Regulations.[3])

Following the continued demand for public trial of those internees not released on 22 August, the Attorney-General, Dr Evatt, who had returned to Australia from his overseas supply mission, called for an investigation. He wanted the matter cleared up. A sub-committee of three military officers headed by Lieutenant-Colonel Prentice was quickly appointed to review the remaining internments. It was decided to have all but four released under restrictions. A further review must have been made, probably by Evatt himself, for by 19 October that year only three of the New South Welshmen were still interned—Stephensen, Cahill and Kirtley, who had been sent to Loveday on 16 September.

Eric Stephensen, Downe, Matthews, Hooper and Arnold were freed on 12 September. Miss Walton interviewed Dr Evatt in Canberra on 2 September with J. S. Rosevear present and was told that

Valentine Crowley, Masey and Rice had 'nothing to worry about'. On 12 September Rosevear told Mrs Rice that the trio would be freed in a fortnight. In fact they were not released until 19 October, shortly after a hurried visit from Major Tyrell. Arnold had returned to camp several days after his release, asking to be reinterned, and this was officially done on 23 September. He was released again on 19 October.

Although Dr Evatt wanted the internments cleared up there were limits to his patience, or, as most Australia Firsters saw it, there were no limits to his vindictiveness. Cahill, Kirtley and Stephensen, annoyingly, would not accept limitations on their freedom of movement and expression. As these restrictions were a condition of their release, they were held in custody. The restrictions applied until March 1944 to all freed internees. In that month the enquiry into internments was promised.[4] Cahill and Kirtley were held until February 1944, and Stephensen had to wait until the end of the war. (In Britain Sir Oswald Moseley, interned in 1940, was freed in November 1943.)

On the evidence of his statements to Parliament, Evatt saw Stephensen, Kirtley and Cahill as the hard core of the movement despite the fact that Kirtley for one was not even a member. Kirtley's extremely strong statements about 'gutless Australians' in private letters to Stephensen, so liable to be read out of context, damned him throughout. Had he not written the letters it is hard to imagine him having been interned. Later he explained that he had used overstatement in his letters 'for the purpose of stress'.

Cahill was seen by Evatt as a man who proposed setting up a semi-secret organization within the army to achieve 'complete national independence'. This was based on his letter dated 31 December 1941, addressed to Downe but not posted, found in Cahill's effects when police searched his belongings on 10 March. Cahill and Kirtley were to have been released from Loveday on 11 January 1944, but as they refused to sign the restriction order they were returned to camp and not finally released, but then 'without strings', until 6 February 1944.

At Loveday about December 1942, after Stephensen had been there three months, the authorities confronted him with the Western Australian, Quicke. According to Stephensen, and there is no reason to think otherwise, there was no recognition on either side. Quicke was given the bed next to Stephensen and they became friendly. Quicke painted a portrait of Stephensen which was subsequently entered, without gaining a prize, for the 1945 Archibald Prize.

Stephensen was involved in a meeting of internees at Loveday

called to discuss rations and payment of cooks. He told the gathering,
which included German prisoners of war, that there were Australian
prisoners in Japanese hands and Australian prisoners in German
hands, and suggested referring camp complaints to the Swiss consul
as the protecting power for the German, Italian and Japanese prisoners. His remarks carried the unfortunate implication that pressure
could be brought to bear through the Japanese and German governments. A report stressing this was made to the camp commandant,
Major Hill, who taxed Stephensen with it the following day. Stephensen denied any such implication. Graf, a German, the camp leader or
internees' representative, opposed Stephensen's suggestion that the
Swiss consul should be approached to get action over the ration
entitlement. Stephensen saw this as a move by Graf to ingratiate himself by pretending to be anti-Nazi. Whatever the explanation, Graf
was released before Stephensen. It was also alleged against Stephensen that in a lecture to several hundred men in the camp about gold
digging in Australia he said Australia's future depended on whether
her deliverers, Hitler and Mussolini, succeeded. Stephensen's reply
to this charge, when it was put to him a year later, was that the compound was full of 'lunatics' who would make up reports to curry
favour with the authorities and gain early release.

Stephensen later came under bitter left-wing criticism for his
friendship with some camp Nazis. He did not go out of his way to
avoid them as he had done in the case of von Skerst at Liverpool.
There he claimed to have sat at the same table as this editor of the
German periodical *Die Brücke* for twenty-one months without once
having spoken to him. He suspected the authorities of having put von
Skerst close to him in the hope of obtaining further evidence of his
supposed German affiliations. Explaining his choice of companions
at Loveday he said later: 'I selected my acquaintances in internment
camps on their personal qualities and not on their political beliefs.'
One of his acquaintances was a British Fascist, Mortimer Alexander,
although Stephensen denied he knew Alexander's past at the time.
Alexander was imprisoned for ten months in Sydney for having
issued a pamphlet on national socialism. After serving his term he
was transferred to an internment camp. Stephensen found some of
the anti-Fascists held in his section of the camp hostile to him. He
claimed to have given them—Communists and Jews was his description—no provocation.

Tribune published an account, which it said came from an Italian
anti-Fascist internee, about the behaviour of Australia First men at
Loveday. The writer claimed that Rud Mills, who met Stephensen

for the first time at the camp, was prominent in openly advocating a Japanese victory. The writer also repeated the claim that Stephensen told a camp meeting that if the internees did not receive suitable treatment, the German government could retaliate on Australians held in their camps. Stephensen, who was transferred from Loveday in May 1943, completed his three and a half years' internment at Tatura. While there he sent the commandant a letter seeking his release, complaining that his detention was the result of the conspiracy of 'certain Jews and Communists'. He expected in due course 'unconditional release, full public exoneration, compensation, punishment of those responsible for conspiring to mislead the Minister of the Army, and the opportunity to serve my country in a position of responsibility.' Stephensen was never exonerated or compensated or given any public position.

Rud Mills was released from Loveday on 17 December 1942 after appearing before a tribunal in July which recommended his release without restriction, but not before a brush with an officer of the camp guard who, he claimed, without cause insulted him and then bashed him with a rifle.

Mrs Walsh also appeared before a tribunal. During a lengthy hearing it emerged that the Walshes had a dog called 'Hitler' (according to one witness) or sarcastically called 'Adolf Benito' (according to Mrs Walsh). Disappointed by the tribunal, Mrs Walsh tried a hunger strike. Within two days she was taken to Concord Hospital and the following day freed without restrictions, but had to return to hospital six weeks later after her husband died. She was another—like Stephensen, Kirtley, Bath and probably several others—who firmly believed that Dr Evatt was the villain of the piece.

11

Parliament

BY AN IRONY that must surely have been appreciated at least by Stephensen and Masey, the two men in the government who had most to do with their incarcerations were themselves strongly inclined to nationalism. To make it worse, some of those leading the Opposition attack on the Curtin government's handling of the case were determined Anglophiles and imperial apologists.

That Dr Evatt, whose entry into federal politics Stephensen had welcomed in 1940 and whose historical studies he had praised in the *Publicist*, should be the one to keep him confined and deny him public trial—for at no time did he get a chance to plead his case before a court—must have added to Stephensen's anguish. He could be a little more forgiving towards Forde, the Minister for the Army, who had approved his internment in the first instance. Evatt was a greater disappointment.[1] Stephensen, after his release, maintained a continual diatribe against Evatt calling him 'dirty Bertie' and 'only a lout with a veneer of higher education'. The effect of this harangue, like that against 'Communists and Jews', became dulled by repetition.

Evatt pushed through the Statute of Westminster Adoption Bill late in 1942, against bitter opposition. Harrison claimed that the public regarded such legislation as 'tantamount to finally cutting adrift from the Empire'. Evatt replied that it dealt with 'five narrow, difficult, technical points of legal import and nothing else.' Although the legislation had little practical effect, it had considerable symbolic content and such symbols of nationalist intent counted for much in the eyes of Australia First.

Forde had shown his lack of sympathy with the imperial connection back in 1936. This was in a parliamentary reference to discrimination against Japanese textile manufacturers to favour similar but dearer goods from Britain—a matter which also greatly stirred the *Publicist*. Debating this policy on 9 October 1936, Forde complained that the government (led by J. A. Lyons) was trying to throttle criticism by labelling it anti-British. Forde commented: 'I stand first for Australian interests and second for British interests.' In May 1940 he queried the appointment of an Englishman, Sir Charles Burnett, as Chief of Air Staff, R.A.A.F., instead of an Australian.

The third principal figure in the administration which was responsible for the internments was the Prime Minister, John Curtin, although there is little evidence that he was able to devote much of his time to that particular problem. Malcolm Ellis has claimed that Curtin knew nothing about the internments until some days after they had taken place.[2] Whether or not he was much involved, it could hardly be said that Curtin was a man pledged to nurture the imperial connection. The only public statement about Curtin's part in the affair was made in 1956 by Evatt, who said it had been on Curtin's initiative that the whole of the jurisdiction over internment was taken from Military Intelligence and given to a civil organization. Curtin's first comment in Parliament was on 27 March 1942 when, after having suffered a goading from Calwell over the appointment of MacKay, he remarked that the government would direct the civil authority to formulate charges on the evidence that was available. The internees should be given every opportunity to establish their innocence, if they were innocent. The Solicitor-General (Knowles), Curtin added, was considering the matter. This was generally taken as a promise of a trial for the internees, and press reports in April strengthened the impression that charges were forthcoming. Yet on 6 May Forde told a deputation led by Blackburn that no charges were to be laid against the Sydney men. It looked as if Curtin had gone back on his word but with Evatt away he was necessarily in the hands of advisers such as Knowles.

Forde and Evatt, as far as can be determined, were both unwilling participants in the whole business. Forde was presented with the responsibility for the initial arrests by the action of Colonel Moseley in Perth and Colonel Powell in Sydney. Section 13 of the National Security Act allowed these officers to order the arrests, and subsection 2 required a report of the arrests and the circumstances to be sent to the Attorney-General, yet in view of the disclaimers of Beasley this apparently was not done.

Evatt left Australia secretly for the United States some time in the two days before the arrests. He did not return until 21 June and on his return the process of reviewing cases against the internees and their consequent release was speeded up. Evatt had many other matters of greater moment to occupy him.

Forde did little more than accept the recommendations of Military Intelligence and act as their mouthpiece in Parliament. On 2 September 1942 he announced in Parliament that several paragraphs had appeared in newspapers stating that members of the Australia First movement had been interned (probably a reference to reports of Blackburn's speech on 25 March), and after this it seemed likely that some questions would be asked so he telephoned the Deputy Chief of General Staff (Major-General S. F. Rowell) in Melbourne to discuss the matter. He already had a report prepared by the Director of Military Intelligence. Forde said that Rowell thought that a statement should be made, though not broadcast or cabled overseas. There is a little confusion in Forde's various statements here. In 1946 he said in Parliament that the internments had been a definite recommendation of the Chief of General Staff (Lieutenant-General V. A. H. Sturdee); in 1942 he had referred to the Deputy Chief.

Forde could hardly have rejected the advice offered to him by the Army. In such matters a Minister must inevitably be almost completely in the power of his administrative subordinates; this is part of politics. The report which he read to Parliament was virtually an accusation of treason. It bunched together all the internees, though the substance of the allegations referred only to the four in Western Australia. Later it was realized and admitted in Parliament that there was no connection between those in Perth and those in Sydney. It was further allowed that the whole affair had been grossly inflated. Later still it became clear that the military officers had made serious errors in their selection of internees. None of this could have comforted Forde, but he was stuck with his officers and did not take refuge in condemning them. Evatt in his turn, when the muddle fell into his lap, stood by Forde. He told Parliament that after his return from abroad there was a reorganization of the security services in March with a director-general and six State deputy directors appointed. While he was away this service was run by the Minister for the Army. He (Evatt) assumed responsibility on his return. When he found nine of the New South Wales internees demanding trial and refusing to appear before a National Security tribunal, he called for an investigation. As a consequence all but P. R. Stephensen, Cahill and Kirtley had been released. Evatt's critics have claimed that this trio was kept in custody to help justify the original detentions. The truth or otherwise of this allegation is difficult to determine, but if their offence was sufficiently serious to warrant continued internment then surely there was enough evidence to justify a charge and trial. If their offence was not serious they should have been freed. This is to reduce the choice to the simplest terms: rarely are politicians offered such a luxury.

Did Evatt fail Stephensen because the latter's seeming Fascism (to put it as kindly as possible) made him too abhorrent to be allowed freedom? Did Evatt feel that Stephensen could not be trusted to keep out of trouble if released? Or (most likely of all alternatives) was it simply the recalcitrance of the three internees in refusing to accept release on restriction, claiming that to do so was an admission of guilt? Finally, was Stephensen justified in maintaining that the internments were engineered by communists and Jews? Exactly which communists and which Jews he never announced in public, although he listed some names, without convincing argument, in private correspondence. He failed even in private correspondence to explain how their pressure was applied and how Dr Evatt came to be in their hands.

Surprisingly, Stephensen admitted that the authorities were justified in making the original arrests though not in continuing the detentions once the facts were known. For his part, Evatt admitted that mistakes had been made by Military Intelligence. Fourteen years after the event, as Leader of the Opposition, he told Parliament that 'the beautiful recommendations [for internment] in lovely red ink, which were made by Military Intelligence as administered in those conditions, and which the Minister had only to sign, were not to be relied upon.' In the same debate E. G. Whitlam, who had discussed the subject with his father (Crown Solicitor until 1949) noted that 'the fault of the Labour Government at the time, if there was a fault, was in acting upon the recommendations of military security.' In 1950 Senator Armstrong (A.L.P.) said that the security forces had made 'a tragic mistake', that the Australia First movement 'comprised men who were able to prove their complete innocence so far as the safety of Australia was concerned.'

Although by late 1942 Evatt was starting to admit that some mistakes might possibly have been made, he maintained for some years that there was a core of evil-doers who were enthusiastically pro-Japanese, pro-Hitler and pro-Fascist. For evidence of this he appeared to rely mainly on letters exchanged by Stephensen and Kirtley, many referring to the likelihood of British defeat. He put this strongly in a debate on 10 September 1942. When next the matter was raised in the House (28 January 1943), Calwell, after calling Forde's initial alarm a 'mare's nest', went on to criticize Evatt for his use of these letters to blacken all internees. Calwell was one of those to press for an enquiry into the internments, and he was perhaps the first to do so publicly. On 20 May 1942 he proposed an enquiry of the sort granted in 1920 to the I.W.W. men imprisoned in 1916. Two years later, in 1944, the United Australia Party and the Country Party took up the same cry for an official investigation into an apparent injustice. During these years the released internees had been busy circulating their side of the case, adding to the political pressure for a review of their treatment and consideration of compensation.

Eventually Dr Evatt announced on 2 May 1944 outside Parliament that a federal bankruptcy judge, Thomas Stuart Clyne, had been appointed to report on the internment of Australia First members. Evatt said that the Director-General of Security, Brigadier Simpson, would prepare a submission for Mr Justice Clyne's review.

Evatt's announcement was the signal for a round of recriminations and, when the full text of his statement is examined, Evatt himself must be held largely responsible. He must also have suggested, or at least authorized, a statement by Simpson, a personal friend, which was no better timed. In their statements Evatt and Simpson tried to defend the Curtin government's action. They did this at the very time that a commissioner had been appointed expressly to see if the action was justified. Evatt's was the more prejudicial, suggesting even the course Clyne might take in his report:

Any person rushing in to make party political capital out of these cases will find, after the full facts are disclosed, that he is on the side of a group, the leaders of which were prepared to stab Australia in the back during the period of our greatest peril. The safety of Australian soldiers and the Australian people could have been placed in greater peril had their agitation and propaganda been successful. It is quite consistent with this that some of the group were duped or misled. Mr. Justice Clyne will, I hope, carefully distinguish in his report as to all the individuals concerned directly or indirectly in the leadership of what was undoubtedly a quisling, a subversive, an anti-Australian and an anti-British group.

Less offensively, Simpson said he believed the Security Service would be able to show before the Clyne Inquiry that, co-existent with national safety, the government had been humane and considerate to the maximum degree. He added that neither Evatt nor the Security Service had taken any part in the internments but 'if the responsibility had been mine at the time these internments took place I feel that I would unhesitatingly have made the same recommendations as were made to the then Minister for the Army.'

Masey and Kirtley took immediate issue, Masey complaining that the statements showed that an attempt was still being made to link the Australia First movement with the unrelated group in Perth. He added that he was grateful to M.P.s such as Blackburn, Calwell, Rosevear, Sir Frederick Stewart and J. P. Abbott who had put up a fight to secure justice for the internees. Kirtley denied Simpson's contention that the treatment of internees had been humane and considerate. He cited the instance of his twelve-year-old son who came to see him at Liverpool the day after he had been taken to South Australia, and was simply told his father was not there and packed off home.*

The following day Bath joined in with a demand for a Royal Commission with a High Court judge presiding. He objected to Evatt's 'pre-judgment' of Clyne's findings. Several internees, he also complained, had been brow-beaten before National Security tribunals, and endeavours had been made to induce internees to sign quittances of various kinds before their release. He suggested seven points of enquiry for a Royal Commission:

1. Whether any internees from NSW were connected with the Australia First Movement.
2. Whether any were involved in any plot as outlined by Forde.
3. Whether any were guilty of subversive acts.
4. Whether there was any connection between the W.A. subversion and any NSW internee.
5. On what grounds internments were made.
6. Whether the anonymous extracts read by Evatt were all written by the internees, whether the extracts gave a fair representation of the import of the letters.
7. If there was any dereliction of duty by Security, who were the guilty parties, and what was the source of their information.

Bath commented: 'If the full facts came out, the country will be shocked to its core by what is revealed and by a new knowledge of the extent to which the concentration camp has been used in Australia.'

A fortnight after Evatt's announcement the University of Sydney's Professor John Anderson, the philosopher who had so much influence on the city's intellectual 'tone', criticized the treatment—imprisonment without trial—of the Australia First men as a symptom of the exercise of dictatorial powers which no claim of war emergency could justify.

* His son's memory of this incident suggests that the camp guards at least were not quite so callous. His son recalls visiting the camp on that occasion with Mrs Harley Matthews and being told with some compassion by a guard NCO that his father had been transferred to Loveday camp.

Two politicians in particular, Blackburn and Calwell, emerged from the debate over Australia First with enhanced reputations. They had nothing to gain in party advancement, and very little in electoral kudos, from bothering themselves about the treatment of men for whom the labour movement could have little sympathy.

It was Blackburn who, right from the start, mistrusted the accuracy of the information supplied to the government. It took other M.P.s many months, some of them years, to come around to the point of view Blackburn expressed in his first reference to the matter in Parliament: 'I do not believe that the persons were in any way in sympathy with the Japanese.' Some who later sprang to the defence of the internees when party advantage strongly dictated this course had made rather less perceptive opening remarks. Eric Harrison, on 27 March, had referred to the Australia First movement as 'this traitorous movement the like of which I as never been known in Australia before.' Blackburn was commended for his part in the affair by individuals like Bullock and by such unlikely journals as the *Bulletin*, which rarely bothered to commend actions of Labor M.P.s, and by the Roman Catholic *Tribune* of Melbourne. (Blackburn was a rationalist.) A foundation member of the Australian Council for Civil Liberties and its president from 1940 to his death in 1944, he had always been concerned by matters affecting the personal liberties of citizens. Years before the internments he had seen the dangers implicit in the National Security regulations. Paul Hasluck, compiler of the civil section of Australia's 1939–45 war histories, commented that Blackburn was qualified to protest at the regulations 'by a lifetime of political scrupulousness and intellectual integrity in maintaining democratic liberties as he saw them.'

Not only was Blackburn the man first to make public the government's action, but he continued thereafter to press for trial or release. Evatt later acknowledged the part he played. Apart from his commendable public pressure Blackburn did much privately. He went with Mrs Keith Bath and the movement's secretary, Mrs Sheila Rice, for an interview with Forde in Canberra on 6 May 1942. It was at this interview that Forde said for the first time that no charges would be laid against the men from New South Wales. Blackburn ensured that a letter from Forde seeking expedition of the hearing of tribunal appeals was forwarded. However within two days the tribunal went into recess for eighteen days because its military prosecutor, H. J. H. Henchman, was required in the Supreme Court for Mrs Pankhurst Walsh's habeas corpus application. One of the tribunal, Andrew Watt K.C., was also appearing in the Divorce Court in a case that lasted from 14 to 26 May. Two months were thus to elapse between the time Mrs Bath saw Forde and 7 July, the day her husband went before the tribunal.

Calwell was not as centrally concerned as Blackburn. His interest in the case appeared initially to be sparked by the involvement of MacKay, whom he distrusted. From then on he harried Forde, Beasley and Evatt, asking when, if ever, the internees were to be brought to trial. He made it his business to plumb the reasons behind the internments, consulting, among others, Major Ted Hattam of the Commonwealth Investigation Branch in Melbourne. It was not long before he was sure that if there had been any plot, which he doubted, it existed only in Western Australia, and anyway, the holding of people without trial was opposed to everything for which Labor stood. In 1965 Calwell said that at the time of Forde's announcement he did not take it seriously and never had. He has attempted to explain Evatt's dilemma in an action taken by Bath against the Commonwealth for compensation in 1947. In an obituary comment[3] Calwell said that Evatt was not responsible for the Commonwealth's invoking the Statute of Limitations to fend off this action, but was bound to back up the decision. Evatt had tried hard to find some compromise but the Australia Firsters insisted on total justice. This would have involved the Commonwealth in a confession that it had acted mistakenly and unfairly. 'This was the only occasion,' wrote Calwell, 'on which Dr. Evatt was not at the forefront in an issue involving civil rights.'

Another clue to Evatt's role has been provided by J. J. Dedman, war-time Labor Minister for War Organization of Industry and later Post-war Reconstruction, in an article discussing Australian negotiations with the United States over Manus Island in 1946.[4] At the time, Labor (and Dr Evatt as Minister for External Affairs) was widely criticized for driving the Americans and all their equipment away from this considerable war-time naval and air base. Dedman explained, twenty years after the event, that the U.S. terms for continuing their occupancy of Manus Island were quite unacceptable: Australia was to meet the entire maintenance cost while America was to pay nothing; America could at any time take over full control and deny the facilities of the base to third parties such as Britain. This 'take-all, give nothing' proposition was rightly rejected by the Labor government. The surprise was, according to Dedman, that Evatt completely omitted to tell the Australian people of the Americans' terms. Dedman added: 'However much I did and do appreciate his great achievements, I never did rank him very high as an advocate in Parliament of the policies in which he and his colleagues so firmly believed.'

J. S. Rosevear and H. L. Anthony, the outspoken Country Party member for Richmond, were concerned about the flimsy evidence against the Western Australians and the way 'Hardt' operated.

Two Labor M.P.s to persist with the description of Australia Firsters as 'quislings' were the party's 'wild men', E. J. Ward and L. C. Haylen. Haylen, who had not been a member of Parliament at the time of the internments, apparently had some knowledge of W. J. Miles and knew Stephensen fairly well. As a playwright and novelist in his leisure time from journalism he quickly saw the melo-drama of the situation in Perth as presented by Moseley and Richards. In 1944 he told Parliament that there were saboteurs and there were stooges in the Australia First movement and 'no good purpose' was served in separating them. After asking what would have happened had the government failed to take swift measures against the men, he added: 'The Japanese planned to make a thrust down the coast of Western Australia. The plot "blew up" in that State because that was the key centre. I am satisfied that the members of the Australia First Movement were fully aware of where the Japanese planned to strike.' This was even stronger than 'Hardt' had dared to pitch his story. On a more circumstantial note, Haylen continued:

> Until the security officers gathered in these men, a quisling walked down George Street, Sydney, every day, stick in hand, called at a certain place and obtained money for carrying on his activities. He spread a little gossip here and there and made derogatory remarks about this and that. The proprietor of *The Publicist* went out of his way to shove the newspaper into the hands of the public. Copies were left in trams and ferries. Even during the Depression, when quite substantial newspapers were experiencing difficulties in carrying on, this man was printing more and more papers every week. Where was the money coming from? . . . surely members do not think that the wily Japanese imagined that all Australians were incorruptible.

Subsequently Haylen claimed that the reference to George Street was not a correct report of his speech.[5] He had not corrected the Hansard proofs. And, he added, some of the comment referred to J. H. C. Sleeman, managing editor of the notorious *Beckett's Budget*.

Ward said that the Opposition, in attacking the government's action, was defending quislings. As one of his bugbears, Eric Harrison, had been a recent speaker, he switched to what was for him a familiar target, the New Guard. 'Quite possibly,' he said, 'the Australia First Movement with which these quislings were associated originated in the New Guard . . . The New Guard did not suggest assassination but they did prepare a list of prominent persons in this country . . . intending to place them in Berrima gaol.' This jibe was not the last time the Australia First movement and the New Guard were linked, although they had little or nothing in common: one was a huge mass movement mainly of the Sydney middle class inspired by fear of left-wing labour; the other was minute in membership, also of the middle class, but inspired by a variety of kinds of nationalist fervour. The New Guard was led by ex-officers imbued with imperial ideals; the Australia First movement was fired largely by distrust of imperial motives. An historian of the New Guard, John James, has privately commented to me that Australia First looked to him 'rather like a drama guild being suddenly involved in international politics'. James agrees there has been general confusion between the two groups despite their separation by ten years in time and a world in ideas. Possibly only one man, Tom Walsh, had belonged to both, because of their common anti-communism.

Not only the Left but the parliamentary Right had its extremists who lost balance over the affair. The peripheral involvement of communists allowed the 'red menace' hobbyhorse to get yet another outing: the Communist Party had persistently campaigned to have Miles and Stephensen and their associates interned and the *Publicist* banned. The *Bulletin* of 20 May 1942 claimed that two 'Leninists' had told a meeting at Griffith that the Legal Rights Committee of New South Wales (one manifestation of the Communist Party) had supplied the authorities with information that led to government action against Australia First. Some Opposition M.P.s spoke in Parliament for internees they knew personally. Bernard Corser (Wide Bay) was a friend of Stephensen while several N.S.W. members knew Masey and Bath.

From attacking the movement and its treachery in the first debates after the internment, Eric Harrison switched to criticizing the government's handling of the case which soon became 'the greatest travesty of justice in the history of this country'. Harrison, plentifully provided with information from Bath and possibly other internees, brought much useful detail into the debate but went too far. He claimed (19 July 1944) that the initial parliamentary statement by Forde was 'nothing more or less than a paraphrase of the indictment of Bukharin and other Rightists and Trotskyites at the Moscow Trials of 1938.' In some instances, he added, actual phrases tallied. The same similarity was also seen by the *Bulletin* (31 October 1945) and noted by

Malcolm Ellis, a *Bulletin* journalist, in his survey of Australian communism, *The Garden Path* (1949).[6] It is more than likely that Ellis originally drew it to Harrison's attention.

A close examination of the Moscow indictment does nothing to support this startling thesis. Ellis noted that the English edition of the official Soviet report of the Moscow proceedings was available in Australia at the time Forde's statement was drafted. It is difficult not to regard the Ellis-Harrison theory with precisely the same degree of scepticism as Haylen's statement and the fantastic plans hatched in Perth.

Ellis claimed that Australia First took its name from the heading to John Curtin's federal election campaign advertisements in 1937, although an inspection of the masthead of the first number of the *Publicist* in July 1936 quickly disposes of this, quite apart from the appearance of the same slogan on stationery used by W. J. Miles in World War I.

More down to earth in his attitude to Australia First than most parliamentarians was the Country Party member for Bendigo, G. J. Rankin, who described it all as 'a case of much ado about nothing. I believe that these few cranks—for I think they are cranks, who were not extremely dangerous to the community—are of no consequence compared with the safety of Australia.'

12

Inquiry

SEVENTEEN DAYS after Dr Evatt announced that there would be a Commission of Inquiry the Commissioner, Mr Justice Clyne, began proceedings in Sydney. It was not a Royal Commission, but rather a Commission of Inquiry authorized by the National Security regulations, although there was little practical difference. (A psychiatric panel might have been more to the point but, in the manner of that time and this, lawyers were set the task of probing men's minds.)

At one or other stage of the proceedings, a lawyer represented each internee except Cahill, who spoke for himself, and three Western Australians, Bullock, Quicke and Williams (still in custody). Some eminent barristers were involved, notably the King's Counsel W. R. Dovey, J. W. Shand and J. E. Cassidy. Dovey, a personal friend of Evatt, assisted the Commissioner. Shand, with H. J. H. Henchman, who had been involved in internee appeal tribunals, represented the Department of the Army and the Security Services. Cassidy appeared for Masey, Salier, Bath, Hooper and Watts. The Stephensens retained W. H. Downing.

Mr Justice Clyne had chaired a Victorian Royal Commission into industrial assurance in 1938, and became chairman in 1940 of the Victorian tribunal hearing applications for release from interned aliens. Dr Evatt asked him to look into the Australia First internments under six headings:

1. Whether the detention in March, April and May 1942 under Regulation 26 of the National Security (General) Regulations of certain persons connected with the 'Australia First Movement' group, as recommended by Army authorities, was justified;
2. Whether the said persons were given a proper opportunity of appealing against their detention to the appropriate appeal tri-

bunal, and whether those who did appeal had their case fairly and justly considered;

3. Whether the continuance of the original detention was justified, and whether the restrictions imposed upon any of the said persons after release were just and reasonable in the circumstances;

4. Whether it is proper that any further action should be taken in respect of any of the said persons;

5. Whether in the case of any of the said persons, it is proper that they should receive any compensation from the Commonwealth, and, if so, what amount, and

6. All matters which, in the opinion of the said Commissioner, are relevant to any of the above matters, or should, in his opinion, be dealt with or reported upon by him.

In the early stages of the legal haggling that occupied the first fourteen days of the sixty-nine sitting days of the Inquiry, counsel for several internees complained that the terms were too limited and the scope of the Inquiry too narrow. There was little justification for these complaints, particularly in view of part 6 of Clyne's charge. Clyne himself dealt firmly with such objections, stating plainly that he could and would include any matter that he thought should be dealt with.

Another complaint, and one more justified, was of excessive delay. This was probably inevitable in view of the number of internees involved, the vast corps of lawyers (sixteen), the necessity to transfer hearings at times between Sydney and Melbourne, and the other calls on the Commissioner's time. Clyne gave ninety-five days to bankruptcy cases during the term of the Inquiry and also undertook a brief special investigation for Curtin of statements attributed to the South Australian Crown Solicitor, A. J. Hannan, that his letters were being intercepted and his telephone tapped. (This occupied about one week and resulted in the finding that the allegations had no basis.) Some of the delays during the Inquiry were caused by counsel for the internees seeking time to digest the mountain of documents involved.

The hearing began in Sydney on 19 June 1944 and did not finish until 17 May 1945, in Melbourne. Of the sixty-nine sitting days, thirty-eight were given to hearing witnesses and final addresses took seventeen. The text ran to 2,514 foolscap pages. Nobody could fairly complain that the presentation of his case was hampered by anything other than the intractability of the evidence or the performance of his lawyer.

After sitting in Sydney and Melbourne to settle procedure a jumble of exhibits was put before the Commission—reports, letters, books, circulars and 124 extracts from the *Publicist*; the Commission heard Dovey's submission,[1] listened to Downing's reading of the depositions of the lower court hearing in Perth, and then, at long last, took evidence. This was on 18 September.

First witnesses were Sergeant Swasbrick and Lieutenant-Colonel Powell. The sequence then was: a term in Melbourne for evidence from Mills and Stephensen (then held at Tatura), back to Sydney to hear from Captain Blood and the New South Wales internees, to Melbourne for the evidence of the Western Australians and finally hearings in both Sydney and Melbourne for addresses by counsel. Having the Western Australian Intelligence officers give their evidence in Melbourne meant they were not exposed to cross-examination by Cassidy K.C. and other counsel for the Sydney internees. This important task had to be borne by Downing and by T. J. Hughes, representing Nancy Krakouer.

Apart from a few press comments and federal Parliament's periodic worrying of the matter, the Commission provided the first real opportunity for internees to air their case. Newspaper coverage of the proceedings was ample, allowing for the newsprint shortage, although a little unbalanced because security revelations provided most of the headlines.

The internees could hardly be blamed for engaging in early manoeuvres in an attempt to attract public sympathy. Could there have been such an element, a little pardonable playing to the gallery, in the plea for reinternment by Harley Matthews on the third day of the hearing? Matthews told Clyne that he felt apprehensive about his personal safety as a result of J. G. Coyle's (Dovey's junior) saying the day before that Matthews had stated he would like to get active assistance for the Nazi cause in Australia. A legitimate ploy, it failed to produce the maximum reaction when Clyne declined to canvass the matter.

The next day G. T. Rice informed Dovey that he wanted nothing to do with the Inquiry, and he left. This, too, was taken calmly by the Commissioner with the comment, 'his departure will not save us much time'. Rice apparently reconsidered, as he appeared on 6 February 1945, represented by Shannon, to give evidence.

On the second day in Melbourne, Security, through H. J. H. Henchman, gave warning that not all the relevant Intelligence files could be produced. Some could be for the Commissioner's eyes only. This possible source of friction did not, in the event, become a serious issue. Counsel did not demand that any secret documents or reports be revealed. Enough emerged to suggest on what kind of evidence the internments were based. Several witnesses were protected by the

Commissioner's ruling that their names be withheld from publication. One was a woman employed at the German Chamber of Commerce in Sydney and the other was a Sydney journalist doing undercover work.

Whether the Commission as constituted was ideally fitted for its task is a question worth considering. Remarks passed on 25 August 1944 suggest that something was lacking. Clyne and Coyle admitted themselves baffled by a reference to an 'R.P.A. member'. Though Clyne for one was clearly not uninterested in history, generally a fugitive virtue in a law court, his interests apparently did not encompass the 1890s when the Rationalist Press Association was being formed or the decade or so later when, partly through the endeavours of W. J. Miles, its organization spread to Sydney. It is true that judges and barristers are not required to be masters of all subjects to come before them, nor could this be expected. Their peculiar talent is to draw information from witnesses and gauge what weight to give it. But when they find themselves puzzled by such a reference it is surely their duty to take the matter further and inform themselves fully. As it happened, the development of the RPA in Australia was quite important in the story of Miles. And without Miles there would have been no *Publicist* and therefore no nucleus for an Australia First movement.

As the Inquiry wore on and internees learned when to take cover, almost all of them tended to become more Anglophilic than was normal. To be anti-British, to shun the 'Poms', was natural for a minority in a young colony or a new federation of independent States and indeed if there had been any hesitancy about publicly admitting such mother-hatred, Archibald's *Bulletin* should have cured it. But it tended to become an unstated maxim at the Inquiry that Anglophobia, in however mild a form, was heretical if not seditious. Occasionally a burst of emotion by an internee broke through this guard bringing back some reality to the proceedings. It is significant that it was Gordon Rice, the most 'working class' of the New South Welshmen, who was least given to this dissimulation. Shand commented that Rice, when giving evidence, kept using the term 'Pommie' instead of 'English'. The Commissioner asked whether Rice objected to 'English'. Rice admitted that 'Pommie' was a larrikin term but added: 'I called them worse than that when Larwood and others were here, throwing the ball at us instead of bowling.'

One of the few issues at stake not gone over with loving repetition was whether the internees who appealed to the tribunal had their cases fairly considered. No clear picture emerged of procedure at the tribunals, which came under criticism from most of those appearing before them. Mr Justice Clyne did once mention the possibility of having the chairman of the New South Wales tribunal, Mr Justice Pike, called to help determine whether proceedings had been fair. However he went on to add (and this probably summed up his opinion) that one would hardly think a reputable tribunal would deal unfairly with the internees. So the idea of calling in Pike was dropped.

It did not take long for the central issue to emerge. This was that the N.S.W. internments were a direct consequence of the message from Perth. Though earlier internment had been considered and restrictions recommended, but not authorized, there would have been no internments on 10 March if the message had not been sent the day before. Once this was established, it was important for the internees to prove that there was no connection between the Perth group and the Sydney movement so that the message could be shown to be misguided. Richards's report of 20 March 1942 helped to establish this.

Security produced correspondence between Miles in Sydney and Mrs O'Loughlin in Perth. This did suggest they had like minds on many matters, though dissimilar temperaments, but it was quite insufficient to prove any organizational link between Western Australia and New South Wales. Anyway Miles was dead and Mrs O'Loughlin had not been arrested. Bullock, Quicke and Krakouer had indeed written to Sydney, either seeking information or suggesting affiliation, but nothing concrete resulted. Security was quite unable to prove any connection between the New South Wales internees and the sort of assassination plot outlined by Forde. Security was thus forced to defend the internments by painting in the blackest terms the characters of those interned as shown in their private letters, whether written in 1936 or 1942, or in their conversations or speeches, reported with varying degrees of accuracy. Thus much of the hearing was taken up with haggling over what a witness meant by such and such a phrase used in a letter to his brother (who could read between the lines) or his girlfriend (who was there to be impressed). There was no evidence of any dealing with the Japanese by any internee. Stephensen, it was shown, had met some Japanese at their Sydney consulate at pre-war receptions, but then so had many other Australians whose loyalty was not impugned.

The preoccupation of A. R. Mills with Nordic mythology and his early meetings with Nazis, including Hitler, in Germany proved so tantalizing and suggestive that he was kept for the best part of three days in the witness stand. He was far from being the most popular witness. Stephensen was kept for five and a half days and Blood entered his fifth day. It was this inflexible officer who figured in what, to some, was the most hilarious incident of the Inquiry, when he was being questioned by Cassidy K.C. During a five-hour stretch of cross-examination by Cassidy, Blood said that among other reasons for recommending the internment of Watts and others were their *Public-ist* articles. He was then offered a quotation and asked whether there was enough in it to warrant internment of its author. After praising the magnificent manner in which Hitler had built up Germany after World War I, the proffered passage ended by describing Hitler as a 'highly competent, cool, well-informed functionary with an agreeable manner', adding that the world lived on in hopes that 'we may yet live to see Herr Hitler a gentler figure in a happier world'. These closing words brought laughter, followed by Captain Blood's incautious comment: 'It is hardly what I'd call a Churchill speech.' Unhappily for the captain that was precisely what it was— an extract from page 268 of Churchill's *Great Contemporaries* (1937), provided for Cassidy's use by Masey. There was little enough other humour in the proceedings. Cassidy attempted a repeat performance with a quotation from a Curtin speech on September 1938, to the effect that the total of Australian resources must be available for its own defence. Blood approached the trap and then backed out with the remark: 'I do not fall for the same trick twice.'

New material uncovered by the Commission came largely from the Intelligence officers. What Stephensen and his associates had been doing and saying was to a great extent already public knowledge. What was novel was how Army Intelligence worked. It was revealed how puzzled constables received assignments such as investigating Odinism, how quickly other constables learned to stiffen up a report on a suspect with careful selections from correspondence in which the innocuous became the seditious, and how unsubstantiated opinions (like Matthews wanting to aid the Nazi cause and Bath verging on the fanatical in his beliefs) became 'Holy Writ' once they were enshrined in the files. Small wonder that Dovey, though his purpose was to defend the government, could quote with apparent approval the words of Cassidy about 'the blundering ineptitude of certain individual military officers'.

Even allowing for the three years that elapsed between the action and the remembrance, it is startling to note the wide divergence in testimony by the different officers about the way it was decided who should be arrested. This was a vital point in Intelligence testimony. Why Bath and not Ludowici? Why Matthews and not Lang? Why Watts and not Mudie or Malcolm Smith? What about Cummins?

Four of the men concerned in the midnight police headquarters conference at which these decisions were made, Detective-Sergeant Swasbrick, Lieutenant-Colonel Powell, Major Tyrell and Captain Newman, gave evidence.

Swasbrick testified that Tyrell went to his 'Australia First' index, picked out fourteen names of persons whom he recommended should be arrested, and gave them to Powell, who had to make the decision. Later Swasbrick altered ground to refer to a list of twenty names from which four, five or six, mainly women, were deleted. Powell's version was that it had been decided definitely to arrest one man and probably two or three more. The others were to have their premises searched and reports were to be relayed to him via Watkins or Swasbrick for a decision whether or not to arrest. Reports came in that morning and the arrest of the remainder was ordered. Tyrell said that when Powell told him he would 'arrest the lot' he (Tyrell) said there was no need to do that and suggested the detention of a certain number, though he could not be sure how many. Newman's version was that it had been decided to arrest all the men on the list and search the premises of half a dozen others. He was not aware of any reports being telephoned back after the searches. The more questions that were asked about this sequence of events, the more tangled became the skein of circumstance.

For some reason officers of the Commonwealth Investigation Branch in New South Wales were not called before the Commission, and it is more than likely that Mr Justice Clyne did not see branch reports. The limited evidence available suggests that Dr Evatt was probably responsible for this. Major Hattam, an acting inspector of the branch in Melbourne, was called to give evidence, principally concerning Mills.

Stephensen, brought down to Melbourne for the Inquiry from Tatura camp, was thoroughly and relentlessly escorted through his evidence by Shand K.C., closely followed by the Commissioner. He had little scope for manoeuvre.

One easy path open to him, to heap the blame onto the dead Miles, he did not take, to his great personal credit. He went instead to the other extreme of attempting to justify and defend embarrassing statements made by Miles and Hardy Wilson. He proved the most stubborn of witnesses. He kept repeating that he was not anti-British and denied that his *Publicist* articles were written to create hostility between Britain and Australia. When pressed, he admitted that in making a decision whether or not a man should be interned it would prima facie be important to determine if he had attempted to bring

Britain into contempt and disrepute in time of war. Anyone who advocated giving in to Japan without fighting should be locked up. He was surprised, he told Shand, to learn of a letter, exhibited in the case, that he had written to W. D. Cookes of Melbourne on 23 January 1942, saying that if the United States and Britain abandoned Australia to concentrate on Hitler, Australia would have to sign a separate peace with Japan. He explained that the situation was purely hypothetical, adding that a separate peace was not the same as a negotiated peace.* When Shand resurrected a phrase used by Stephensen in an article published in 1938 about 'Britain's next aggressive war', Stephensen dodged by saying that this was 'just a bit of journalese, a loosely used adjective'.

Stephensen's partial deafness at times led to misunderstanding, as in: 'Have you a contempt for Churchill?'—'No, I have a respect for clergymen.'

Some of his private correspondence, when made public, was seen to be phrased unfortunately. In a letter to Kirtley on 20 April 1941 he noted: 'Adolf spent his 52nd birthday in Salonica. What a man!' In this, he told Shand, he was not expressing admiration but astonishment and surprise, respect for an opponent. Shand brought out letters written by Hardy Wilson, a man Stephensen described as 'a great Australian patriot' though one 'obsessed against Jews because he thinks that they are having a bad influence on art.' Wilson, in a letter said by Shand to have been addressed to Miles but later admitted to have been addressed to Sir Arthur Streeton (a mistake that Stephensen saw as evidence that a plot against him was being engineered), wrote that if the Japanese were to win the war he could 'help a lot making peace with the confidence of the Japanese'. In this same letter (dated 30 December 1941) he remarked that John Curtin was 'a blind tool under the Jewish influence of the U.S.A.' Shand asked Stephensen if he agreed. Curtin, responded Stephensen, was a blind tool in the hands of the Labor Party.

Stephensen agreed with Dovey's proposition that when the presence of an individual in the community was likely to affect the safety of the community, any doubt, from the point of view of common sense, should be resolved in the favour of the community. He would agree with this as long as it were done secretly and not publicly, as long as names were not divulged.

* A Melbourne man was given four weeks' gaol in April 1942 on a charge, laid under the National Security Act, that he tried to influence public opinion prejudicially to the conduct of the war by asking people to sign a petition to Mr Curtin urging him to negotiate with the Japanese rulers to end the war (*Sydney Morning Herald*, 24 April 1942).

The early *Publicist* 'advertisement' that began 'Wanted 500,000 young Australians' was offered to Stephensen by Shand for possible repudiation, to find its author 'proud of it'. Later in the Inquiry Masey found it 'offensive' while Hooper thought it should not have been published.

Stephensen denied a suggestion by Shand that he had told a meeting at Loveday, largely made up of Italian and German prisoners of war, that Australia was being robbed by England and America. This was a 'monstrous fabrication'. Harried further about his opinions on the subject, he finally turned defiant and maintained that Britain 'quite rightly' had been making use of Australia for her own selfish ends throughout all Australia's history. To be certain he had heard correctly Mr Justice Clyne asked what exactly was 'quite right'— Stephensen's statement that it was a fact or that Britain was right in doing it? Stephensen replied that it was quite right for the British to make use of the colonies for their own selfish ends. Would Stephensen agree that to spread such a suggestion about would serve to alienate the allegiance of Australians to England? Oh no, replied Stephensen, there was no allegiance of Australians to England. Australians should reciprocate and 'take the English down a bit'. This admission of opinion was closer to his true feelings than all the protestations about having no antagonism to Britain and talk about it being his 'second home'.

Clyne remarked that there was stronger evidence against W. D. Cookes than against any of the men interned. Stephensen asserted that Cookes was 'a very good Australian citizen, a very loyal man to Australia'. What exactly Security had against Cookes was not fully revealed. His letters to Miles and to various German firms were read but he was not questioned on them after his personal physician, Dr M. D. Silverberg of Collins Street, Melbourne, gave evidence that a court appearance would endanger his health. Earlier, a Commonwealth medical officer, Dr F. R. Kerr, had said there was no reason why Cookes should not attend to answer questions. However Mr Justice Clyne accepted Dovey's suggestion that in all the circumstances, including Cookes's apparent disinclination to appear, his presence should not be insisted on.

Several matters that one would have expected to get more attention went without argument. One was why Ian Mudie, a long-time contributor of poetry to the *Publicist* and, more importantly, an executive member of the Australia First movement, escaped arrest and internment? Several times, though only idly, this question was put. It was never satisfactorily answered, although it was suggested that he was outside New South Wales at the time and thus the concern of another military command. Mudie himself does not know why. Another unanswered question was why a report of the arrests as required by the Act was not sent to the Attorney-General. That a report had not been sent might never have been suspected outside the Attorney-General's Department had not Beasley, the acting Minister, twice denied knowledge of the whole affair in Parliament. In his final address, Downing, counsel for Stephensen, maintained that no evidence had been produced that the required report had been made, and as the terms laid down in section 13 had thus not been fully met the arrests were wrongful. Clyne thought the report may have gone to one of the Attorney-General's officers, but Downing insisted that the report must be to the Minister. Dovey attempted to come to the rescue by suggesting that Knowles, the Solicitor-General, had apparently examined the report, adding that the Solicitor-General for the time being might take the place of the Attorney-General during his absence. Downing maintained his position and there the matter rested. It was not again referred to and it was not discussed in Clyne's report. That the internees, who were well aware of the apparent omission, did not take legal action based upon it suggests that their advisers (and an opinion on possible litigation was obtained at one stage from Garfield Barwick K.C.) saw no prospect of success.

All manner of schemes for court action to redress grievances were mulled over in the years after the war, especially by Stephensen and Bath, both supremely optimistic about their chances long after almost all the others had given up hope. In the event, nothing was carried through the courts although actions were begun, one by Bath and one by Stephensen.

As well as the questions left unanswered there was one unasked, notable in that it was one which anyone trying to understand the genesis of the Australia First movement would seek to have explained. The unexplored mystery was why that most unlikely of groups, the Women's Guild of Empire, or even former members of such an imperially oriented body, should wish to associate with the *Publicist* group, widely known for its extreme coolness to imperial ties. The answer might be found in an investigation of Mrs Walsh's motives. Did she urge the formation of the movement because she was temporarily at a loose end after her break with the guild? Was she casting around for some new cause? Or was it because of her strong sympathies with Japan, believing that the *Publicist* people thought the same way? Nobody at the Inquiry appeared at all curious as to why these two groups, apparently so incompatible, joined forces.

In his opening recital of the 'facts' leading to the arrests and intern-ments, Dovey referred to Mrs Walsh and her connections with the Japanese. Stephensen could not deny outright Shand's claim that Mrs Walsh was pro-Japanese. There was some mention in evidence by Rice and Tinker-Giles about the circumstances of Mrs Walsh's departure from the movement, but apart from this the motives that impelled her and her association went unexplored. There had been, of course, time and sufficient alteration in political conditions since 1937, when the guild and the *Publicist* had crossed swords, for a *détente* in 1941 to be plausible.

Brief evidence was given by Mrs Marjorie Corby and Mrs Vera Parkinson, those politically unsophisticated associates of Mrs Walsh, who stayed with the movement after she left. Mrs Corby claimed that she knew nothing of Australia First until Mrs Walsh asked if its inaugural meeting could be held at her flat. Mrs Parkinson said her membership of the movement 'arose out of my five years' service in the Guild of Empire'. She attended most of the meetings of the Australia First executive and heard nothing subversive; of her fellow officials she thought 'how much nicer and more respectable they were than the Communist interjectors from whom we suffered so constantly and I thought I would rather be an Australia First than a Communist, thank you.' She saw the movement as an extension of the social work she had done among the unemployed in Sydney industrial suburbs in the Depression. Clyne did not discuss their involvement beyond recording that the movement was formed when it was suggested 'by some persons who were members of an association called the Woman's Guild of Empire, which was at the time in abeyance' that there should be a merger between the Guild and the *Publicist* group. Mrs Walsh, according to Dovey, was interned not because of her Australia First activities but for 'pro-enemy sympathies, utterances and subversive talk and conduct'. A probing of her strange associa-tion with Stephensen was not attempted.

Another oddity was a reference in a report put before the Com-mission in which Inspector Watkins advised his Commissioner, MacKay, about a telephone call made on the night of the arrests by A. M. Sticpewich, Secretary of the Police Department. According to Downing's reading of the report, Sticpewich rang police headquar-ters to get an assurance that the military and not the police were taking responsibility for the arrests. Dovey said that this action was quite formal and there is little if anything to suggest otherwise. However, Stephensen later suggested in a letter to Bath that Sticpe-wich, who, he claimed 'managed to keep well under cover during the

Klein [*sic*] Inquiry', was a possible party to the 'Jewish-Communist' plot behind the internments.

Mr Justice Clyne ended proceedings in Melbourne on 17 May 1945 with the remark: 'It is a very onerous task ahead of me.'

While the Commission was still proceeding, Parliament had been giving it intermittent attention. On 19 July 1944 Eric Harrison urged a widening of the terms of reference and a speeding of the Inquiry. In the process he canvassed the justice of some of the internments and was censured by Dr Evatt, who had done much the same two months before, for prejudging the issues.

A remark made by Captain Blood at the Commission on 9 November 1944 was picked up by the ebullient Archie Cameron, member for Barker. Asked why the communists who created the disturbance at Adyar Hall had not been sent for internment, Blood replied, after trying to hedge, that it was because of a ministerial order of 1941 that no more communists were to be submitted for internment. Cameron asked Evatt whether this was so, to be told that no such thing had been said in reference to the Labor government. Persisting with his questions, Cameron quoted a section of the transcript. Forde stalled by saying that enquiries would be made. About a week later he admitted the correctness of Cameron's extracts from Blood's statement, but denied that any such ministerial direction had been given.

It is hard to resist the conclusion that although Blood may have misunderstood or misinterpreted ministerial directions sufficiently for Forde to be able with a clear conscience to deny the exact words used, the first Curtin cabinet had in fact laid down some such principle following the embarrassing Ratliff and Thomas case. According to the Council for Civil Liberties, Evatt required Commonwealth officials to seek his personal sanction before starting prosecutions in such cases, thus withdrawing the previous delegated authority. A survey of June 1942 added: 'And no prosecution of an anti-fascist has in fact been authorized by him since the Government took office.'

On 12 September 1945 Beasley, the Minister for Defence, laid the Clyne report on the table of the House. There was no full debate on it until March 1946.

13

Judgment

MR JUSTICE CLYNE had been asked to enquire into matters relating to the detention of 'certain persons connected with the "Australia First" Movement group'. However the title of his report refers to the detention of 'certain members of the "Australia First Movement" group'—not quite the same thing. Clyne himself found that Matthews and Kirtley were not members and that Bath had not been finally accepted by the movement as a member, so it was hardly a beginning to inspire confidence in the report.

His report set out the main facts in a fairly workmanlike manner, with no flagrant injustices done to any internee. This is not to say there were no mistakes—these are not difficult to find. But if injustice was done it was not in the minor errors but in the general assumption that subversive thinking was enough to 'justify' detention. Subversive, of course, was a word capable of being used, and in fact was used, to cover a wide set of situations.

Clyne said that Kirtley had strong views which could only be regarded as subversive, but he did not suggest that Kirtley's thinking had ever been or was ever likely to have been translated into action. What Kirtley thought, which was principally revealed in his private correspondence, was enough to damn him. Clyne noted that Kirtley, according to his letters, had a tremendous contempt for Australians, who were 'gutless swine', saw the country's leaders as fools and scoundrels and its soldiers as 99 per cent mercenaries, and he held a low opinion of Churchill and Roosevelt. Kirtley did indeed write these things, and more, in his correspondence with Stephensen. He must have had some regrets later that he ever put such words to paper; they were picked up and used by all opponents of Australia First who were attempting to prove what a dastardly set of people had been interned; they were used by police in Intelligence reports, by Evatt and others in Parliament and again by Clyne in his report.

Captain Blood's submission of 13 March 1942, seeking internment for those arrested on or about 10 March, commented that Kirtley's correspondence, intercepted by the censor, showed him to be 'almost intensely anti-British and anti-Australian, and, in consequence, guilty of subversive activities.' The Commissioner failed to question the unstated minor premise of this syllogism.

Cross-examined by Shand during the Inquiry, Kirtley did not attempt to deny having written the pungent phrases so often held against him, but he did time and time again rightly object to the use being made of such extracts. He admitted that 'gutless swine' was an overstatement used to stress his point; he admitted also that he had been proved wrong about the Australian people who had in the event 'come up to scratch', and he considered they deserved an apology. Surely an important point was that such remarks were made in private correspondence. This did not appear to weigh any more with Clyne than with Blood.

Kirtley was ill, often inclined to misanthropy, a creature of violent gusts of emotion, and what he wrote in private to Stephensen could harm nobody, however unpopular the opinions expressed. He was justified in objecting to questions designed to discover his state of mind in the days before internment. Shand asked what he thought of Curtin's leadership and Kirtley replied: 'Does it matter what I thought?' To other questions he replied: 'Why should I select my words in a private letter? What does it matter?'

Kirtley did not join the movement; he was sent an application form for membership but replied that he had enough on his hands for the present. He had a temporary job at Woy Woy police station, about fifty miles north of Sydney, and only rarely made the trip to the city. However turbulent may have been his thoughts, he lived quietly with his invalid mother. Some of his feelings, no doubt, had an outlet in his unpublished novel, 'Corroboree'. He enrolled as a police reservist and could hardly have been regarded as a threat to the Commonwealth. It is quite possible that he would be living there still, perhaps maintaining a characteristically bitter correspondence with friends, had he not been interned in 1942. No case of any consequence was made out to prove him a menace to the country's security, yet together with Cahill he received the second-longest term behind barbed wire. Those letters to Stephensen earned him internment for one year eleven months.

The Commissioner came closest to considering the relevance of a

man's private thoughts and opinions to his loyalty in his comment
that the activities of some of the members of the movement were
likely to have created ill-will and hostility in the community. Had
Kirtley proclaimed in public, in wartime, his private opinion that
Australians were 'gutless swine', or if his opinion was spread about
by others, ill-will would probably have resulted, thus justifying restriction or detention. But Kirtley held his counsel; he did not attend
meetings; he just wrote letters. Apart from a handful of unexceptionable articles on Pacific strategy in the *Publicist* he did nothing to aid
the Australia First movement and took no part in its propaganda.

Kirtley stood out because of the vehemence of his opinions, but
he was no more guilty than his fellow-internees of any overt action
against his country's defences. None of the sixteen did anything more
harmful than stir up political and racial feeling. The *Publicist* had to
pass the censor, and this should have been enough of a check on its
encouragement of community divisions at a time of national emergency. National Security legislation could have been used to stop
further meetings of the movement. As it happened, according to
most estimates of the position, the cancellation of the Manly meeting
caused the movement to wait until the war's end before resuming
active campaigning. This may not have been so apparent at the time
to mistrustful Intelligence officers made more apprehensive by the
melodramatic message from Perth.

After extensive research into the Clyne report, Masey and Bath
uncovered numerous errors of fact and instances of unsupported
opinions. They thought, for example, that Clyne was not being fair
when he noted that generally the movement was hostile to the Jewish
race. In a private commentary, now in my possession, they noted that
while Stephensen and what they called three obscure members,
Arnold, Graham and Mills, were anti-Jewish, the movement itself
had no views. Evidence at the Inquiry bears this out. Clyne observed
that members of the movement were 'a strangely assorted set, some of
whom were prone to adopt extreme opinions on any subject.' Detailing some of their views he noted that one member had a 'strong antipathy to the Christian religion'. This was hardly a matter which one
would have thought to come within the scope of his charter.

Clyne quoted two *Publicist* passages as examples of the movement's antagonism towards the United Kingdom and the United
States, and admiration of Japan. One was Stephensen's 1936 advertisement 'Wanted 500,000 young Australians'. The other was Miles's
article of August 1936, 'We have nothing to fear from the Japanese'.
He did not point out the year they had been written—hardly conclu-

sive proof of the *Publicist*'s war-time attitudes, which after all were what mattered.

Clyne's report began with a short account, set in a sketchy historical background, of the formation of the movement, its connection with the *Publicist* and a reference to the opinions expressed in that journal. He went on to discuss the Yabber Club, public meetings, the arrests in Western Australia, the cipher message and consequent Sydney action and, after some general observations, details were given for each of the sixteen individuals.

Clyne concluded that the army had not been justified in recommending the detention under regulation 26 of Bath, Clarence Crowley, Hooper, Masey, Matthews, Salier, Tinker-Giles and Watts. He also found that all internees were given a proper opportunity for appealing against their detention, and that appeals before the tribunal were fairly and justly considered. Compensation was due to seven of the eight men unjustifiably held and to the widow of the eighth. He suggested sums ranging from £350 (Masey) to £500 (Bath) and £700 (Matthews).

In Parliament on 5 October Forde briefly announced that Clyne's recommendations had been approved and were being put into effect. He looked back to the internments as having taken place at a time when Japanese invasion was imminent. There was no chance then for a 'wait-and-see' policy. Failure to act would have been inexcusable.

He exonerated the eight internees Clyne had found to be unjustifiably interned, saying: 'On behalf of the Government, I now publicly declare that Messrs K. P. Bath, Clarence Crowley, S. B. Hooper, E. C. de la Roche Masey, Harley Matthews, C. W. Salier, W. F. Tinker-Giles and Martin F. Watts were in fact wrongly detained and were not disloyal.'

Apart from the objections already raised, the most disputable conclusion in Clyne's report was his statement that the Western Australians had seriously intended their 'fantastic and extravagant' designs. Allowing that Thomas was 'not a passive investigator', Clyne still considered that the four people had actually been planning to assist the Japanese. This, of course, is a matter of opinion, and the Commissioner called the Western Australians before him to give evidence —to find them 'very unsatisfactory'. In one of the few memorable passages of his report he remarked of them: 'It is difficult to imagine what moved these puny conspirators to such ambitious and dangerous designs.' A more apt comment might have been that of T. J. Hughes: 'No Thomas, no conspiracy.'

The ex-internees can conveniently be divided into the 'goats' and the 'sheep' on the basis of Clyne's findings.

THE 'GOATS'

Arnold. Clyne found that Arnold was strongly biased in favour of Germany and was ready and willing to advocate a separate peace with Germany and Japan.

This 'separate peace' was to be the strongest allegation made against the men from New South Wales. During the Inquiry it received most attention when the draft manifesto of the movement containing three points of a national defence policy, including 'Australia's right to make peace', was being investigated. Showing how easily he could see the sinister in the straightforward, Mr Justice Clyne revealingly remarked that the manifesto's proposals 'indicate to what lengths some member or members were prepared to go'. The judge had himself taken an active part with Shand in questioning Stephensen on the manifesto. When pinned down Stephensen said he could not remember whose idea this third point had been, but he had prepared its phrasing. It had been discarded as it was 'liable to be misunderstood'. Point 3 hardly warranted the attention it received as point 2, on Australian national independence, came to much the same thing, including the sentence: 'The Australian Government, representing only the Australian people, has the responsibility of upholding Australia's independent status in all international discussions and negotiations, for both war and peace.' Stephensen observed that a 'separate peace' was not the same as a 'negotiated peace'. In forming the Australia First movement he had never intended to have anything to do with a negotiated peace. According to several internees the notion of a separate peace was proposed by Mrs Walsh and constituted a major cause of the rift leading to her departure.

Evidence against Arnold cited by the Commissioner consisted, as for Kirtley, of private letters. Some were sent to the German Consul-General, Asmis, but this was before the war. Arnold, who was anti-Semitic, had some strange ideas, but it is debatable whether the Commissioner was justified in holding that these ideas, however regrettable, constituted a sound reason for internment.

Cahill. Leslie Kevin Cahill was regarded as an unreliable witness and one the Intelligence officers were justified in recommending for detention. A wide-ranging set of questions on the possibilities of the overthrow of the government, put to him by Shand, brought replies that were taken seriously—though Cahill was hardly a man whose opinions were to be taken too literally. Within certain limits Shand seemed to be able to get Cahill to say almost anything: he was quite ready to romance on any topic; because of its turmoil his mind needed little to send it out on new and exciting paths.

The Commission had before it an Australia First leaflet with some notes Cahill admitted scribbling on the back. These notes listed names and numbers: Cahill 1, Lang 2, Mudie 3, Masey 4, Tinker 5, Crowley 6 and Collins 7. Underneath each was a code word representing a State capital. Shand eagerly followed this up and after numerous wrong turnings managed to get Cahill to admit that although he could not recall what had been in his mind at the time the list could have been meant as a 'Council of Seven' for a possible national revolution for Australian independence. He had, he said, used codes of various kinds when he was in the Communist Party but not when he was in the Australia First movement.

In the jumble of Cahill's evidence were the rudiments of a coherent nationalist argument and when he felt he was on solid ground he could dig in his toes. Although the Commission was sensitive to criticism of Britain, a fact quickly sensed and acted on by more astute witnesses, Cahill firmly maintained that Australia had been 'oppressed and impoverished' by the British government. He cited the Bank of England and the Manchester Chamber of Commerce as two British institutions which had acted against our best interests. Then, in the middle of questions about British influence, he was asked without warning about anti-Semitism, and, equally casually, replied: 'I am anti-Semitic.'

Cahill maintained that the communists were gaining control of Parliament at the time of the Inquiry (November 1944) and when asked about his revolutionary intentions usually managed to relate them to his desire to combat this. Mr Justice Clyne said he was unable to accept Cahill's denial that he had enlisted in order to form some semi-secret organization within the services to bring about complete national independence. If the Commissioner could regard the intentions of the Western Australian group as recorded in the 'Hardt'-Bullock proclamation as serious, then it followed that Cahill was other than a crackpot.

Valentine Crowley. The Commissioner was certainly far less happy about Valentine than about his brother Clarence, whom he cleared. Valentine Crowley, he said, was an unsatisfactory witness and a person who had been properly detained. Accepting Intelligence evidence of Crowley's remarks at the Yabber Club, the Commissioner said there was little doubt that Crowley was extremely hostile to Britain and indeed, if the reports were to be believed, this could hardly be disputed. Statements in this vein cited in the report by the Commissioner included:

'The sooner Germany bombed England the better.'

'Wherever the English flag was flown it brought poverty, corrugated iron and dirt.'

'England was buggered, and he [Crowley] was only waiting for the rain of bombs to start and they [England] would be forced into submission.'

Clyne said he could not accept the suggestion that such remarks were made merely to provoke discussion. Further, he was dubious about Crowley's conversion from republicanism in 1936 to monarchism not very many years later, a change attributed to Miles's persuasion.

Simply being anti-British was not enough to justify detention, but it was a great help. For Clyne the clincher was, in Crowley's case, that 'in my opinion, he was ready at a critical time during the war to cause hostility between Britain and Australia, and, by stirring up strife, to impair the war effort of Australia.' Captain Blood had accused Crowley of 'many disloyal remarks'. In his analysis of the Clyne report, Masey, who admitted that Crowley was well known for his 'provocative and unusual views', summed up: 'Crowley's case is a vital one as it throws into strong relief the distinction between restraining action and suppressing opinions'.

The heretical opinions held by Crowley were, in general, similar to those propounded in the editorials of Archibald's *Bulletin* in the nineties. Any slights Crowley might have offered on the English connection could easily have been matched, and many times surpassed, by those earlier nationalists. There was no suggestion of his ever having been pro-Japanese, either before or during the Pacific war, or of having been pro-Nazi; he showed no sympathy with the antagonism exhibited by Miles to the Jews; his republican views came, he claimed, from the six years he had spent under the republican system of the United States. Some of the strong anti-British opinions attributed to him in reports by Intelligence agents at the Yabber Club he called 'pure fabrication'. One agent, as we have seen, told the Commission that he relied on memory to jot down afterwards what had been said at club gatherings, and an earlier (pre-1940) agent had been found unreliable. The Commissioner decided there was 'no sufficient reason why the substance of the reports of these speeches made by the investigators should not be accepted.'

Some of Crowley's private letters were held against him—letters to Miles (principally one in 1936 advocating republicanism) and one to an old boyhood friend, Jack Beasley, M.H.R. The letter to Beasley, dated 3 July 1941, contained this passage: 'My real opinion is that as we have not adopted the Statute of Westminster we are still an English colony and all Australians who leave Australia to go to England's war lose all national status and cannot expect any more consideration.' Under questioning by Shand he refused to retract this. Nevertheless he did consent to his son, while under age, joining the army in 1940, he did offer his car for use by army H.Q. in Sydney and he did become air raid warden at Mosman.

Downe. A trooper in the 11th Armoured Car Regiment at Tamworth at the time of his arrest, Clive Kirkwood Downe was found to be justifiably interned. The Commissioner reported: 'Downe's conduct justified the conclusion that he was a zealous supporter of Stephensen, prepared to advocate a change of leadership in Australia under the control of the Australia First Movement. In any event, his conduct was such as to excite strong suspicion'. Downe, in his early thirties when arrested, had been a staunch though not active supporter of the movement, a reader of the *Publicist* since 1937 and one who attended many of the movement's public meetings. An advertisement in the *Sydney Morning Herald* first introduced him to the *Publicist,* whose nationalist sentiments he found to his taste. He tried to join the R.A.A.F. in 1940 but had been rejected because of defective eyesight. Soon after the Pacific war began he joined the A.I.F. Before he left for camp he believed, or so he told the Commission, that the Australia First movement was going to go into recess until after the war. Two letters provided the core of the case against him. One addressed to him, but not sent, was written by Cahill, in whose possession it was found. Cahill put forward his idea for some sort of secret organization of Australia Firsters in the services, to obtain 'complete national independence, if necessary with the force of arms'. A letter Downe sent to Stephensen appeared to confirm the suspicions aroused by Cahill's letter. Downe asked Stephensen for twelve membership forms and a supply of the movement's manifestos. He explained to the Commission that this request followed a discussion with a fellow-soldier named Cornell who was disappointed with the existing political parties and wanted the forms to send to friends in the country. Apart from this, the main documentary evidence against Downe came from some personal diaries. One entry, dated 11 February 1942, came under particular scrutiny: 'Malaya won by the Japanese; we withdraw to Singapore which is now under attack. Defeat here inevitable. Australia will not be invaded if it is not to become an outer base for America.' This was immediately interpreted to mean that we should not allow the United States to establish bases. Downe also commented in his diary that the Americans were prepared to adopt only those measures and plans essential for their own survival and not for Australia's, despite their high-sounding but empty boasting. This defensible proposition—that any country is primarily concerned with its own survival—was held against him. It was put to Downe that publicly broadcasting such an opinion would have done some harm. So indeed it might, to a small extent, at a time when the Americans were allies and already had troops in our country. However Downe's opinion was kept to his private diary.

On his release from internment in September 1942, at which time he was discharged from the army, Downe was told to live outside Sydney at Moss Vale. After some protest, and declarations that he did not intend to accept such a restriction, he agreed to go to Moss Vale until he received an answer to an appeal he had sent to Dr Evatt. After three weeks there he was told that he could, if he wished, re-enlist. He did so under a new army number and eventually saw action at Bougainville.

Downe's case was, for some unknown reason, not canvassed by Captain Blood in his submission of 13 March. In the parliamentary debate that followed the tabling of the Commissioner's report, A. W. Fadden, the Country Party leader, claimed that Colonel Prentice, Chief Intelligence Officer in New South Wales at the time of Downe's arrest, had later (December 1944) offered Downe a posting to one of the army's most secret units. This unit, according to Fadden, was 'so secret that its members are sworn to refrain from mentioning that they have been members of it, even after they have been discharged from service.' M. H. Ellis has claimed that Downe was cleared at a supplementary enquiry which he (Ellis) was personally responsible for instituting.[1] This is the sole reference to such an enquiry; the Attorney-General's Department and the Department of Army know nothing of it.

Kirtley. A few points remain to be made about Kirtley. The Commissioner thought him 'an intense admirer of Japan', quoting a lengthy article written for the March 1940 *Publicist* in which he said 'only the weak or sinister can accuse the Japanese of being disrupters of peace'. A passage from a letter of 2 March 1942 was also cited: 'The fact is that we are Japan's for the taking.' This, like Miles's interminable defence of his theory of the 'biological inevitability' of war, was hardly an expression of desire, but rather an opinion of what was possible. Neither the quotations nor the references to Kirtley's belief that the Chinese were the aggressors in the Sino-Japanese war were sufficient buttress for Clyne's belief that Kirtley admired Japan. Kirtley was not a man to do much admiring of anything.

Mills. Alexander Rud Mills, the Melbourne solicitor, was at a disadvantage among the internees because of his association with Nazi organizations in the thirties and his continued antipathy to Jews.[2] This more than outbalanced the fact that his only link with the Australia First movement was to send 10s 6d to Cahill as a subscription. The Commissioner found that Mills was not—despite Captain Blood's contrary claim—the movement's Melbourne agent, but thought him justifiably detained in view of his past record even though 'after the outbreak of war he had not disclosed in his conduct any hostility to the allied cause'. This was hardly a confident justification for Mills's arrest.

Rice. Gordon Thomas Rice was a foundation member of the movement; Clyne called him 'a very unsatisfactory witness' and one who was 'properly detained'. Rice had been pulled in well beyond his depth in cross-examination. Two documents were much used against him—the script of an undelivered speech and some pencilled remarks on a pamphlet. He showed a fairly rudimentary Anglophobia in keeping with his lack of political sophistication. The Commissioner questioned his preference for 'Commonwealth of Nations' over the word 'Empire'.

Eric Stephensen. Army Intelligence found it hard to develop a strong case against Eric Dudley Stephensen. He was a member of the movement, but more importantly—and this was enough to put him behind barbed wire—he was a brother of P. R. Stephensen and under his influence in political matters. The Commissioner decided that Eric was ready to give full support to anything suggested by his elder brother. Eric Stephensen, aged twenty-seven at the time he gave evidence, had been to all the Australia First meetings. He had come to Sydney in September 1941, having saved enough money by working at a Cardwell, North Queensland, timber mill to finance a course at the Julian Ashton art school in Sydney. He had had some correspondence about Percy with their younger brother Ted who had enlisted in the R.A.A.F. Ted maintained that Percy was a bad influence, a narrow, clever revolutionary, and thought Eric had come too strongly under his influence. Eric joined the army three weeks after release from internment; at the time of the Commission he was attached to the 6th Australian Ambulance Corps.

P. R. Stephensen. Naturally he was the central figure in the Inquiry. If he were cleared it would be almost impossible to justify the detention of his colleagues. If he were blackened his associates were likely to share in the disapprobation to the extent of their association with him. In dealing with him, the Commissioner did not break with the assumptions that appeared to underlie the whole Inquiry: if no overt act of sabotage against Australia's defence could be proved (and none were, even in Perth) then disloyalty could be found to lie in disaffection with imperial ties, or in praise of Japan (even before December 1941) or in praise of Germany (even before September 1939). Operating on these principles it was easy to deal with Stephensen. Any reading of the evidence would provide examples in plenty of hostility to Britain, admiration for the Nazi régime and admiration for Japan. Mr Justice Clyne could not resist the irrelevant remark that Stephensen, a Rhodes Scholar, had 'done little to realise the aspirations of Cecil Rhodes since leaving Oxford'.

THE 'SHEEP'

Matthews. Of the eight 'sheep' exonerated by the Commissioner, the one for whom internment had been the greatest injustice was surely Harley Matthews. Like Kirtley, he did not belong to the movement but, unlike Kirtley, he did not discuss war strategy or the failings of his fellows in letters to Stephensen. He had, however, written to Hooper, and several passages attracted attention—for example that Mrs Walsh, Billy Hughes, 'Secret Fund' Nelson (a Miners' Federation official) and 'all the imported union heads' were 'saboteurs' of Australia First. He explained that he meant that these people had no regard for Australia First. Mr Justice Clyne recorded this explanation without comment and cleared Matthews as loyal, adding that Intelligence officers had blundered badly.

Masey. Edward Cory de la Roche Masey was another who, in the Commissioner's opinion, should not have been detained—at worst he was 'perhaps indiscreet' and had 'extreme views' upon the right to freedom of speech. Masey, a keen student of economic and political affairs, was one of the most level-headed of the internees. His only real mistake was joining the Australia First movement, which he had done without enthusiasm. Faced with such determined moderation and fair-mindedness, Clyne could hardly do other than give him a clean sheet.

Bath. Clyne found that Keith Bath also should not have been detained. He had been associated with the movement only in its final months; there was nothing subversive in his papers and nothing to indicate association with either Germans or Japanese. Clyne evidently dismissed the fanciful claim by Captain Blood that Bath was 'verging on the fanatical in his beliefs'.

Clarence Crowley. He admitted to the worst that Captain Blood could say against him: that he had maintained an association with the *Publicist,* had joined the movement and kept copies of its literature. His part in the activities of the movement had been much less important than those of his elder brother, and the Commissioner found him to have been unjustifiably interned. Their backgrounds had been very different. Clarence spent his early and middle years farming in Victoria and Queensland, finally selling up in 1921 to buy city property and settle in Sydney. Valentine began as an electrical engineer in Victoria, then lived in New Zealand, the United States, Germany and Britain before returning to Australia in 1912, later moving to live in Sydney about 1920. The placid Clarence regarded his brother as an 'impulsive sort of fellow'. He told the Commission that he did not even know what his brother's religion was.

Hooper. Of the triumvirate which took over the *Publicist* from Miles, Sydney Benjamin Hooper was the first to be released. A long-standing Australian nationalist, his position was clear and uncomplicated, and this was how Clyne saw it, finding that he had been mistakenly interned. Hooper's objections to instances of British domination of Australia did not constitute disloyalty. Hooper, aged seventy-five at the time of the Inquiry, was an old friend of Miles. An employee of the Union Bank for forty years, he spent his early life in outback towns of New South Wales, eventually becoming manager of the George Street, Sydney, branch. His first conscious nationalism, he told the Commission, came when he took issue as a boy with his father, an Englishman, about the formation of an Australian navy. While his father thought Australia should simply pay the Royal Navy to send ships to the Pacific, he preferred Australia to establish and maintain her own fleet. This issue was in fact one of the first of any magnitude to cause dissension between the new Commonwealth and its mother country.

Captain Blood said little about Hooper in his report of 13 March other than to note his close connection with the *Publicist,* his attendance at the Yabber Club and membership of the movement. Closer in sympathy to Miles than to Stephensen, Hooper helped, though only in small ways, to shape *Publicist* policies. It was he who introduced Morley Roberts to Miles. He held Miles in high regard and did not change this opinion when pressed at the Commission. 'He was the most serious as well as the most honest man I ever met', he told Henchman. Some of Miles's intransigence about Germany and Japan rubbed off onto Hooper. The Commission was told that Hooper had written in June 1939 to the woman author of an article about Hitler in the Sydney *Sun*. Hooper stated, *inter alia,* 'it was indeed a pleasure to have such a rarely courageous and independently minded expression of view to set off against the depressing chorus of anti-Hitler pronouncements in the Press and on the air.'

Mr Justice Clyne found that Hooper was always ready to place the interests of Australia before those of the Empire, but he examined the matter no further.

Salier. Cecil Walter Salier, who did not give evidence before the Commission although represented by counsel (Cassidy), was easily dealt with. All Captain Blood had been able to say against him was that he was a member of the movement, was 'clearly associated' with it and was 'definitely in contact with the executive officers'. Salier, an old rationalist associate of Miles, had written for the *Publicist* under his own name or as 'H. B. Thomas', usually about nationalist figures in Australia's past, such as John Dunmore Lang ('a forerunner of Australia First'). He also tackled Pacific problems. In 1937 he wrote that 'taken broadly, the idea of a Japanese invasion in force of Australia is baseless'—an opinion that subsequent events did nothing to disprove.

Dovey's opening address to the Inquiry noted that Salier was 'thoroughly respectable, honest and upright'. Although Salier had been led to believe that it was right to cultivate a spirit of mutual understanding between Australia and Japan, said Dovey, he did not appear to have been active in the movement, where he was a listener rather than a participant. The Commissioner accepted this picture. He had little alternative. Cassidy obtained from Captain Blood as near an admission as any counsel got about any internee that the only suggestion of disloyalty about Salier was his association with the movement, nothing more.

Tinker-Giles and Watts. Both Walter Frederick Tinker-Giles and Martin Francis Watts were exonerated; nothing of any substance could be held against them. The Commissioner found that having held executive office in the movement was not sufficient reason for detention. Though Watts was on the executive, the Pike tribunal had noted that he had never actually signed up as a member of the movement. Watts died during the Commission hearing. He was found to have been a loyal subject of the King; his antipathy towards the Jews, as shown clearly in his articles in the *Publicist,* was not mentioned.

In assessing the findings of the Clyne Commission, there is the difficulty of the gap between the summary of the facts and the recommendations. (Dr Sondra Silverman, during research at the Australian National University, studied the Clyne report in detail and saw in it 'fuzziness par excellence'.[3]) In few cases, and certainly not in Stephensen's, is any connection made; the argument is not carried through; unstated assumptions provide the sole bridge. If Clyne had decided what actions, statements or thoughts justified internments, nowhere are these criteria revealed. In the key case of Stephensen, all that was given was a bare statement of his views on Germany, Italy and Japan, his toying with the idea of a separate peace, and then the flat statement that there was 'substantial' reason for his detention being recommended. We are left to deduce that these reasons were his pre-war expressions of admiration of Nazis and Japanese, his hatred of Britain and his notion of a separate peace with Japan. His 'Hitler—what a man!' comment to Kirtley must also have counted heavily. Were there other, more objectionable, matters contained in security documents tabled before the Commission but not made public? There is little to suggest this.

In one attempt to explain his reasoning, Clyne mentioned that views similar to those held by Stephensen were likely to cause dissension in the community. This remark deserved expansion it did not get. Some provocative speeches by Stephensen, if less hot-headed than those of Cahill and Mrs Walsh during their brief terms as organizers in the movement, did arouse and annoy some of his audience. However, most of those who were incited and annoyed had gone to the public meetings as political opponents, many of them only too willing to cause an upset. Some were communists, bitterly opposed to Stephensen. Had there been more meetings further civil disturbances like that at Adyar Hall could have been expected, but was this not a matter for the civil police, however heavily engaged their activities elsewhere? Was Stephensen to be denied the right of free speech in war-time because it enraged his opponents? Stephensen and Masey both firmly maintained in public speeches that the war emergency made the freest expression of opinions more than ever necessary, though Stephensen also wrote, in April 1941, that in time of war there was not a full scope for oppositionists.

Can a democracy stand unfettered freedom of expression in war-time? Can minorities be allowed to ventilate dissent at such times of national crisis? If we are dealing with the real world, one in which compromises are the rule and adherence to principle the exception, the answer must be: it all depends on the circumstances. In June 1941, in England, a member of the British Union of Fascists, Elsie

Orrin, was sentenced to gaol for five years for having told two soldiers that Hitler was a better ruler than Churchill. No Australia First internee was ever accused of having publicly stated anything so 'disloyal'. (The Western Australians, of course, were accused of having made plans to greet the invading Japanese.) In April 1943 another British Fascist, William Craven, was sentenced to a life term for having written to the German Legation in Dublin stating his sympathy with, and willingness to aid, the enemy. Mistrust of certain British and American motives constituted the most extreme of the statements held against the New South Wales internees. Did this mistrust, expressed only by a few and then usually in private, warrant more than proscription of meetings and either the banning or heavier censorship of the *Publicist*?

Mr Justice Clyne, summing up, dealt in his report with the various terms of his appointment. He found that Forde had been bound to order the internments in view of the army's recommendation. However the army had not been justified in recommending the detention of Bath, Clarence Crowley, Hooper, Masey, Matthews, Salier, Tinker-Giles and Watts. He found no evidence that those appealing against their detentions had not been dealt with fairly and justly by the appeal tribunal. The continued detention of the internees not excepted in the first finding was justified, as were the restrictions imposed on those released.

At the time the Commission was announced Dr Evatt had stated that if Mr Justice Clyne recommended prosecutions in the ordinary courts, such advice would be followed. However Clyne found that no further action should be taken. Those wrongly detained were entitled to a public declaration that they had been wrongly detained and were not disloyal.

The report having been completed and the last internee, Stephensen, freed after three years, five months and one week in internment camps, the matter was now back with the (Chifley) government.

14

Finale

AFTER THE government accepted Clyne's recommendations, and the Opposition, led by R. G. Menzies, in no way significantly challenged his findings or assumptions, those internees who had been 'black-washed' (to use Stephensen's phrase) were left to ventilate their grumblings privately. The Western Australians faded right out of the picture, never to be heard of publicly again, at least in any political role. For the New South Wales internees, even some of those exonerated, the matter was far from closed.

Seething at Clyne's findings, Stephensen nevertheless refrained from canvassing his disagreements publicly until as late as 1959. He hoped for a further enquiry, like that into the I.W.W. arrests of 1916, to get to 'the real truth'. Stephensen, Masey, Hooper and Bath spared little effort spurring on M.P.s to take up their case when the Clyne report came before Parliament in mid-March 1946. These 'friendly' M.P.s were mainly members of the new Liberal Party, formed in 1945 to replace the old disunited United Australia Party, and the Country Party. Streams of material went to them and to the newspapers. It was a time of high hopes: justice would come at last. Writs of all kinds were planned with zest—against the government, against various newspapers, against B. Burgoyne Chapman for his booklet *The Compleat Anti-Semite* (Melbourne 1946)—but somehow these never passed the planning stage.

One idea was for consolidated action by all New South Wales internees against the Commonwealth on the ground that the Attorney-General had not been notified of the arrests as required by the National Security Act. The planners saw it as a matter mainly of legal argument. This suited Stephensen who was not looking forward to another prolonged bout of cross-examination.

After his release Stephensen went to live as a recluse on a farm at Warburton East, fifty-five miles from Melbourne. Though privately declaring himself 'quite knocked out' of politics, this did not stop him from spurring on his colleagues in Sydney. He made one brief trip to Sydney in mid-1948 to see Hooper and others. He himself was hampered by the effort he had to make to meet the debts incurred by legal representation. Bath kept in touch, advising him what was being attempted and done in Sydney. Stephensen thought that any public moves were better left to the eight 'sheep'.

Although the attack mounted on the government during the debate on the Clyne report was well documented and carefully planned, it suffered because it was not clear exactly what the internees wanted. There was no united front. Stephensen sought a new, broader enquiry, Evatt's downfall, complete vindication of the Australia First movement and payment by the government of the legal costs of all internees. Bath appeared primarily concerned about the paucity of his compensation which he considered insufficient to make it publicly clear that he had been vindicated. Matthews, no less upset over his treatment, had no specific plans. Others by their silence showed that they merely wished to forget.

Those most insistent on 'justice' pinned their hopes on Parliament. Bath had already circularized M.P.s before the 1943 federal election with a complaint about his treatment. Now, in 1946, with Clyne's report showing that they would not be defending a bunch of out-and-out Fascists, M.P.s were more ready to listen.

On 12 March 1946, the day before the Clyne Report was due for debate, Bath, Masey and Clarence Crowley drove to Canberra to confer with Opposition speakers. Masey's sixty-eight-page study of the internments was not ready in time, but Stephensen had sent a far more tendentious twenty-two-page memorandum to his old friend Corser, the Country Party Whip.

The deputy Leader of the Opposition, E. J. Harrison, opening the debate on 13 March, said it was evident that had even the most superficial enquiry been made between the time of the arrests and the day of Forde's statement it would have been clear that the happenings in Western Australia were of no importance to Australia's security. What these Western Australians had said were 'the gabblings of three or four windbags who had not the means even to stop a tram or kill a rabbit.' Harrison wrongly referred to Bath as an ex-serviceman and to Bullock as a former communist.

Defending his actions, Forde said his statement of 26 March 1942 had been drafted by Army Intelligence officers. What would have been his position, he asked, had he refused to act on the definite recommendation (for internment) by the Chief of the General Staff, and the Japanese *had* invaded? Forde pointed to the example of the threat to Britain in 1940: overnight about 3,000 aliens were rounded up and shipped to Australia; most were later found to be 'harmless'. (This was a reference to the *Dunera* men.)

Menzies, the Opposition Leader, had not shown much public interest in the fate of the Australia First men although he had had extensive correspondence with Hooper and Bath. When he took part in the resumed debate on 14 March 1946 he contented himself with a mild 'lawyer-like' correction of Mr Justice Clyne and a plea for more adequate compensation. He concentrated his remarks on the case of Harley Matthews, whose arrest was the least defensible. He admitted that the arrests and detentions could have occurred under any political administration. In correcting the Commissioner, he pointed out that while the report stated that neither the arrest nor the detention of Matthews was justified, nevertheless it went on to include Matthews among those who should not have been detained but whose arrest was justified. This was 'pure inadvertence' on Clyne's part. Menzies added that the compensation offered did not come anywhere near enough to cover the damage done to the reputations of the exonerated men. He called for the 'closest and fullest' enquiry by a tribunal.

E. J. Ward, in truculent mood, complained that the Opposition had restricted their complaints to injustices suffered by internees; they had omitted to condemn the Australia First movement which had been undoubtedly Fascist. L. C. Haylen, the only other government speaker that day, said that perhaps a Security officer might have been a little over-zealous; however Dr Evatt and his ministerial colleagues need offer no excuse for what they had done, which had been for the greater good of the greater number.

For the Opposition, Sir Earle Page remarked that the outstanding feature of the whole affair was that a Labor government had acted on the evidence manufactured by a police agent, 'a Government pimp named Thomas'.

Archie Cameron suggested that Military Intelligence officers had security responsibilities for which they were not trained, and inevitably mistakes were made. Australia First men had not been the only British-born subjects to be interned without charge. He added that some branches of the Returned Servicemen's League in his electorate (Barker, S.A.) had asked the government to publish in the *Gazette* the names of everyone interned for the duration of the war.

The government, he said, had rightly rejected the idea as the publication of such a list could do irreparable damage to many people against whom no charge had been, or could be, laid.

Three Opposition M.P.s who, like the government members Blackburn (who died in 1944) and Calwell, had followed the internments right through from the start, were next to speak. H. L. Anthony enumerated the ten-point manifesto of the Australia First movement to show how unexceptionable it was and how easy for anyone to support. Sir Frederick Stewart, who knew Bath and Masey personally, asked for 'more appropriate justice' than had been given to those exonerated. As the Commissioner had stated, it was impossible to place a monetary value on the pain and loss of social prestige thus caused and it was the government's responsibility to determine what should be paid apart from the compensation already suggested, which only covered loss of earnings and costs incurred.

J. P. Abbott (C.P., New England) had, unlike some of his more opportunist colleagues, a word of praise for Dr Evatt who, he said, had acted promptly when he returned from overseas. Of Blood, Abbott said in Parliament on 14 March 1946 that 'none of his evidence which was given against the members of the Australia First Movement is worth a damn. He is a tainted witness'.

Fadden, the Country Party leader, the final speaker that night, moved an amendment that a commission be appointed to assess compensation to cover loss of income and status incurred by internees. To head such a commission he proposed a High Court judge and as members a government and an Opposition M.P. This amendment was defeated by forty votes to twenty on party lines the next day, following a reply from Dr Evatt who continued to maintain that the 'inner core' of the Australia First movement was 'enthusiastically pro-Japanese, pro-Hitler and Fascist'. Its members seemed, he said, to have been prepared to do everything to indicate that they regarded a Japanese invasion as a good thing. As for the exonerated men, 'no one dare point a finger' at them. Evatt quoted extracts of letters, as he had done in September 1942, to back up his 'inner core' charge. In 1942 the letters he used had been written by Miles, Kirtley, Cahill and Stephensen. Now he added one from Arnold. (Miles and Kirtley were not members of the movement; Cahill dissociated himself from it months before the arrests, and Army Intelligence knew about Arnold long before the movement was formed. Moreover, there was nothing in the Clyne Report to support the charge.)

Administration of National Security regulations, Evatt continued, had been of great anxiety to the government. On his return from overseas in 1942 he had reviewed the machinery and amended regulations to deal with defects in appeal tribunals, thus making it obligatory for them to tell the detainee the essence of the charge against him. A few M.P.s had kept these matters prominently before Parliament and 'in doing so, they did their duty'. Several newspapers had also kept the matters before the public eye but 'their motive in doing so does not matter'.

Evatt conceded that Harley Matthews rightly felt bitter about what was undeniably an injustice. When Matthews rejected recourse to an appeal tribunal because it was 'secret' he appointed a special tribunal of Security officers, and as a result Matthews was quickly freed because there was nothing against him.

This parliamentary debate was virtually the last time the internments received any sustained attention in the House of Representatives. The case had been a handy weapon for the Opposition before the September 1946 elections. By the next elections in 1949 Labor's bank nationalization plans pushed most other issues into the background.

Opposition promises to the internees were not fulfilled. Their cases were not brought up in the 1946 Budget debate and did not become an important issue at the 1946 elections. Perhaps Liberal and Country Party M.P.s could see little electoral advantage to be gained.

Labor was victorious in 1946, winning forty-three seats to the thirty-one held by the Opposition and independent M.P.s. A vigorous Liberal–Country Party campaign promising to lower taxes and deal with the housing shortage and industrial strikes failed to weaken public support for Labor under J. B. Chifley. If in a few electorates Australia First was at times mentioned, it was clearly a non-starter as a national issue. Had the Liberals won the election they would have been faced with a demand from Bath to honour a promise they had given him in writing, though in terms more than a little ambiguous—on 2 September 1946 the chief executive officer of the New South Wales Liberal Party, F. R. Burton, had written to him: 'If the Liberal Party should be returned to power I think the interest Mr. Menzies has so far shown in seeing that justice is done in respect to yourself and your colleagues is some assurance that justice will be done.'

When the Liberals came to power with a big majority in 1949 this half-promise may have been regarded as a little out of date. At any rate nothing was done to reopen the case. The internees' political friends were indeed fair-weather friends. Stephensen was not greatly surprised, as he had never expected much of Menzies. Parliament did again return to the subject but only fleetingly and incidentally. When the Australian Security Intelligence Organization set up by Chifley in 1949 was being discussed by the House in 1955 and 1956, several members thought the events of 1942 had some application. Ward noted that the Deputy Chief of the organization was Detective-Sergeant Richards, largely on whose advice the Australia First internments were made.

Keith Bath had long been thinking of litigation against the Commonwealth. He had decided to delay any legal challenge until after the 1946 elections, hoping that if Menzies was voted into power he would obtain justice. When Chifley was returned, Bath sought £25,000 for unlawful arrest and wrongful imprisonment in a High Court writ, attaching the Commonwealth and Lieutenant-Colonel Powell. Bath had been set down for £500 compensation in the Clyne recommendations, but he was offered this sum only if he signed a quittance absolving the government from further claims. He held his ground, refused to sign and then received his £500 unconditionally. At one stage Evatt sent H. G. Alderman K.C. to see if Bath would accept £1,000 to end the matter. Alderman thought this a generous offer. Bath refused as he had made up his mind to test his case in the High Court. His £25,000 claim, based on an opinion from Garfield Barwick K.C., was lodged on 7 May 1947. The Commonwealth entered two defences, initially claiming that the arrest had been lawful, and later amending this by pleading the Statute of Limitations which required such claims to be brought within four years. Thus as Bath was arrested on 10 March 1942 his action could be barred after 10 March 1946. Bath had foreseen this possibility. He withdrew his writ on 5 April 1948. Angered over the government's use of the statute, he shortly afterwards issued an eight-page pamphlet entitled *Injustice within the Law* in which he claimed that Evatt had purposely delayed the parliamentary debate on the Clyne Report until the four-year term had expired.

Both sides of Parliament found Bath difficult to silence. Firmly convinced that a technical point had denied him compensation for the injury to his reputation and prospects, he battled on for years. M.P.s must have come to dread his approach. His optimism lasted long after most other people would have given up—he saw his cause as one of flagrant injustice that must surely be righted and he even came to enjoy his status as a grievously wronged citizen. Many another man would have rationalized his misfortune with the thought that the world is full of injustice,[1] and the best one can hope for is to be free again and able to work on restoring one's position. As Shand K.C. remarked during the Clyne Inquiry: 'We all suffer injustices more or less in wartime.'

When the Liberals dashed Bath's hopes he turned on Menzies in a one-page circular to federal Liberal and Country Party M.P.s in May 1952 asking them: 'What is the value of Mr. Menzies' word?' He had renewed his High Court damages claim after the change of government in 1949, and this brought an offer from the Prime Minister to negotiate.

I made my submissions [he explained in his circular] which went forward for consideration without the benefit of negotiation. Back has come the answer. Not a penny am I offered for the injury to my reputation. I am requested to discontinue my claim and take a small ex-gratia sum of money for something totally different. If I do not accept within 14 days the Commonwealth will plead the Statute of Limitations to keep me out of court. This is a complete somersault. Mr. Menzies, seemingly, concurs even after careful consideration. If this is so, what then is the value of his word?

A week earlier Bath had sent a seven-page document, dated 19 May 1952, to Fadden, Earle Page, Harrison and Anthony suggesting that they form themselves into an 'unofficial select committee' to advise cabinet, to 'see that justice is done'.

Bath's siege of Parliament was not lifted until 1954, when to end the whole affair one high-pressure day of insistence at Canberra, lobbying the Prime Minister and the Solicitor-General, brought him £2,500 in final settlement.

Neither Bath nor the Solicitor-General, K. H. Bailey, was to refer publicly to the terms of settlement. Thus it was that in 1965 Calwell could still call for justice to Bath, quite unaware that Bath had eleven years before signed all his claims away. He received, through persistence, far greater compensation than any other internee. As it was kept secret the added sum did nothing to help in the public vindication of his name.

Bath's case was not typical. It was by his own efforts that he came to occupy the centre of the stage. Many of the other ex-internees asked for nothing more than to be left alone.* If they had complaints —and some undoubtedly harboured grievances against either the government, Army Intelligence or internment camp guards—they

---

* One man, not mentioned in this book, who has claimed he was interned because of his activities in the Australia First movement, appeared in public early in 1968 as 'chief adviser of the Nazi Party in Queensland'. An interview with him was published in the *Sunday Truth*, 3 March 1968. He has written to me saying that he was interned with T. P. Graham at Tatura.

voiced them privately. The stuffing had been knocked out of them. Even the hitherto irrepressible Bullock was quelled, and today limits his public advocacies to the reform of the Adelaide flower market and the virtues of polyunsaturated fats and oils. His feeling is that he deserved what he got for being carried away by his enthusiasms and falling for 'Hardt''s talk.

Rud Mills was not willing to let the matter rest. Like Bath, but with less effect, he maintained a continual correspondence with Canberra, refusing to accept advice given him in 1944 by Brigadier Simpson that he was not legally entitled to compensation. For a time Stephensen believed Mills was preparing a book about the internments. This was in 1946. In 1961 Mills was still talking about a book; he died in 1964 without one having been published. It is almost certain it did not get beyond the wishful stage. His chaotic ideas changed little in his final years. He remained obsessively anti-Jewish, anti-Christian and anti-black.

Masey worked away for a while on a documentation (which has proved invaluable for the present study) but only referred publicly to his experience in a symposium on 'Liberty in Australia'. There he recorded with admirable restraint that some of the military officers who made recommendations for internment to the Minister for the Army 'were not well equipped to judge a suspect's eligibility for detention'. In October 1945 Masey had canvassed the case briefly in *Smith's Weekly*, claiming that press censorship had kept the truth from the public.

Hooper busied himself in 1945-6 with an extensive correspondence with Knowles over the implementation of the Clyne Report. Hooper pointed out, fairly, that Clyne had stated that those found to be wrongly detained were entitled to a public declaration to that effect, and such a declaration 'should afford them some measure of redress'. Despite this, Forde had made his declaration a few moments before a four-month parliamentary recess. As a result it failed to achieve significant publicity and the public was virtually unaware the declaration had been made. Forde should have withdrawn the unjustified allegations made in his speech of 26 March 1942. Not only had he failed to do this but he had aggravated the wrong done by further misstatements at the time of the release of the Commissioner's report. One of these was that some members of the Australia First movement were 'found guilty of conspiracy against their own country' whereas in fact no member of the movement was even charged, let alone convicted.

Hooper joined Bath in publishing a consolidated reprint of the three 1942 issues of the *Publicist*, to provide a 'durable historical record' to help prove that the *Publicist* represented a 'completely loyal and patriotic Australian activity'. These were the three issues produced by Stephensen, Hooper and Crowley when they took over as co-owners after Miles's death. Articles by Mrs Watts and Miss Phoebe Walton were omitted from the reprint 'solely for reasons of economy'. (Women contributors had not been interned.)

Publication of this booklet and its public sale for 2s sent the Sydney communists into a flurry until the limited purpose of the venture was realized. Here, it appeared to them, was the hated *Publicist* back again in business. Had not the internees learned their lesson? A Mosman Communist Party branch circular of September 1946 called for the booklet to be taken off local bookstalls. Communists had always paid close heed to Australia First activities and should have been in a position to know the facts, but among those after the war to misrepresent what had happened in 1942 was Frank Hardy,[2] who wrote that the *Publicist* had been banned and Stephensen interned after having published in it a frankly pro-Japanese article.

At first Stephensen had not been keen on the idea of a *Publicist* reprint. He was pinning his hopes on the anticipated book by Mills. He also thought Masey was bringing out a pamphlet and envisaged its use by candidates opposing Evatt and Forde in 1946. However, neither project came to anything, nor did the big newspaper campaign he expected in Western Australia urging a new trial for Bullock and Williams. For a while everything Stephensen touched seemed to fall apart. He had been toying with the idea of asking Kenneth Slessor or, failing him, Ross Gollan of the *Sydney Morning Herald,* to edit a sixty-four-page brochure reprinting the main documents in the case plus a brief commentary. Slessor was thought to be likely to undertake this work for £100. Something went astray and Slessor was not even approached.

Harley Matthews had one grand slam with a whole front page of *Smith's Weekly* in September 1945 to tell his story. *Smith's* editor added the comment that soon after Matthews had been detained he (the editor) went to Military Intelligence and told them he would stake his life on Matthews's loyalty. He was told: 'We've got it on him.' About the same time two M.P.s, Sir Frederick Stewart and W. V. McCall, visited Victoria Barracks to obtain details about Masey's internment, to be told that the army had a document incriminating him in treasonable acts. A little later Masey's solicitor was told by the army that they had evidence enough to hang Masey and all the New South Welshmen.

With Australia First dead and buried, eager cultural nationalists with the proselytizing urge still had the Jindyworobak movement as a possible outlet for their energies. Ian Mudie, who had been in both camps, felt he should stay out of Jindyworobak for a time at least. In 1944 he wrote to Rex Ingamells:

Best if you leave me out of the Jindy pamphlet. I'm really a late-comer into the movement and I find that most people look on me as being more or less merely associated. They look on me as AF. Therefore my name, too prominently associated, would probably cause a suspicion that Jindy is a political dingo in a literary kangaroo's clothing.[3]

Though he escaped detention Mudie felt fully involved. His poem of 1943, 'If this be treason', was a pointed and unapologetic reference to the internments.[4]

Mudie's friendship with Stephensen continued until the latter's death in 1965. He once asked Stephensen, after the war, about the prospects for a revival of Australia First. The reply he received was roughly in these terms: 'What's the use? Everything we were after has been achieved. It would look like getting on someone else's bandwagon.' In 1946 Stephensen wrote to Hooper: 'In many directions I see the fruits of my sowing reaped by others. National consciousness was stimulated greatly by my efforts. Now let others stimulate it, for I am silenced.'

After the war, particularly in the first few vibrant years, there was in Australia an intense surge of interest in things Australian. The imperial nexus had clearly suffered a body-blow: it is now almost completely shattered. Australia acquired a new confidence unself-consciously, as more people began to write, paint, compose, build and discuss in their own unforced native idiom. The Statute of Westminster had been ratified; especially under Dr Evatt as Minister for External Affairs, the country grew to have its own distinctive foreign policy, and hallowed imperial terms such as 'Far East' became replaced by the more realistic 'Near North'. There was a new atmosphere of self-sufficiency but one that lacked any elements of wrongheaded isolationism. All this should have been welcomed by the old Australia Firsters but if they were pleased by the more self-reliant post-war community they successfully kept their joy to themselves. They were in no mood to respond.

Kirtley, in particular, lost none of his bitterness. After the war he returned for a time to Ettalong Beach, Woy Woy, where he had lived for eleven years before his internment. But he did not know what to do with himself until the Melbourne literary enthusiast J. K. Moir 'collected' him and staked him to a hand press at Ferntree Gully, where he became the Mountainside Press, producing luxury limited editions. Those years behind the wire, he told me, 'destroyed in me something that was really good, my love of my native land, and for that I am very sorry I cannot forgive.' He believed it wisest to avoid taking part in community affairs. One should give the state nothing but should not oppose it, as 'martyrdom is a comic state of tragedy.'

Of the women connected with Australia First, only Dora Watts kept up any public activity after the war; she recently published a racist booklet, *The Dangerous Myth of Racial Equality*, which was distributed by the radical right-wing League of Rights. Mrs Walsh, who died in 1961, did nothing controversial after release from internment in October 1942, except that in December 1960, at the age of seventy-two, she was received into the Roman Catholic Church. Looking back in 1951 on her busy life, she told a journalist from *People,* which at that time set its sights on a literate public, that 'the only wholly successful thing in my life was my marriage.'[5]

During the eleven years after his release spent in Victorian country towns, Stephensen kept well clear of politics. At Warburton he set his hands to growing potatoes but this did not pay the bills. His mainstay was literary work, still principally for Frank Clune. After several years he moved to Bethanga, in north-eastern Victoria, where, among other old friends, was Miles Franklin. Another visitor was Manning Clark, the historian, who has seen him as 'a very angry man, driven by a Dionysian-like frenzy and yet a member of a great tradition.'[6] At Bethanga Stephensen became involved in local civic affairs. Then, having finished his share of a joint biography (with Clune) of Jorgen Jorgenson, he made his first tentative step back to the sort of world in which he once occupied so undeniable a place as publisher, editor and promoter. He published a lengthy, argumentative (the old arguments over again) review of novels by Tom Hungerford and Helen Fowler in the *Austrovert*.[7]

This, in 1952, was his first signed contribution to any publication since his internment a decade earlier. Soon afterwards he went to live in Melbourne, where in 1954 the Sydney printer and bibliophile Walter Stone, a Labor nationalist, and until then a stranger, persuaded him to set down his recollections of the Fanfrolico Press days. Stone's own press published this first and only Stephensen autobiography, *Kookaburras and Satyrs*. The book stirred up some controversy, aired in Stone's periodical *Biblionews,* about his days in England. Jack Lindsay asserted that Stephensen had developed anti-Semitism to justify himself after losing a considerable sum of Edward Goldston's money in the Mandrake Press. Stephensen, he added, had been an ardent admirer of Trotsky. Denying both charges, Stephensen said that he had had at the time, and retained, a warm regard for Goldston and supposed it was reciprocated.

By 1956 Stephensen was ready to return to Sydney and Stone threw a welcome-back party. Stephensen was still supporting himself by helping Clune and doing other 'ghost' and editorial work. By 1959 he was sufficiently rehabilitated to be asked to go on a Commonwealth Literary Fund lecture tour of South Australia where he was accompanied by his old friend Ian Mudie. (These lectures were published as *Nationalism in Australian Literature*.) He also gave C.L.F. lectures in Queensland in 1961. His theme in these lectures was in the *Publicist*'s (literary) tradition of 'anything England can do, Australia can do better'. As Geoffrey Dutton, no more an Anglophile than Stephensen, pointed out, this might have caused a stir in 1937 but not any more.

Stephensen gradually settled into Sydney literary society and did so without modifying any of his opinions. At parties at friends' houses he showed himself as willing as ever to bait Jews or gibe at English accents. Yet the man retained to the last a compelling personal charm and rarely gave lasting offence.

In his last years Stephensen produced a flotilla of books, several of them in collaboration with retired sea captains. Apart from the Jorgenson biography, published as *The Viking of Van Diemen's Land* (1954), he produced *The Cape Horn Breed* (1956), *Sail Ho!* (1961), *Commodore* (1961), *Sydney Sails* (1962) and *The Pirates of the Brig Cyprus* (1962). His lengthy *Sydney Harbour* was published posthumously in 1966.

In 1960 he was employed for four months by the major Sydney publishing firm of Angus and Robertson Ltd. He had been appointed to the firm's editorial department by the managing director, Walter Burns, without the consent of the publishing director, G. A. Ferguson. This was a time of bitter controversy about the direction the firm should be taking, and the result was internal disorganization and serious disruption of publishing. A. W. Sheppard, a Sydney bookseller, commented[8] that Angus and Robertson that year probably produced fewer important books than in any previous year of their seventy-two years' history.

Stephensen, installed as Manuscript Procurement Officer by Burns, was given the task of finding novels suitable for paperback publication in large quantities. None of this fiction was published. Stephensen left Angus and Robertson in November, shortly before his sponsor, Burns, was defeated at the company's annual general meeting in December. There was no ill feeling between Stephensen and Angus and Robertson. Following this brief episode the firm dealt with him in his private capacity as an editor and agent.

In 1959 Donald Horne's lively Sydney fortnightly magazine, the *Observer*, published Stephenson's account of his interment. It was headed: 'How Dr. Evatt put me in gaol'. It contained no surprise revelations. Stephensen explained that he was awaiting the official verdict, to be delivered by the war historian Paul Hasluck, whose first volume of the civil section of the official war record appeared in 1952. This carried the story up to 1941, including the Ratliff and Thomas incident but not Australia First. Stephensen was looking to volume 2, 'The Government and the People, 1942-45', to clear him. But this volume has not yet appeared although the research into and writing of the section referring to Australia First was completed before Stephensen's death in 1965. Hasluck was not willing to make available in advance his Australia First 'verdict', that is if he has in fact formed a judgment on the episode. Stephensen threatened to sue Hasluck if the account libelled him.

In his *Observer* article Stephensen failed to explain exactly how Evatt was culpable. He made some valid criticisms of Evatt's conduct after his return from overseas in 1942, but pushed his theories too far. He gave himself rather too much importance in claiming that Evatt fled to the United States on the day of the Sydney arrests 'just to cover his tracks'.

Brian Fitzpatrick, in a reply in the following issue of the *Observer*, suggested that Stephensen, after his miserable experience of internment, had got everything out of perspective. Fitzpatrick defended the Australian Council for Civil Liberties, which Stephensen had not attacked, from the charge that it had failed to intervene on behalf of Australia First. Fitzpatrick, the Council's general secretary, said that there had been no specific request for help. 'We had to be careful not to acquire a reputation as busybodies', he explained. He offered no rousing defence of Dr Evatt, but commented that 'in so far as the article is an attack on Dr. Evatt, and in so far as I was in Dr. Evatt's confidence in the war years when Mr. Stephensen was interned, I am not in a position to reply.'

Stephensen kept the argument alive for a further issue by asking Fitzpatrick: 'Do the watchdogs of liberty bark only on request?' This was a fair enough comment but Stephensen went on to spoil it: 'How could a prisoner, held by machine guns and bayonets behind barb-wire [sic] in one of Evatt's Australian concentration camps ask an outside organization to act on his behalf?' In fact the internees managed to do quite a lot while still in camp through their limited postal rights and weekly visit of friends and relations. Fitzpatrick was clearly unsympathetic to the cause of the internees, as his *Smith's Weekly* article of 13 June 1942 proves, but he did not, in the style of the *Tribune*, openly rejoice in the repressive action taken against them.

Stephensen, Evatt and Fitzpatrick all died in 1965, within seven months of each other, with the question of Dr. Evatt's involvement still unresolved.[9]

Stephensen died, penniless, in dramatic circumstances, collapsing after having resumed his seat following one of his most flamboyant and brilliant literary addresses—dealing with *Lady Chatterley's Lover*—given in Sydney. According to Walter Stone, who delivered the panegyric at his funeral several days later, the representative of the Rhodes Scholars' Fellowship left the Northern Suburbs Crematorium when he discovered it was to be an agnostic and not a Christian service.

Looking back over the whole episode, from the founding of the *Publicist* in 1936 to the death almost thirty years later of the main spokesman for this raucously chauvinistic movement, several things are quite plain. Australia First's advocacy was legitimate but it was misdirected by Miles. There was no need for it to be concerned with defending the Axis powers. Even with this, the movement was an irritant, a talking-shop and little more. C. E. W. Bean, the historian of World War I, wrote: 'I cannot imagine the Australia First Movement . . . ever constituted any great threat to our safety'.

During his researches into fringe groups in British politics George Thayer, an American political scientist, noted that 'the people who take part in fringe group activities may be eccentric, narrow-minded, intolerant, and even mentally unstable, but none that I ever met would qualify as people dangerous to public safety.'[10] Australia First was definitely a fringe group; it publicly admitted its minority status. However, it went off the rails when, as so often happens, its ethnocentrism took in anti-Semitism and other authoritarian attitudes, but it hardly deserved the severe treatment handed out by Military Intelligence.

There was, it is fairly plain, no deliberate government plot involved in obtaining the internments, only a series of ill-advised decisions by little men who momentarily possessed great power. Another series of accidents served to delay the release of those clearly entitled to regain their freedom.

The greatest damage caused was to the civil liberties of the sixteen men from New South Wales and Victoria and the three men and one woman from Western Australia. The cause of Australian self-reliance remained unharmed. While the personal tragedy of the internees was being played out, everything was conspiring to bring about just the sort of national fervour which they had aimed to promote. Their cause was one which hardly needed public meetings and polemical pamphlets. If Australians in general had so loose a grip on their nationality that it required frequent and angry affirmation—to adapt Shils's phrase on hyperpatriotism[11]—their cause was indeed lost. The Sydney composer Malcolm Williamson has seen this clearly. On his return to Australia late in 1967 after fifteen years abroad, he commented: 'We must be terribly proud to be Australian; but we must also, I think, shut up about it. We are recognizably Australian when we say nothing.'[12]

The sinking of the *Repulse* and the *Prince of Wales* by Japanese aircraft off Malaya on 10 December 1941, and the fall of Singapore on 15 February 1942, promoted the cause of Australian national self-dependence more than all the propaganda of the *Publicist* and all the meetings of the Australia First movement combined. These two war-time defeats were clear proof that Australia could no longer depend on Britain to guarantee self-survival. The Empire looked shaky then; it has gone altogether now and without much doubt the scapegoat of any present-day Australian nationalist movement would be no longer Britain but the country's new protector, the United States of America.

The Australia First affair touched many departments of our national life. Many of the main issues remain unresolved, perhaps never to be resolved in terms of neat formulae. Just how far can the individual be left free in war-time? Even if he does nothing overt to aid an enemy, may he safely confide seeming sympathies with the enemy in private correspondence or personal diaries? How far should democracies adopt authoritarian community rules in time of emergency? When a community is thought by the rulers to be 'in danger' (and there can be no doubt that Australia in March 1942 was in very real and present danger), is panic action destroying civil liberties excusable? Should the community later repent at leisure and recompense those who were innocent sufferers? I leave the answers to others, for I have attempted to follow Dr Elton's precept which regards it as an error to 'study the past for the light it throws on the present'.[13]

If I am forced to sum up a complicated situation in the search for a central message it would be that we have seen how a small group of politically active people with few friends in government could be removed from sight and hearing as a result of what, quickly enough, was seen to be a foolish mistake. It certainly cannot be ignored that 1942 was a time of definite danger for Australia. There was no precedent for the handling of dissident opinion on such an occasion for there had never been such a threat before. Drastic measures may well have been justified.

Further, the aftermath of the internments revealed yet again (as had the I.W.W. gaolings in 1916[14]) the enormous reluctance of the machinery of government to admit it may have been at fault in allowing such an unambiguous assault on personal liberty. Should civil libertarians in this country need any more cautionary tales, then this is one.

Notes

1 NATIONALISM

1 Joseph Furphy, *Such is Life* (Sydney, 1944): 'This recordless land . . . is committed to no usages of petrified injustice; she is clogged by no fealty to shadowy idols, enshrined by Ignorance and upheld by misplaced homage alone; she is cursed by no memories of fanaticism and persecution; she is innocent of hereditary national jealousy, and free from the envy of sister states.' (p. 81)

2 T. G. H. Strehlow, *An Australian Viewpoint*, p. 35.

3 Brian Fitzpatrick, *The Australian People* (Melbourne, 1951), p. 28.

2 MILES

1 *Publicist*, August 1936, p. 13.

2 Miles undertook all the risks of publishing this novel which Xavier Herbert, after years of disappointment, was beginning to doubt would ever get published. Miles entered it for the 1938 Commonwealth Sesqui-centenary literary prize, which it won. Later editions were taken over by Angus and Robertson who used the Stafford Printery type that Miles had kept from his original edition of 2,000 copies.

3 Beatrice Miles is at present living at the Little Sisters of the Poor Convent in Randwick.

3 STEPHENSEN

1 The *Bulletin*, 16 June 1962, reported that Stephenson referred in a lecture to a University of Queensland audience to his 'thirty years' war', starting in 1932, for the defence of Australian literature against attempts to undermine it.

2 House of Commons, *Parliamentary Debates*, 1925, vol. 189, p. 1621.

3 *Isis*, 16 May 1964, p. 8.

4 Hal Porter, 'Melbourne in the Thirties', *London Magazine*, September 1965, p. 31.

5 John Kirtley, 'My friend Baylebridge', *Southerly*, no. 3, 1955, p. 135.

4 THE PUBLICIST

1 One biographer of Baume, Arthur Manning, in *Larger Than Life* (Sydney, 1967), notes how out of step Baume was with his contemporaries on Nazism.

2 Bedford had some ideas that must have pleased Miles. In his autobiography *Nought to Thirty-Three*, published posthumously in 1944, he commented (p. 292): 'All the wild imperialists and title-hunters committed us to the Boer

War; and Australia equipped armies for a dispute that wasn't Australia's business. The precedent dragged us into the World War also, and we must be careful that we break the habit before another foreign war begins.'
3 See accounts of the incident in Edgar Snow, *Scorched Earth* (London, 1941) and Agnes Smedley, *Battle Hymn of China* (London, 1944).
4 Neil Clerehan, *Hemisphere*, vol. 9, no. 1, 1965, p. 13.
5 There was another outburst in the same vein in the *Publicist*, January 1941: 'Australia's greatest political need is for a non-elected leading class or caste, self-appointed—an order of indigenous knightage or samurai—self-dedicated to the idea of the preservation and strengthening of Australia. When such an order arises in Australia, fanatical, maybe, in its origins, it will be the true Australia First Party'.
6 *Publicist*, March 1938, p. 7.

5 WAR-TIME

1 Ralph Gibson, *My Years in the Communist Party*, p. 80.
2 *Parl. Deb.* (L.A. N.S.W.), 25 February 1942, p. 2696.
3 *Sydney Morning Herald*, 17 February 1942, p.7.
4 Clyne Inquiry evidence, p. 1943.
5 This episode and the *Publicist*'s attitude to it has been fully detailed by the scheme's sponsor, Dr I. N. Steinberg in *Australia—The Unpromised Land?* (London, 1948).

6 MOVEMENT

1 The Japanese subsidized a number of U.S. magazines in the immediate pre-war years; see J. L. Morrison, 'Editor for Sale', *Journalism Quarterly*, Summer 1966, p. 34–42. A former radical, Joseph Hilton Smyth, received $5000 a month for his publication *The Living Age*. In April 1940 he wrote a piece on Japan's 2600th 'birthday' (commemorating the founding of the Japanese Empire in 660 B.C. by the Emperor Jimmu). In the *Publicist*, February 1940, Stephensen wrote on Japan's 2600th anniversary. There is no evidence that Stephensen took money from the Japanese.
2 Ian Mudie on ABC radio on 20 November 1966: 'The real nationalist is the man who is most dissatisfied with his country.'
3 *Sydney Morning Herald*, 20 November 1941, p. 14.
4 Sir Thomas Gordon, knighted in 1938, had extensive shipping interests. He represented the British Ministry of Transport in Australia, 1939–46, and was Australia's Director of Shipping, 1942–5. There is a strong presumption that he had been a member of the New Guard. He died in 1949.

7 MELBOURNE

1 In addition, according to Valentine Crowley, Cyril Brown, an Adelaide Jindyworobak poet whose booklet *Writing for Australia* was published in 1956, sent £50 to help the final issues of the *Publicist*.

8 PERTH

1 Richards was an important witness in the Petrov Royal Commission of 1954–5. He was then Deputy-Director of the Australian Security Intelligence Organisation.

9 ROUND-UP

1 Brian Fitzpatrick has noted, in *The Australian Commonwealth*, p. 134, that, up to 1956, none of the Commonwealth police forces was set up by statute after debate in Parliament.

2 Lady Street tells of her experiences on this committee in her autobiography, *Truth or Repose* (Sydney, 1966), pp. 261–3.

3 In a letter to me Smith conjectures: 'I can only guess that even the security authorities were not that stupid and knew that I had fairly powerful friends who, whatever they thought of AF, would know I was not disloyal and would move on my behalf.'

4 A Japanese officer, Major Haishida, had spent a week in Adelaide in October 1941—under continual military observation. See the *News*, 5 September, 11 September, 5 October 1945 for details of Nazi, Fascist and Japanese interest in South Australia.

5 H. Homburg, *South Australian Lutherans and Wartime Rumours*, p. 36. Homburg was a member of the S.A. House of Assembly in 1906–15 and 1927–30. Subject to a war-time attack because of his German origins—though he was himself born in Adelaide—he resigned his office as Attorney-General in 1915. Homburg interested himself in the Australia First case in correspondence with Bath.

6 *Canberra Times*, 27 March 1942, p. 1.

10 INTERNMENT

1 However Ernest Scott discussed internment camps during World War I in *Australia During the War*, pp. 114–37. He pointed out (p. 66) that censorship during the war forbade any mention of the camps. For World War II a brief account of the camp at Loveday, *Internment in South Australia*, was published in 1946, but it made no mention of the Australia First internees.

2 Could some of these baseless charges have been encouraged by a statement of the Postmaster-General, H. V. C. Thorby, in May 1940 that Australians should not hesitate to tell tales on their neighbours and should report their suspicions?

3 See Court of Appeal decision in *R. v. Secretary for Home Affairs, ex p. Budd,* 58 T.L.R. 212. Also relevant is the earlier House of Lords decision in *Liversidge* v. *Anderson, 58 T.L.R. 35.*

4 Ironically, there was one notable occasion when the restriction on former internees associating with one another was publicly flouted. Menzies and Evatt both delivered papers at the January 1944 Summer School of the Australian Institute of Political Science. As a director of the Institute Masey was present; so were Hooper and Valentine Crowley who had every right to attend. On the Sunday afternoon of the school Masey, in company with Curtin, Evatt, Menzies and others, was guest at a cocktail party at Government House, given by the Governor-General, Lord Gowrie.

11 PARLIAMENT

1 Stephensen wrote to Evatt in 1941, probably soon after the latter was installed as External Affairs Minister, offering his services as a 'special propagandist'. This offer was either ignored or swiftly rejected.

2 Letter in *Nation*, 9 March 1963, p. 17.

3 *Australian*, 6 November 1965.

4 J. J. Dedman, 'Encounter over Manus', *Australian Outlook*, August 1966, pp. 135–53.

5 In a letter to me, 27 April 1966.

6 Ellis's account here of Australia First seems more concerned with scoring points off Brian Fitzpatrick, secretary of the Australian Council for Civil Liberties, and sneering at Dr Evatt than soberly recording the facts.

12 INQUIRY

1 Dovey submitted that 'there can be little doubt that some of these members of the Australia First Movement were avowed defeatists, avowed anti-English, anti-United States of America, anti-Semitists, pro-Fascists, pro-

Nazi and pro-Japanese; and all of those at a time when this country was at war with Germany and Japan'. The information presented by Dovey and Coyle included the opinion of Military Intelligence that the Australia First movement 'appeared to be on the lines of Lindbergh's America First Movement'. Although there were some similarities between these two isolationist bodies, such a comparison tends to obscure the fact that the U.S. organization tapped such a substantial strain of that country's thinking that it had a powerful influence on Roosevelt's war-time policies before Pearl Harbor. Australia First had no effect on Australian policies.

13   JUDGMENT

1 Letter to *Nation*, 9 March 1963.
2 In some 'observations' recorded in 1952, Mills noted: 'I did see Hitler in 1933 . . . he was a striking person. He appeared to me to be able, kindly and devoted to his country. But that does not make me disloyal.'
3 *Nation*, 9 February 1963, p. 17.

14   FINALE

1 H. J. Laski in *Liberty in the Modern State* (London, 1937), had commented: 'In wartime, any plea for reasonableness is at a discount.' (p. 173)
2 *Guardian*, 31 July 1952.
3 Mudie to Ingamells, 5 April 1944, Rex Ingamells Letters.
4 This poem begins:
> 'So this is treason, that a love of land
> strengthen and circle in our hearts
> through every hour of every day?
> So this is treason, that our minds
> should stir to none but native breeze'.
5 *People*, 9 May 1951.
6 *Comment*, January 1967, a review of Craig McGregor's *Portrait of Australia*.
7 *Austrovert*, no. 7, 1952.   8 *Nation*, 3 December 1960, p. 21.
9 Yet Alan Dalziel in his aptly titled *Evatt the Enigma* (Melbourne, 1967) believes that Dr. Evatt was unhappy about the whole affair. He conjectures that the internments would not have happened if Evatt had been in Australia at the time (pp. 24, 27). Dalziel says that Clyne told Evatt shortly before his death in 1967 that he had acted in a way that reflected great credit on him.
10 G. Thayer, *The British Political Fringe*, p. 238.
11 E. A. Shils, *Torment of Secrecy*, p. 81.
12 Malcolm Williamson, ABC 'Guest of Honour' broadcast, 24 September 1967. In his radio address Williamson makes this further interesting comment which is rather closer to Stephensen's position: 'I think the true enemies of Australia are not the Communists, or people with coloured skins, but rather the over-refined, crypto-English Australians who want to blunt the really sharp edges of the Australian character'.
13 G. R. Elton, *The Practice of History* (Sydney, 1967), p. 48.
14 See Ian Turner, *Sydney's Burning* (Melbourne, 1967).

Bibliography

I OFFICIAL SOURCES

Inquiry into matters relating to the detention of certain members of the 'Australian First Movement' group. Report of Commissioner [Mr Justice Clyne]. Canberra, 1946.

Irish Republican Brotherhood Internees. Report on Cases by Mr. Justice Harvey. Melbourne, 1918.

Commonwealth: *Parliamentary Debates*, vol. 82, 8 August 1917; vol. 161, 8 September 1939; vol. 163, 17 April 1940; vol. 165, 12 December 1940; vol. 168, 24 September 1941; vol. 169, 25 November 1941; vol. 170, 6 March 1942; vol. 171, 20 May 1942; vol. 172, 2 September 1942; vol. 173, 28 January 1943; vol. 174, 5 March 1944; vol. 178, 31 March 1944; vol. 179, 18 July 1944; vol. 180, 24 November 1944; vol. 181, 27 February 1945; vol. 184, 24 July 1945; vol. 185, 5 October 1945; vol. 186, 13 March 1946; vol. 196, 7 April 1948; vol. 207, 11 May 1950. *New Series,* vol. 7, 13 September 1955; vol. 8, 19 October 1955; vol. 13, 24 October 1956.

New South Wales: *Parliamentary Debates*, 1942, vol. 167, pp. 2694, 2696.

Western Australia: *Votes and Proceedings of the Legislative Council*, 1942, vol. 3, pp. 2780, 3035.

Law Reports

Ex parte Stephensen [1942] 59 N.S.W.W.N. 118.
Ex parte Walsh [1942] A.L.R. 359; 59 N.S.W.W.N. 115.
Lloyd v. *Wallach* (1915) 20 C.L.R. 299.
Little v. *Commonwealth* (1947) 75 C L.R. 94.
R. v. *Clift, ex parte P*– [1941] S.A.S.R. 41.

187

II UNPUBLISHED SOURCES

Australian Labor Party, Federal Parliamentary Minutes (held by federal parliamentary A.L.P.).

Bath, Keith, Papers (in possession of author).

Herbert, Xavier, Letters (National Library of Australia, Canberra).

Ingamells, Rex, Letters (La Trobe Library, Melbourne).

Mackaness, George, Letters (National Library of Australia, Canberra).

Masey, Edward, Australia-First Internments/Compensation, duplicated, 12 June 1946; notes on debate in the House of Representatives 13–15 March 1946 (in possession of author).

——, Notes on the Australia-First Internments, 16 February 1946 (typescript in possession of author).

—— and Bath, Keith, An analysis of Mr Justice Clyne's report, based on the evidence; typed and handwritten annotation to the Clyne report, undated, probably 1946 (in possession of author).

Miles, W. J., Letters (in possession of W. W. Stone, Sydney).

Miller, Morris E., Letters (National Library of Australia, Canberra).

Mills, A. R., Papers (in possession of Mrs E. L. Mills, Upwey, Victoria).

Molesworth, V., Papers (Mitchell Library, Sydney).

Souter, Gavin, biography of Beatrice Miles (in possession of Gavin Souter, Sydney).

Stephensen, P. R., Letters (in possession of W. W. Stone, Sydney).

——, The Political Aspects of the 'Australia-First' Internments, some notes, compiled 27 February 1946, pencilled revision October 1951 (typescript in possession of author).

Waite, George, Papers (Mitchell Library, Sydney).

III NEWSPAPERS

Advertiser (Adelaide)
Advocate (Melbourne)
Argus (Melbourne)
Australian (Canberra)
Canberra Times
Century (Sydney)
Daily Mirror (Sydney)
Daily News (Sydney)
Daily Standard (Brisbane)
Daily Telegraph (Sydney)
Farrago (Melbourne)
Forward (Sydney)
Guardian (Melbourne)

Murrumbidgee Irrigator (Leeton)
News (Adelaide)
Progress (Sydney)
Smith's Weekly (Sydney)
Sun (Sydney)
Sunday Telegraph (Sydney)
Sunday Worker (London)
Sydney Morning Herald
The Times
Tribune (Sydney)
West Australian (Perth)
Who's for Australia (Sydney)
Workers' Weekly (Sydney)

IV PERIODICALS

Angle (Melbourne)
Austral-Asiatic Bulletin
  (Melbourne)
Australian Law Journal (Sydney)
Australian Quarterly (Sydney)
Australian Rhodes Review
  (Melbourne)
Austrovert (Melbourne)
Biblionews (Sydney)
Book News (Sydney)
Bulletin (Sydney) 'Political
  Points', 8 April 1942; 'Plain
  English', 15 April 1942;
  leading articles on 1 April,
  20 May, 1 July, 2 Septem-
  ber 1942; 27 September, 8
  November 1944; 10, 31 Oc-
  tober 1945.
A Comment (Melbourne)
Comment (Sydney)
Communist Review (London)
Design (Melbourne)

Empire Gazette (Sydney)
Galmahra (Brisbane)
Independent Sydney Secularist
Liberator (Sydney)
Literary Guide (London)
London Aphrodite
Meanjin Papers (Brisbane)
Nation (Sydney)
National Socialist (Sydney)
Observer (Sydney)
People (Sydney)
Political Quarterly (London)
Publicist (Sydney)
Right (San Francisco)
Ross's Monthly (Sydney)
Salt (Melbourne)
Socialist (Melbourne)
Southerly (Sydney)
Stephensen's Circular (Sydney)
Twentieth Century (Melbourne)
Wharfie (Sydney)
World Peace (Sydney)

V SELECTED ARTICLES

'Ek Dum' [M. H. Ellis], 'The Australia First Affair', *Bulletin*, 7
  June, 14 June 1950.
Fitzpatrick, Brian, 'Rights of Labor—and of "The Publicist"',
  Smith's Weekly, 13 June 1942.
Masey, Edward, 'Can We Afford Reduced Taxation?', *Australian
  National Review*, December 1938.
———, 'Social Services and War', *Australian Quarterly*, December
  1939.
———, 'The Clash in Cotton', *Publicist*, July 1936.
———, 'Vast Open Spaces', ibid., August 1936.
———, 'Alfred Deakin', ibid., September 1936.
———, 'The Drift to the Cities', ibid., October 1936.
———, 'Australian Trade Policy', ibid., January 1937.
———, 'The Trade Treaty with Japan', ibid., February 1937.
———, 'Depression and Finance', ibid., August 1940.
———, 'Our War Economy', ibid., September 1940.

————, 'Australia's Taxation System', ibid., November 1940 to February 1941.

————, 'Decadence and Resurgence', ibid., November 1941.

————, 'Credit and the War', ibid., December 1941.

————, 'Australia's Birthrate Problem', ibid., February to March 1942.

Miles, W. J., 'Sir Oliver Lodge', *Sydney Rationalist Annual*, August 1914.

Silverman, Sondra, 'A Poser for Liberals', *Nation*, 9 February 1963.

Stephensen, P. R., 'The Democratic Arcadia—Some Reflections on the Australian Labour Movement', *Communist Review*, vol. 6, no. 10, 1926.

————, 'Book Publishing in Australia', *Australian Rhodes Review*, no. 2, 1934.

————, 'The Decline and Fall of the British Empire', *Australian Rhodes Review*, no. 3, 1937.

————, 'A Reasoned Case Against Semitism', *Australian Quarterly*, March 1940.

VI   BOOKS AND PAMPHLETS

Australian Institute of Political Science, *Liberty in Australia* (21st Summer School, Canberra). Sydney, [1955].

Bath, Keith, *Injustice within the Law*. Sydney, 1948.

Baylebridge, William (ed. P. R. Stephensen), *This Vital Flesh*. Sydney, 1961.

Bean, C. E. W., *War Aims of a Plain Australian*. Sydney, 1943.

Belloc, Hilaire, *The Jews*. London, 1922.

Bisset, (Sir) James (in collaboration with P. R. Stephensen), *Tramps and Ladies: My Early Years in Steamers*. London, 1960.

———— (————), *Sail Ho! My Early Years at Sea*. London, 1961.

———— (————), *Commodore: War, Peace and Big Ships*. London, 1961.

Bread and Cheese Club, *Miles Franklin—A Tribute*. Melbourne, 1955.

Brown, Cyril, *Writing for Australia: A Nationalist Tradition in Australian Literature?* Melbourne, 1956.

Catts, Dorothy M. (comp.), *James Howard Catts, M.H.R.* Sydney, 1953.

Chapman, B. Burgoyne, *The Compleat Anti-Semite*. 2nd ed., Sydney, 1945.

Childe, Vere Gordon, *How Labour Governs: A Study of Workers'*

Representation in Australia. 1st ed., London, 1923; 2nd ed. (ed. F. B. Smith), Melbourne, 1964.

Clune, F. P. and Stephensen, P. R., *The Viking of Van Diemen's Land: The Stormy Life of Jorgen Jorgensen*. Sydney, 1954.

—— and ——, *The Pirates of the Brig 'Cyprus'*. London, 1962.

Coleman, Peter, *Obscenity, Blasphemy, Sedition: Censorship in Australia*. Brisbane [1962].

Council for Civil Liberties, Australian, *Liberty and the Labour Government*. Melbourne, 1942.

——, *The War and Civil Rights*. Melbourne, 1940.

Cross, Colin, *The Fascists in Britain*. London, 1961.

Duncan, W. G. K. (ed.), *Australian Foreign Policy*. Sydney, 1938.

Egan, Beresford (with Preface by P. R. Stephensen), *The Sink of Solitude*. London, 1928.

Ellis, Malcolm, *The Garden Path: The Story of the Saturation of the Australian Labour Movement by Communism*. Sydney, 1949.

Fellowship of Australian Writers, *The Australian Author*. Sydney, 1935.

Fernandez, Brian, *Australia Awake and other Poems*. Riverton, S.A., 1941.

Fitzpatrick, Brian, *The Australian Commonwealth: A Picture of the Community 1901–1955*. Melbourne, 1956.

Fox, Len, *Australia and the Jews*. Sydney, 1939.

Gibson, Ralph, *Stop this Fascist Propaganda*. Melbourne, [1942].

——, *My Years in the Communist Party*. Melbourne, 1966.

Green, H. M., *A History of Australian Literature*. 2 vols. Sydney, 1961.

Hartz, Louis, *The Founding of New Societies*. New York, 1964.

Hasluck, P. M. C., *The Government and the People 1939–1941*. Canberra, 1952.

Homburg, H., *South Australian Lutherans and Wartime Rumours*. Adelaide, 1947.

Huxley, Aldous (ed.), *The Letters of D. H. Lawrence*. London, 1932.

Hyden, Walford, *Pavlova*. London, 1931.

Ingamells, R. C. and Tilbrook, I., *Conditional Culture*. Adelaide, 1938.

Internment in South Australia. Adelaide, 1946. (Published by the Loveday camp's commandant, Lieutenant-Colonel E. T. Dean.)

Jauncey, L. C., *The Story of Conscription in Australia*. London, 1935.

Jones, W. H. (as told to P. R. Stephensen), *The Cape Horn Breed: My Experiences as an Apprentice in Sail in the Full-rigged Ship 'British Isles'*. London, 1956.

Key, V. O. jun., *Politics, Parties and Pressure Groups*. New York, 1960.

Kisch, E., *Australian Landfall*. London, 1937.

Lamshed, Max, *The River's Bounty: A History of Barmera and its People*. Barmera, S.A., 1952.

Lawrence, D. H. (ed. H. T. Moore), *Collected Letters*. 2 vols. London, 1962.

Lindsay, Jack, *Life Rarely Tells*. London, 1958.

———, *The Roaring Twenties: Literary Life in Sydney, New South Wales, in the Years 1921–6*. London, 1960.

———, *Fanfrolico and After*. London, 1962.

Lindsay, Philip, *I'd Live the Same Life Over*. London, 1941.

MacCallum, M. W., *Australia First*. Sydney, 1921.

McLeod, A. L. (ed.), *The Pattern of Australian Culture*. New York, 1963.

Mander, A. E., *The Making of the Australians*. Melbourne, 1958.

Matthews, Harley, *Patriot's Progress*. Adelaide, 1965.

Miles, W. J., *The Myth of the Resurrection of Jesus, The Christ*. Sydney, 1914.

Miller, E. Morris, *Australian Literature*, vol. 2. Melbourne, 1940.

Mudie, Ian, *This is Australia*. Adelaide, 1941.

———, *Poems 1943–1944*. Melbourne, 1945.

Nehls, E., *D. H. Lawrence: A Composite Biography*. 3 vols. Wisconsin, 1959.

Nelson, Tom, *The Hungry Mile*. Sydney, 1957.

Pankhurst, Adela, *Put up the Sword*. Melbourne, 1915.

———, *see also* Walsh, Adela.

Price, C. A., *German Settlers in South Australia*. Melbourne, 1945.

Robinson, E. E., *The Roosevelt Leadership 1933–1945*. New York, 1955.

Sawer, Geoffrey, *Australian Federal Politics and Law 1929–1949*. Melbourne, 1967.

Scott, Ernest, *Australia During the War* (vol. 11, *Official History of Australia in the War of 1914–1918*). Sydney, 1936.

Shils, Edward, *The Torment of Secrecy: The Background and Consequences of American Security Policies*. Melbourne, 1956.

Smith, Julian, *On the Pacific Front: The Adventures of Egon Kisch in Australia*. Sydney, 1936.

Stephensen, P. R., *Norman Lindsay Does not Care*. London, 1928.
————, *The Bushwhackers: Sketches of Life in the Australian Outback*. London, 1929.
————, *Policeman of the Lord*. London, 1929.
————, *The Well of Sleevelessness*. London, 1929.
————, *Harry Buckland, Master of Hounds*. London, 1931.
————, *The Foundations of Culture in Australia: An Essay towards National Self Respect*. Sydney, 1936.
————, *Life and Work of A. G. Stephens, the Bookfellow*. Sydney, 1940.
————, *William John Miles*. Sydney, 1942.
————, *Kookaburras and Satyrs: Some Recollections of the Fanfrolico Press*. Sydney, 1954.
————, *Philip Dimmock: A Memoir of a Poet*. Sydney, 1958.
————, *Nationalism in Australian Literature* (1959 Commonwealth Literary Fund Lecture). Adelaide, 1959.
————, *The History and Description of Sydney Harbour*. Adelaide, 1966.
———— (comp.), *Sydney Sails: The Story of the Royal Sydney Yacht Squadron's First 100 Years (1862–1962)*. Sydney, 1962.
Strehlow, T. G. H., *An Australian Viewpoint*. Melbourne, 1950.
Walsh, Adela, *Conditions in Japan*. Sydney, 1940.
———— and Walsh, Tom, *Japan as Viewed by Foreigners*. Sydney, 1940.
————, *see also* Pankhurst, Adela.
Watts, Dora, *The Dangerous Myth of Racial Equality: Genocide for the White Races?* Melbourne, [1962].
Whitington, Don, *Ring the Bells: A Dictionary of Australian Federal Politics*. Melbourne, 1956.
Willyan, Charles. *Behind Barbed Wire in Australia*. Murchison, Vic., 1948.

Index

195